The Annotated Prison Writings of Oscar Wilde

The Annotated Prison Writings of Oscar Wilde

EDITED BY Nicholas Frankel

Harvard University Press
Cambridge, Massachusetts
London, England
2018

Text of Wilde's letters and of *De Profundis* © the Estate of Vyvyan Holland 1962, renewed 1990

First printing

Library of Congress Cataloging-in-Publication Data

Names: Wilde, Oscar, 1854–1900, author. | Frankel, Nicholas, 1962– editor.
Title: The annotated prison writings of Oscar Wilde / edited by Nicholas Frankel.
Description: Cambridge, Massachusetts : Harvard University Press, 2018. |
    Includes bibliographical references.
Identifiers: LCCN 2017046439 | ISBN 9780674984387 (alk. paper)
Subjects: LCSH: Wilde, Oscar, 1854–1900—Imprisonment. | Wilde, Oscar, 1854–
    1900—Correspondence.
Classification: LCC PR5812 .F72 2018 | DDC 828/.809—dc23
LC record available at https://lccn.loc.gov/2017046439

Book design by Dean Bornstein

I am no longer the Sirius of Comedy. . . . If I write any more books, it will be to form a library of lamentations . . . written in a style begotten of sorrow . . . in sentences composed in solitude, and punctuated by tears. They will be written exclusively for those who have suffered or are suffering. . . . I shall be an enigma to the world of Pleasure, but a mouthpiece for the world of Pain.

—*Oscar Wilde to Thomas Martin, Reading Prison, Spring 1897*

Contents

Introduction   1

A Note on the Texts   33

Clemency Petition to the Home Secretary, 2 July 1896   41

De Profundis   53

Letter to the *Daily Chronicle*, 27 May 1897   293

The Ballad of Reading Gaol   317

Letter to the *Daily Chronicle*, 23 March 1898   373

Further Reading   385

Illustration Credits   389

Acknowledgments   393

The Annotated Prison Writings of Oscar Wilde

Introduction

On 25 May 1895, Oscar Wilde was sentenced to two years in prison with hard labor for the crime of "gross indecency" with another man. The crime had only recently entered the statute books, introduced at the eleventh hour during parliamentary debate leading to the passage of the 1885 Criminal Law Amendment Act. "Gross indecency" was a catchall phrase, outlawing even private and consensual sexual relations between adult men. The criminal standard was loosely defined and subjective, and the burden of proof dangerously low. For this reason the law soon became known unofficially as the "blackmailer's charter." Astonishingly, this statute was not fully abolished until 2003, when the United Kingdom finally accorded sex between men the same legal status as heterosexual sex.[1] It would not be until 2017 that Wilde and other men convicted under this statute were issued formal—usually posthumous—pardons by the British government.

After two highly publicized criminal trials—the first ended in a hung jury—featuring a series of intrusive investigations into Wilde's personal life, including his letters and his personal, literary, and sexual dealings with a number of men, Wilde was found guilty on seven counts of gross indecency and received the severest sentence allowable by law.[2] At the time of Wilde's incarceration, conditions in British prisons were especially harsh, and the cruelty of the late-Victorian prison system—which subjected inmates to a regime of "hard labour, hard board, and hard fare," in accordance with the 1865 and 1877 Prison Acts—was coming into disrepute. Prisoners were kept isolated in separate cells, forbidden to communicate or associate with one another, and their diet and living conditions were calibrated at the minimum necessary to maintain life. The 1885 statute left to judges' discretion whether to impose hard labor, but in practice criminals sentenced to even short periods in prison were routinely given hard labor to intensify their punishment. For an initial period at least, Wilde was expected to spend six hours per day climbing the prison treadwheel (an ascent of 8,640 feet, equivalent to climbing Chicago's Willis Tower six times) or longer still mindlessly turning a mechanical crank or picking oakum in his cell. The prison regime—which was to be made more humane by an act of Parliament shortly after Wilde completed his sentence, partly as a result of Wilde's own imprisonment—has been called "the most severe system of secondary punishment in English history," amounting to "scarcely veiled torture."[3] It was designed to destroy the spirit of even the toughest offenders, and mental breakdowns were frequent.

Wilde had approached the prospect of imprisonment bravely. Within days of his arrival at London's Pentonville Prison, however, newspapers reported that he had broken down both physically and mentally and that officials were becoming anxious on his account. In early June he was taken off the treadwheel and moved to Pentonville's infirmary before being reassigned to "second-class hard labour" (oakum picking). But press reports that he was infirm, losing weight, and going violently insane alarmed those in the highest echelons of the British establishment. Probably as a consequence, Wilde was moved first to Wandsworth Prison, in South London, where his condition only deteriorated further. In November 1895, following a series of official investigations into his health and well-being, he was moved again, this time to the supposedly less onerous regional prison at Reading, Berkshire, forty miles west of London. At a "country prison," the Prison Commission's advisers recommended, Wilde might be allowed "a cell larger than the usual size," "such association with other prisoners as may be deemed advisable or desirable," some "variation of employment," "minor relaxations of the full rigour and discipline of prison life," and even "outdoor exercise with some garden work, with a view of a more wholesome state

Reading Prison, exterior, circa 1900.

of his tissues being induced and his mind being thereby roused."[4] But officials were not just concerned with Wilde's health. They were mindful too that his sufferings would attract less attention at a regional prison from London-based journalists and prison reformers.

The imprisoned aesthete would spend the final eighteen months of his sentence at Reading, and during the first nine of them there was no letup in the intensity of his punishment. He remained in solitary confinement, unable to associate with fellow prisoners, picking oakum in his tiny cell for hours on end. His health continued to deteriorate, giving rise to the very real fears of insanity that are palpable in the petition he wrote to the home secretary in July 1896, pleading for a remission of his sentence.

The reasons for his mental deterioration were partly personal: his removal to Reading coincided with the conclusion of bankruptcy proceedings at which the scale of his financial recklessness in the years leading up to his conviction was made public. Two weeks after his arrival at Reading, moreover, he was informed that his wife, Constance, and children had taken the last name "Holland" in an effort to dissociate themselves from his scandal. Within a couple of months, it became clear that his marriage was at an end. One of the assets listed at his bankruptcy was his life interest in his wife's marriage settlement (investments in her own name bestowed on her by her family at the time of her marriage, guaranteeing her an independent income), and over the course of 1896 a fierce dispute erupted between his wife and his representatives over the fate of this asset. Constance wanted to buy the life interest to secure income for the couple's children in the event of her death, but Wilde's representatives, his friends More Adey and Robert Ross, determined foolishly upon securing it for Wilde himself. As the year progressed, Wilde became increasingly anxious that his wife would bring a divorce action and that he would be subjected to new criminal proceedings for committing sodomy, a graver crime than that of gross indecency.[5] In the event, neither of these feared outcomes came to pass. But toward the end of his sentence, Constance successfully nullified his parental rights, an act that he called "a blow appalling . . . [and] so terrible that to expunge it from the scroll of History and Life I would gladly remain in this lonely cell for . . . ten years if needs be."[6] Two days before his release, he signed a painful and humiliating Deed of Separation, strictly limiting his future dealings with his wife and children in exchange for a financial allowance of roughly £12 per month upon his release. He was never to see his wife or children again.

Illness also played a part in Wilde's deterioration. In his petition of July 1896, he alludes to the lack of attentive treatment for a painful abscess in his right ear. He had begun suffering from the condition before his conviction, and it would eventually contribute to his death from meningoencephalitis in 1900. The ear had discharged fluid throughout his imprisonment to this point, he was losing his hearing, and he feared that the condition would spread to his other ear too. When his friend and editor Frank Harris asked him in June 1896 why the Reading authorities didn't give him cotton wool or something else to put in the ear, Wilde replied, "If you think one dare disturb a doctor or a warder for an earache, you don't know much about prison. You would pay for it."[7] His head was splitting and pain kept him awake at night, he told a warder in March 1897, two months before his release.[8]

The pain was emotional as well as physical. Three months after Wilde's arrival at Reading, Constance journeyed unexpectedly and compassionately from her home in Italy, where she had exiled herself, to break the news that Wilde's beloved mother had died some weeks previously. "Her death was so terrible to me," he writes in *De Profundis* (p. 145 below), "that I, once a lord of language, have no words in which to express my anguish and my shame. . . . She and my father had bequeathed me a name they had made noble and honoured not merely in Literature, Art, Archaeology and Science, but in the public history of my own country in its evolution as a nation. I had disgraced that name eternally. I had made it a low byword among low people. I had dragged it through the very mire. I had given it to brutes that they might make it brutal, and to fools that they might turn it into a synonym for folly. What I suffered then, and still suffer, is not for pen to write or paper to record." Two years later, Constance too would be dead, from complications arising from surgery to correct a long-standing, painful, and poorly understood condition now recognized to have been multiple sclerosis.[9]

If personal reasons contributed to Wilde's deterioration at Reading, so too did the continued harsh treatment meted out by prison authorities. In *De Profundis*, he details the humiliating circumstances in which he was taken by train to Reading, on 20 November 1895. He was dressed in prison garb, manacled between two policemen, exposed to public ridicule, and spat at by crowds while waiting on the platform at London's Clapham Junction station. "For half an hour I stood there in the grey November rain," he writes, "surrounded by a jeering mob. For a year after that was done to me I wept every day at the same hour and for the same space of time" (p. 235 below). The experience was so distressing that, as late as April 1897, with his release less than a month away, Wilde petitioned the home secretary requesting that he neither be transferred again nor made "to undergo any similar exhibition to public gaze."[10]

The governor of Reading Prison, Lieutenant-Colonel Henry Isaacson, assured him on his arrival that he would never again be subjected to so harrowing an experience, but evidently Wilde wanted a further guarantee. One can readily understand why. Compassionate assurances aside, Isaacson—whom Wilde would later describe as "a mulberry-faced dictator"—proved himself the cruelest and most merciless of Wilde's overseers.[11] Isaacson was an unyielding stickler for regulations, and prisoners under his jurisdiction were punished severely for even the smallest infractions. The two letters that Wilde wrote to the *Daily Chronicle* upon his release, printed on pp. 293–315 and 373–83 below, testify eloquently to the rigidity and cruelty of the prison regulations as well as the punishments awaiting the disobedient. One of Wilde's warders later suggested that many prison rules appeared to have been made with no other object than to be broken, so that an excuse might be found for inflicting additional punishment.[12] Another warder testified to Wilde's "inability to comply with the regulation tasks allotted to his class of prisoner," such as keeping his prison cell scrupulously clean and well-ordered, or picking his required daily quantity of oakum.[13] Wilde was often caught talking or late in rising, and he was "no good for anything."[14] He was punished relentlessly and repeatedly for disobedience. Particularly painful was Isaacson's refusal to allow Wilde access to the few books he possessed, even though the Prison Commission had given special permission for Wilde to have them in his cell. Other punishments included the restriction of Wilde's diet to just coarse bread and water and lengthy periods of solitary confinement in a darkened, windowless cell. Isaacson was "not able to enjoy his breakfast unless someone was punished before he ate it," Wilde related after his release.[15] Such testimony is borne out by the fact that, under Isaacson's immediate successor, the number of punishments awarded for petty breaches of prison regulations fell by two-thirds.[16]

By the summer of 1896, it was clear to Wilde's friends and prison administrators alike that something had to be done if he was to survive incarceration with his sanity intact. In June, by special arrangement with the Prison Commission, he was visited by his friend Frank Harris, one of the most widely respected journalists in London, who promised that he would bring about an improvement in Wilde's treatment.[17] Shortly after Harris's visit—and possibly at Harris's instigation—Wilde wrote the moving, desperate clemency petition to the home secretary printed on pp. 41–51 below. The petition documented his treatment over the previous year, and in it Wilde pleaded for some remission in his sentence. Besides conveying his fears of insanity, the petition is remarkable for the note of defiance underpinning it, for Wilde's insistence that his offences were "diseases to be cured by a physician, rather than crimes to be punished by a judge," and for his indictments of a system that, far from rehabilitating prisoners, "hardens their hearts whose hearts it does not break" (pp. 41 and 49 below).[18] Indeed, such punishment "brutalises those who have to carry it out no less than those who have to submit to it," Wilde writes (p. 49 below).

Although the authorities would not sanction a remission of sentence, Wilde's petition met with a largely sympathetic response from Sir Evelyn Ruggles-Brise, the recently appointed head of British prisons.[19] Ruggles-Brise was more progressive and reform-minded than his predecessor, the draconian Major-General Sir Edmund Du Cane, who had overseen the prison system from 1877 to 1895. Upon receipt of Wilde's petition, Ruggles-Brise dispatched a committee of official "visitors" to Reading to inquire closely into Wilde's case. Ruggles-Brise also consulted David Nicolson, the lord chancellor's visitor in lunacy. One important consequence was that, in answer to Wilde's complaint at "the entire privation of literature to one to whom Literature was once the first thing of life" (p. 47 below), Ruggles-Brise on July 27, 1896, instructed the governor of Reading Prison to provide Wilde with foolscap paper, ink, and pen "for use in his leisure moments in his cell"; to relax the rules limiting Wilde to just two books per week and allow him instead "sufficient books to occupy his mind"; and to allow Wilde to request access to any work he liked.[20] Around this time, too, the tyrannical Isaacson was replaced by the far kinder Major James O. Nelson, whom Wilde was later to call "the most Christ-like man I ever met."[21] It has been suggested that "the Prison Commissioners engineered the switch in governorship because they recognized that the continuing conflictual relations between Isaacson and Wilde were a bad omen for the uneventful completion of Oscar Wilde's sentence."[22] Without doubt Isaacson's replacement by Nelson was both timely and momentous where Wilde was concerned.

Wilde memorialized Nelson's benign influence on Reading Prison at the end of his first letter to the *Daily Chronicle,* written less than a week after his release. As Wilde writes, if Nelson could not alter the rules of the prison system, he nonetheless "altered the spirit in which they used to be carried out under his predecessor" (p. 315 below). Nelson's influence can be broadly felt throughout this volume, since his compassionate and generous actions helped rebuild Wilde's self-confidence, not just as a man but as a writer. One of Nelson's first acts was to carry out Ruggles-Brise's instructions by approving the vast bulk of the books Wilde requested, including works by Tennyson, Marlowe, Spencer, Keats, and Chaucer; an edition of the Greek New Testament; a prose translation of Dante's *Divina Commedia;* Renan's *Vie de Jésus (Life of Jesus)* and *Les Apôtres (The Apostles)* in the original French; and essays by Carlyle, Newman, and Emerson. (The influences of Dante, Renan, Newman, Emerson, and the Greek New Testament can all be felt in *De Profundis,* which Wilde would begin composing toward the end of 1896.) Upon arrival, Nelson also issued Wilde a bound manuscript notebook, which he put to good purpose. Two months later Wilde wrote, "I take notes of the books I read, and copy lines and phrases in the poets. . . . I cling to my notebook: it helps me: before I had it my brain was going in very evil circles."[23] Nelson also encouraged Wilde to make full use of his right to call on him, and, according to a mourner at the time of his death, Nelson took great pleasure when Wilde exercised this right on a daily basis.[24] It is no surprise that Nelson—to whom Wilde would refer near the end of his sentence as "my good and kind friend"[25]—was among the first to receive an inscribed copy of Wilde's *The Ballad of Reading Gaol* upon its publication in 1898.

Nelson's "Christ-like" nature is especially important to critical understanding of the lengthiest and most autobiographical of the writings in
this volume, the long letter to Lord Alfred Douglas written in the last six
months of Wilde's sentence, parts of which were published under the
title *De Profundis* in 1905, five years after Wilde's death. Nelson is not
mentioned directly in Wilde's text; he is alluded to in passing only once,
when Wilde says he owes "much to this new personality that has altered
every man's life in this place" and that "for the last seven or eight months,
in spite of a succession of great troubles reaching me from the outside
world almost without intermission, I have been placed in direct contact
with a new spirit working in this prison through men and things, that has
helped me beyond any possibility of expression in words" (p. 229
below). But Nelson undoubtedly had a profound influence on the
work. He was the first—and, arguably, most important—reader of *De
Profundis*. In his official capacity, he reviewed Wilde's composition on a
daily basis, enjoined by the Prison Commission to vet Wilde's correspondence and ensure that he made "no improper use" of the writing
privileges granted him. Unofficially, he was responsible for encouraging
the letter's composition.[26] From the outset he understood that perhaps
the most inhumane elements of Wilde's imprisonment were the constraints upon his imagination and his capacity to communicate. For this
reason Nelson was perfectly content to stretch the instructions he had
been given setting conditions on Wilde's use of writing materials. He
allowed Wilde a greater frequency of correspondence with his friends
outside than prison regulations allowed, and his daily oversight of *De
Profundis* shows that he understood how Wilde might exploit the form
of the personal letter so that it became something far more capacious
and self-expressive than a letter is traditionally regarded as being. Above
all, Nelson quickly understood the psychological and emotional necessity of allowing Wilde to write, over a period of many months, to the
man whom he blamed for his personal downfall, his lover Douglas.

Douglas had been Wilde's nearly constant companion for about three
years before his conviction. During this time Wilde spent long periods

Lord Alfred Douglas, c. 1892, shortly after Wilde first met him.

with Douglas, away from his wife and children, residing in hotels or rented accommodations. Sometimes they shared sexual partners. In January 1893 Wilde told Douglas by letter, "Your slim gilt soul walks between passion and poetry," and "Hyacinthus, whom Apollo loved so madly, was you in Greek days." The letter was signed, "Always, with undying love, Oscar."[27] Just days before his conviction and sentencing, he told Douglas, "If prison and dishonour be my destiny, . . . my love for you and this . . . divine belief that you love me in return will sustain me in my unhappiness."[28]

By late 1896, however, Wilde had turned violently against his lover, consumed with bitterness not just at the part he attributed to Douglas in his personal downfall but also at what he perceived to be Douglas's silence and neglect in the nearly eighteen months he had been behind bars. So far as the latter charge is concerned, at least, Wilde's recriminations are deeply unfair: Douglas had in fact been active on Wilde's behalf, despite being exiled on the European continent, where he had fled at Wilde's insistence for fear of being arrested on charges similar to those Wilde faced. Douglas had written poems and letters to the press, tried organizing petitions, and composed two magazine articles justifying his love for his imprisoned friend. He had wanted to dedicate to Wilde his first volume of poetry, but Wilde learned of this while in prison and managed to prevent it. After Wilde repulsed Douglas's early attempts to communicate, their mutual friends Ross and Adey led Douglas to believe that further attempts would be unwelcome. It is highly likely that Ross and Adey—who wished to bring about a reconciliation between Wilde and his wife—misrepresented Douglas to Wilde in letters and during prison visits. "You were the true author of [my] hideous tragedy," Wilde tells Douglas. "Had *you* been in prison, . . . do you think that I would have allowed you to eat your heart away in darkness and solitude?" (pp. 121 and 160–61 below). If Wilde was to approach the prospect of release with equanimity, it was crucial , as he put it, that he first remove the poisonous adder feeding at his breast.[29]

It is vital to understand that the picture Wilde draws in *De Profundis* of his relationship with Douglas is shaped by the bitterness of his imprisonment. As the critic Regenia Gagnier writes, "If there had not been an Alfred Douglas, Wilde would have had to invent one. . . . Douglas was the image of all unworthy audiences."[30] Wilde paints a compelling and detailed—though by no means reliable—picture of the two men's inseparability in the three years leading up to his imprisonment. The emotional intensity and passion of their relationship is evident, but according to Wilde their love was one-sided and based on a pattern of abuse. Wilde contends that Douglas had lived entirely at his expense, distracting the author from writing new plays; making unreasonable emotional, ethical, and financial demands; and ultimately bringing about Wilde's "utter and discreditable . . . ruin" as both a man and an artist. Only weakness of will had kept Wilde from the permanent break he knew he ought to make (p. 63 below). Wilde tells us that when he began to be persecuted by Douglas's father—the Marquess of Queensberry, who had grown increasingly belligerent in his efforts to separate Wilde from his youngest son—Douglas deliberately stoked his father's ire while urging Wilde to throw caution to the wind. Queensberry's persecution culminated in February 1895 when he left at Wilde's London club a card on which he had scrawled, "For Oscar Wilde, posing somdomite [*sic*],"[31] whereupon Douglas encouraged Wilde to pursue an ill-fated libel suit that ended with Wilde, rather than Queensberry, facing criminal charges. At least some of those charges, Wilde contends, ought more properly to have been laid to Douglas's account. Whatever his past feelings, Wilde writes Douglas, "It would be impossible for me now to have for you any feeling other than that of contempt and scorn" (p. 163 below).

But *De Profundis* is far more than a lengthy indictment of Douglas, and Nelson, as he reviewed Wilde's fresh pages in his office each morning, must have quickly realized that this was no ordinary letter. Composition took place late into the night over many months, with Wilde's plank bed serving as a makeshift writing table. As the manuscript progressed, Wilde's feelings and intentions changed.[32] He shifted his focus away from

Douglas, to consider not just his own past but also his personal and artistic future, possibly by amalgamating into the manuscript other material on which he had been working.[33] In February 1897, with much of the manuscript evidently still unwritten, he wrote to Adey that "It is the most important letter of my life, as it will deal ultimately with my future mental attitude towards life, with the way in which I desire to meet the world again, with the development of my character: with what I have lost, what I have learned, and what I hope to arrive at."[34] We should be mindful, when considering this characterization of the letter, that Wilde knew Nelson would review his written words. But even allowing for the possibility that Wilde's characterization was written partly for Nelson's eyes, the description has a great deal of validity. "At last I see a real goal towards which my soul can go simply, naturally, and rightly," he told Adey. "Before I see you and Robbie, I must finish the letter, that you may understand what I have become, or rather desire to become in nature and aim."[35]

Some of the most impressive parts of Wilde's manuscript deal not with Douglas directly but with Wilde's efforts to cultivate a spirit of love, forgiveness, humility, and acceptance—to appreciate, as he puts it, that "Humanity has been in the prison along with us all" and that "whatever is realised is right" (pp. 229 and 121 below). Being sent to prison, indeed, might prove to be one of "the two great turning-points of my life."[36] Wilde knew that he needed to find it in himself to forgive Douglas, and he came to recognize that his love for the younger man had by no means been extinguished. Toward the end of the letter, Wilde writes that "No one can possibly shut the doors against Love for ever," and he speaks of meeting Douglas "in some quiet foreign town" when "the June roses are all in their wanton opulence" (p. 287 below). These rhapsodic sentences anticipate the emotional reconciliation with Douglas that would take place shortly after Wilde's release, when the two met secretly in Rouen and then scandalized friends and enemies alike by setting up house in Naples, until they were forced apart by their families some months later. "I love him, and have always loved him," Wilde wrote his friend

Reginald Turner from Naples in September 1897. "It was necessary that [Douglas] and I should come together again," he told Ross.[37]

In addition to Wilde's efforts to transcend his bitterness toward Douglas, *De Profundis* is notable for its increasingly philosophical and reflective tone, and some of its most moving passages concern the difficult, transformative truths Wilde says he has painfully come to understand in prison. He tells us that "the secret of life is suffering," that "there is no truth comparable to Sorrow," and that "sorrow, being the supreme emotion of which man is capable, is at once the type and test of all great Art" (pp. 187 and 185 below). Toward the end he tells us that he wants to model his future behavior on the personality of Christ, a purportedly historical account of whose life he had recently been rereading in "that gracious Fifth Gospel," Renan's *Vie de Jésus*.[38] "Christ's place is with the poets," Wilde says, since "his whole conception of Humanity sprang right out of the imagination and can only be realised by it" (p. 199 below). Above all else, he tells us he has rediscovered conviction in himself as an artist. "There is before me so much to do," he writes, "that I would regard it as a terrible tragedy if I died before I was allowed to complete at any rate a little of it" (p. 183 below). Henceforth he would dedicate his talents to "Sorrow . . . and all that it teaches one." If he wrote any more books, he told a warder around the time he was finishing *De Profundis*, it would be "to form a library of lamentations. . . . They will be written exclusively for those who have suffered or are suffering. . . . I shall be an enigma to the world of Pleasure, but a mouth-piece for the world of Pain."[39]

How seriously should we take Wilde's expressions of humility, penitence, and Christian piety, especially given his consciousness that the "Christ-like" Nelson possessed the power to terminate the letter's composition should he judge it improper? To what extent did Wilde write of his unorthodox Christian convictions because he wanted to be redeemed in Nelson's eyes, just as he would be redeemed in the eyes of readers like the one who proclaimed of Wilde's letter on its first publication in 1905, "Hardly in any literature does such a great and bitter cry pierce to the heart"? "The charitable man . . . must take [Wilde's] book for expiation and in it find his martyrdom," this observer decided.[40] This question of intent is likely unanswerable, especially by readers who have never personally experienced the kind of suffering Wilde underwent in prison. The critic Regenia Gagnier reminds us that Wilde's "grandeur and authority of statement" are typical of "prison literature under modern conditions" and that they constitute a necessary "response to the monotony of prison life . . . [which] matches the conditions of mass convict labor under a strong centralized system."[41] But just as importantly, expressions of forgiveness and piety can also be acts of defiance and self-assertion, designed to unsettle the judgments of those at whom they are directed. "My mind may lose its force, my blood its fire, / And my frame perish even in conquering pain," says Byron's Childe Harold,

> But there is that within me which shall tire
> Torture and Time, and breathe when I expire;
> Something unearthly, which they deem not of,
> Like the remembered tone of a mute lyre,
> Shall on their softened spirits sink, and move
> In hearts all rocky now the late remorse of love.[42]

Behind the mask of his self-transformation, Wilde was as defiant and self-assured as ever. In this respect, it is instructive to consider reactions to the 1905 edition among those who knew Wilde personally. George Bernard Shaw proclaimed, "No other Irishman has yet produced as masterful a comedy as *De Profundis*." He considered the work "quite exhilarating and amusing as to Wilde himself" and observed, "The unquenchable spirit of the man is magnificent." Shaw said Wilde "maintains his position and puts society solidly in the wrong," and while "there is pain in it, inconvenience, annoyance," Wilde's text contains "no real tragedy, all comedy."[43] E. V. Lucas—who, in his role as a director of the publishing firm Methuen, was instrumental in the text's first publication—wrote, "It is impossible, except very occasionally, to look upon his testament as more than a literary feat. . . . This is not sorrow, but its dexterously constructed counterfeit."[44] For Lucas, the value of *De Profundis* lay in the "triumph of the literary temperament over the most disadvantageous conditions" as well as the evidence it gives "as to one of the most artificial natures produced by the nineteenth century."[45] As Wilde's friend and sometime-disciple Max Beerbohm explained, "No discerning reader can but regard the book as essentially the artistic essay of an artist. . . . No modern writer has achieved through prose the limpid and lyrical effects that were achieved by Oscar Wilde. One does not seem to be reading a written thing. The words sing. There is nothing of that formality, that hard and cunning precision, which marks so much of the prose that we admire, and rightly admire. The meaning is artificial, but the expression is always magically natural and beautiful."[46]

We should keep in mind that these early readers were responding to a heavily redacted text, from which Wilde's embittered references to Douglas and Queensberry had been cut. Nevertheless, as Beerbohm and Lucas suggest, the power of *De Profundis* derives ultimately from its majestic and impassioned prose. To approach it as a truth-telling document or as an accurate historical record is to mistake Wilde's relish in demonstrating—not least to himself—that he was once again a "lord of language." "The mere handling of pen and ink helps me," Wilde told Adey around the time he commenced the text.[47] "Language requires to be tuned, like a violin," he writes in *De Profundis,* while telling Douglas that he must "make [the letter] out as best you can, blots, corrections, and all" (pp. 265 and 267). By implication the letter was a virtuoso performance. Before prison Wilde had used his gift to entertain and shock or to play gracefully with ideas. In *De Profundis* he uses those same powers to seduce and shock in an entirely different fashion—in the service of persuading readers of the truth and extent of his personal transformation. "Some day the truth will have to be known: not necessarily in my lifetime or in Douglas's," he told Ross, "but I am not prepared to sit in the grotesque pillory they put me into, for all time."[48]

As this remark indicates, Wilde seems to have understood that *De Profundis* is far more than a personal letter to Douglas and that at least

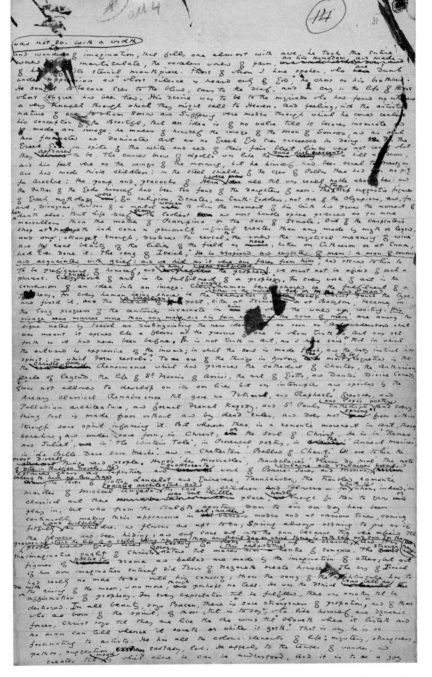

Oscar Wilde, untitled manuscript letter to Lord Alfred Douglas, composed in Reading Prison, 1896–1897, published posthumously as *De Profundis*. Granger.

parts of it possessed a potential readership that included Ross, Adey, and others besides. Probably for this reason, he revised the manuscript meticulously before he left prison, and he may have intended to rework it further. The process of composition "resembles . . . closely what we know of the processes of composition of Wilde's literary works," says one recent editor.[49] By the beginning of April 1897, seven weeks before his release, Wilde had decided that rather than send the manuscript directly to Douglas, he would send it to Ross instead, since he wished Ross to be his literary executor and "to have complete control over my plays, books, and papers."[50] To be sure, Wilde asked Ross to send the manuscript to Douglas after first having a typed copy made "on good paper such as is used for plays."[51] Nonetheless he realized that the letter might one day restore honor to a name that had become "the shield and catspaw of the Queensberrys," and for this reason he gave Ross detailed instructions about passages "good and nice in intention" to be copied in typescript and sent to friends "interested to know something of what is happening to my soul."[52] It is "a sort of message or letter I send them," he told Ross. "Indeed it is an Encyclical Letter, and as the Bulls of the Holy Father are named from their opening words, it may be spoken of as the *Epistola: In Carcere et Vinculis* [Letter: In Prison and in Chains]."[53]

As the scholar Ian Small has observed, Wilde's instructions to Ross present us with "strong grounds for arguing that Wilde intended his manuscript to form (in some way) a literary work, or the basis of a literary work."[54] From the title Wilde half-jokingly supplies, and his reminder to Ross that any income from the sale of his works might be lodged to the credit of his children, one might infer too that Wilde foresaw the publication some day of at least those parts of the letter that did not concern Douglas directly. What is certain is that on the day after Wilde's release from prison, Ross received the manuscript from Wilde personally and at some date thereafter decided to retain the manuscript—whether he did so with Wilde's knowledge and authority can never be known—almost certainly because he realized its immense literary value and knew that sending it to Douglas would incense him and inevitably result in its immediate destruction.[55]

Five years after Wilde's death, Ross gave the letter the title *De Profundis* and published those parts of it that he deemed fit for public consumption, using Wilde's instructions for extracting "good and nice" passages as a guideline. Four years later, in 1909, in an effort to prevent Wilde's recriminations from becoming public in his own or in Douglas's lifetime, and perhaps also to ensure that it would never fall into the hands of Douglas (whom Ross knew to be personally hostile as well as litigious),[56] Ross donated the manuscript to the British Museum with instructions that it remain sealed for a period of fifty years. Only in 1962 was a complete and accurate transcription of Wilde's manuscript published, in *The Letters of Oscar Wilde,* making the unreliable nature of all previous editions self-evident. To be sure, the 1962 publication dispensed with Ross's title and framed *De Profundis* as a personal letter, accenting the depth and complexity of Wilde's feelings for Douglas. But it also highlighted the majesty of Wilde's prose for a new generation and, together with the Wolfenden Report and the partial decriminalization of homosexuality in England and Wales in 1967, helped bring about the restoration of Wilde's reputation that has taken place over the last fifty years. After 1962 biographers began to frame Wilde's criminal conviction almost exclusively in personal and sexual terms, placing Wilde's relations with Douglas squarely at the center of understanding. Richard Ellmann's Pulitzer Prize–winning biography of 1987 lent academic legitimacy and gravitas to this trend: together with the advance of queer studies in academia in the 1980s and 1990s, Ellmann's biography gave rise to a virtual industry of studies focused on Wilde's transgressive sexuality and gender-bending. More than any previous scholar, Ellmann also called attention to the massive literary price that Wilde's conviction exacted. It is perhaps unsurprising that studies of *De Profundis* have proliferated since the 1980s and that, with the exception of *The Picture of Dorian Gray* and *The Importance of Being Earnest,* none of Wilde's works has so thoroughly absorbed the attention of modern critics.

Wilde would have been gratified that *De Profundis* played such a central part in freeing him from the "grotesque pillory" into which he had been put. But *De Profundis* was by no means the only text occupying Wilde's mind at the time of his release. "The prison system is absolutely and entirely wrong. I would give anything to be able to alter it when I go out," he writes (p. 229 below). "I hope to write about prison life and try and change it for others," he told Thomas Martin, a friendly warder, in the weeks before his release.[57] This very warder would be the catalyst for Wilde's first, impressive effort to deliver on that promise.

On 24 May 1897, five days after Wilde's release, the *Daily Chronicle* printed a letter from Martin recounting that he had just been dismissed from his job at Reading Prison for giving a biscuit to a small, crying, hungry child. The child was one of a group of three who, unable to pay a fine, had been imprisoned for snaring rabbits. Wilde, who must have read this letter with alarm, responded quickly. Four days later the *Chronicle* printed the long letter reproduced below on pp. 293–315, subsequently published as a penny-pamphlet titled *Children in Prison and Other Cruelties of Prison Life.*[58] It was the last of Wilde's writings to be published under his own name in his lifetime. The letter began personally, although Wilde took pains to avoid referring to his own sufferings. He had seen the children himself on the Monday prior to his release; the one to whom Martin had given a biscuit was "a tiny little chap," too small even for the regulation prison clothing in which the authorities had attempted to dress him (p. 293 below).

Wilde went on to describe the children's fear and isolation, as well as the terrible injustices to which all British prisoners, adults and children, were subject as a result of the prison system's inherent cruelty. The first and most prominent emotion produced by prison life, he writes, is terror, which "seizes and dominates the child, as it seizes the grown man also, [and] is of course intensified beyond power of expression by the solitary cellular system of our prisons." Of another child prisoner, incarcerated on remand and as yet unconvicted, he writes, "The child's face was like a white wedge of sheer terror. There was in his eyes the terror of a hunted animal. The next morning I heard him . . . crying, and calling to be let out. His cry was for his parents." The letter also details the sufferings of a prisoner named Prince, who Wilde suspected was slowly succumbing to insanity. Unable to sit peacefully or control his erratic mannerisms, Prince was repeatedly flogged and punished until his "wretched face [became] bloated by tears and hysteria almost beyond recognition." Although Prince was just halfway through a six-month sentence, "something should be done at once for him," Wilde said, pleading for the paper to use its influence to have his case examined (pp. 309–13 below).

Although the letter reads as a document of personal witness, Wilde was well aware of the effect his words—and his signature—would have on the general debate about prison reform. The *Daily Chronicle* had for years been a loud advocate for prison reform, helping to bring about a parliamentary inquiry and the resignation of the draconian Du Cane in the days before Wilde's imprisonment. The paper's voice carried far and wide. As important, Wilde realized that his own case had become something of a focal point for the prison-reform movement. William D. Morrison—the chaplain at Wandsworth Prison, where Wilde was held in the late summer and fall of 1895—was one of the system's fiercest critics and had taken a close interest in Wilde's case.[59] Wilde was immensely gratified when, in direct response to his letter, the Irish Nationalist M.P. Michael Davitt took up Prince's case in Parliament. Wilde's letter also elicited leading articles in the *Daily Chronicle* (May 28) and the *Catholic Times* (June 4). A translation and accompanying article were printed in *Le Soir,* a Brussels paper. "The D. C. letter has produced . . . the best effect," Wilde wrote a few days after its appearance.[60] "I think now . . . that I could do *three* articles on Prison Life."[61]

But Wilde's next and most telling contribution to the prison-reform movement was not an article. Within days of his letter's appearance in the *Daily Chronicle,* he began working on the haunting *Ballad of Reading Gaol,* in which he movingly dramatizes in verse how "the fetid breath of living Death / Chokes up" each prison cell and "all, but Lust, is turned to dust / in Humanity's machine" (p. 365 below). Wilde labored intensively over the poem in the six months after his release, eventually completing it in Douglas's company at Naples in the autumn of 1897. Published in February 1898, it would prove to be his best-selling book, running to seven editions and 7,000 copies in England alone in the two and a half years before his death.

That the poem's author meant it to play a part in the debate preceding passage of the 1898 Prisons Act is clear. Shortly after the book's appearance, Wilde wrote a second letter to the *Daily Chronicle* detailing urgently needed reforms and signed it "The Author of *The Ballad of Reading Gaol.*" Three months later, he said, "I have been able to deal a heavy and fatal blow at the monstrous prison-system of English justice."[62] He was gratified when the poem was twice quoted or cited on the floor of Parliament in the run-up to the act's passage, and he even urged his publisher (unsuccessfully) to issue a cheap edition with a preface by Davitt or some other radical politician. "I want the poem to reach the poorer classes," he told his publisher, adding, "The provinces must be made to rise like one man."[63]

Still, though Wilde was gratified by the poem's effects on the prison reform debate, *The Ballad* was much "more . . . than a pamphlet on prison-reform."[64] Wilde intended that it be his literary swan song. The ballad form was at this time undergoing something of a revival, and Wilde was well aware of how socially engaged poets of his day—notably Rudyard Kipling, George Sims, and A. E. Housman—had revitalized the traditional form so as to highlight the horrors and injustices of their moment. During the poem's composition, he told friends that he was "out-Henleying Kipling" and that his new poem was "G. R. Sims at best."[65] At the same time, he recognized an older tradition of literary balladry, invoked by the Pre-Raphaelite writers whom he admired, and exemplified by Samuel Taylor Coleridge's "Rime of the Ancient Mariner" (whose influence, along with that of Thomas Hood's "Dream of Eugene Aram," is detectable in Wilde's ballad). One of the first books he requested when his jailers permitted him wider access was Thomas Percy's *Reliques,* the collection of ancient English ballads and songs, first published in 1765, that had inspired Coleridge a century before Wilde wrote. Although Wilde clearly wanted the poem to speak to his contemporaries of the horrors of prison life, *The Ballad of Reading Gaol* also represents Wilde's effort to write himself into an ancient and venerable literary tradition.

Given Wilde's successes in drama and prose, it is easy to forget that he began his career hoping to leave his mark on English-language poetry. With *The Ballad,* he closed his career leaving exactly such a mark. Although he published the poem under the pseudonym of his Reading Prison cell number, "C. 3. 3."—"It would be better . . . to publish . . . without my name," he told his publisher, Leonard Smithers, "I see it is my name that terrifies"—his contemporaries immediately saw through the pseudonym. The work was proclaimed "a remarkable addition to contemporary poetry," "a very beautiful, very powerful, perhaps a great poem," and the most sincere, realistic, and moving of all Wilde's works.[66] "Literature, to be of the finest quality, must come from the heart as well as the head, must be emotionally human as well as a brilliant thinking," the poet and critic Arthur Symons declared in an astute review for the *Saturday Review.*[67] For Symons *The Ballad* was the work in which Wilde best realized an "extraordinary talent" that had previously little concerned itself with matters of common experience and dwelt "so fantastically alone in a region of intellectual abstractions."[68] Even Wilde's severest literary enemy, the poet W. E. Henley, was forced to admit that parts of *The Ballad* were "instinct and vigorous with veracity" and that "sincerity, veracity, vision even, have their part."[69] In later generations, the poem elicited high praise from, among others, André Maurois, Albert Camus, W. B. Yeats, John Cowper Powys, and Jorge Luis Borges.

Although Wilde self-consciously invoked literary tradition and the ballad form, *The Ballad* is more than the sum of its rather obvious influences. It is a hybrid production, simultaneously personal and literary, combining elements of formal balladry, plangent lyricism, grim realism, and incisive political commentary. Outwardly the poem is focused on, and dedicated to the memory of, Charles Thomas Wooldridge, a murderer and fellow prisoner of Wilde's who was executed at Reading in July 1896. But Wooldridge is a symbolic reflection of Wilde himself, and the poem is at once an eloquent expression of Wilde's own suffering, a defiant statement of his solidarity with other "outcast men," a meditation on the human propensity to inflict pain and violence on those we love ("all men kill the thing they love," Wilde proclaims in the central refrain [p. 371 below]), and above all an indictment of the pitiless and hypocritical criminal-justice system that had imprisoned Wilde. It was a fitting publication with which to end his literary career, and it fulfilled his ambition "to do beautiful work and speak to the world again on an instrument that has . . . gained other strings, and become wider in possibility of range and effect."[70] Within three years of *The Ballad*'s release, Wilde would be dead. Along with the majestic and all-too-human *De Profundis,* it is among the greatest of all his writings.

NOTES

1. The history of the decriminalization of male same-sex relations in the United Kingdom is complex. The 1885 statute against gross indecency was replaced by an almost identical statute in the Sexual Offences Act of 1956. Sex acts between adult men were partially decriminalized in England and Wales by the Sexual Offences Act of 1967, but only for men over the age of twenty-one, an age of consent five years higher than that legislated for heterosexual acts. The military and merchant navy were excluded from this partial decriminalization and "gross indecency" remained a crime for another thirty-six years. As with the English and Welsh legislation of 1967, sex acts between men were partially decriminalized in Scotland and Northern Ireland in 1980 and 1982 respectively, although again with important exclusions and a high age of consent. The age of consent was not equalized until passage of the Sexual Offences (Amendment) Act of 2000, and the crime of gross indecency between men was not repealed until the Sexual Offences Act of 2003.

2. For details of Wilde's trials, see Joseph Bristow, *Oscar Wilde on Trial: The Criminal Proceedings* (New Haven, CT: Yale University Press, forthcoming);

The Real Trial of Oscar Wilde, intro. and commentary by Merlin Holland (New York: Fourth Estate, 2003); and H. Montgomery Hyde, *The Trials of Oscar Wilde,* 2nd ed. (1962; repr., New York: Dover, 1973). For a modern analysis, see Michael S. Foldy, *The Trials of Oscar Wilde: Deviance, Morality, and Late-Victorian Society* (New Haven, CT: Yale University Press, 1997). It has long been suspected that the British government's relentless prosecution of Wilde was motivated by politics or personal vendetta. Some of the witnesses who testified against him were of dubious character and may have been coerced or paid for giving evidence. During the first criminal trial, one witness, Freddie Atkins, was shown to have perjured himself in the dock, while another accuser, Alfred Wood, was shown to have blackmailed Wilde. For the tainting of key witnesses, see Holland, introduction to *The Real Trial of Oscar Wilde,* xxxvii.

3. Sean McConville, *English Local Prisons 1860–1900: Next Only to Death* (London: Routledge, 1995), 187; Sean McConville, "The Victorian Prison: England 1865–1965," in *The Oxford History of the Prison,* ed. N. Morris and D. J. Rothman (New York: Oxford University Press, 1995), 147. Many of the prisons built to facilitate the harsh regime under which Wilde was punished are still in use today, and as McConville observes, twentieth- and twenty-first-century imprisonment in England "has been marked by a tenacious Victorian inheritance" ("The Victorian Prison," 154).

4. David Nicolson and Richard Brayn, Report to the Under-Secretary of State at the Home Office, 29 October 1895, quoted in H. Montgomery Hyde, *Oscar Wilde: The Aftermath* (New York; Farrar Strauss, 1963), 37; also in Ashley H. Robins, *Oscar Wilde: The Great Drama of His Life* (Brighton, UK: Sussex Academic, 2011), 44.

5. Under Victorian law, Wilde's wife was unlikely to secure a divorce only on the grounds of his gross indecency and bankruptcy. To succeed she needed to prove that Wilde had committed sodomy, an offence with which he had never been charged and for which an entirely new criminal prosecution would be likely.

6. *The Complete Letters of Oscar Wilde,* ed. Merlin Holland and Rupert Hart-Davis (New York: Henry Holt, 2000), 821, hereafter cited in notes as *CL.*

7. Frank Harris, *Oscar Wilde, His Life and Confessions* (1916), repr. as *Oscar Wilde* (New York: Dorset, 1989), 197.

8. [Thomas Martin], "The Poet in Prison" (1906), repr. in *Oscar Wilde: Interviews and Recollections,* ed. E. H. Mikhail, 2 vols. (London: Macmillan, 1979), 2:334. See too the remark with which Nicolson and Brayn prefaced their report (n. 4 above): Wilde "does not appear to sleep very well at night" (quoted in Hyde, *Oscar Wilde: The Aftermath,* 36, and in Robins, *Oscar Wilde: The Great Drama of His Life,* 43).

9. See Ashley H. Robins and Merlin Holland, "The Enigmatic Illness and Death of Constance, Wife of Oscar Wilde," *The Lancet* 385, no. 9962 (3–9 January 2015).

10. *CL* 803. In the end, Wilde was transferred on 18 May 1897 by train to Pentonville Prison, from which he was released early the following morning. This time his transfer, like his release, was handled discreetly and humanely.

11. *CL* 983.

12. [Martin], "The Poet in Prison," 333–34.

13. "In the Depths" (1905), repr. in *Oscar Wilde: Interviews and Recollections,* ed. Mikhail, 2:328.

14. Ibid. For Wilde's infractions of prison regulations, see also Harris, *Oscar Wilde,* 203.

15. Wilfred H. Chesson, "A Reminiscence of 1898," *The Bookman* (1911), repr. in *Oscar Wilde: Interviews and Recollections,* ed. Mikhail, 2:376.

16. Hyde, *Oscar Wilde: The Aftermath,* 42.

17. In his capacity as editor of the *Fortnightly Review,* Harris published Wilde's "Pen, Pencil and Poison" (1889), "The Soul of Man under Socialism" (1891), "A Preface to *Dorian Gray*" (1891), and "Poems in Prose" (1894). After he became owner and editor of the *Saturday Review* in late 1894, Harris also published Wilde's "A Few Maxims for the Instruction of the Over-educated" (1894). The *Saturday Review* would be one of the first publications to which a review copy of *The Ballad of Reading Gaol* was sent in 1898.

18. Wilde would later qualify his assertion that his offenses were "diseases to be cured by a physician, rather than crimes to be punished by a judge," saying "they are maladies for physicians to cure, *if they should be cured*" (emphasis added; see p. 127 below).

19. Ruggles-Brise told Harris that Wilde could not be released early, because he had continually breached prison regulations (Harris, *Oscar Wilde*, 202–3). In any event, the historian Sean McConville writes, "A man or a woman sentenced to two years imprisonment served the entire sentence, no matter how good his or her conduct" ("The Victorian Prison," 150).

20. Evelyn Ruggles-Brise, "Instructions Sent to Governor, Reading Prison, in the Case of Oscar Wilde," 27 July 1896, printed in Hyde, *Oscar Wilde: The Aftermath*, 77–78.

21. Chesson, "A Reminiscence of 1898," 376.

22. Robins, *Oscar Wilde: The Great Drama of His Life*, 63.

23. *CL* 666.

24. "I looked forward to those morning talks [and] always allowed Wilde to stay the full quarter of an hour to which a prisoner was entitled . . . or rather I kept him the full time. For it was a pleasure to me" ("T. M." [Thomas Martin?], quoted in the *Manchester Guardian*, 13 October 1914, 5).

25. *CL* 826.

26. The Prison Commission set four conditions on Wilde's allowance of writing materials: that "no communication [be] made to outside persons otherwise than consistently with the ordinary rules"; that "use is not made of writing materials to such a degree as to interfere with [Wilde's] ordinary prison occupation"; that "all writing materials . . . be withdrawn at locking up and all written matter . . . be subject to your inspection"; and that "no improper use [be] made of this privilege" (Ruggles-Brise, "Instructions Sent to Governor, Reading Prison," in Hyde, *Oscar Wilde: The Aftermath*, 77).

27. *CL* 544.

28. *CL* 646.

29. *CL* 729.

30. Regenia Gagnier, *Idylls of the Marketplace: Oscar Wilde and the Victorian Public* (Palo Alto, CA: Stanford University Press, 1986), 180.

31. In his haste and spleen, Queensberry misspelled "sodomite."

32. Although the bulk of the letter was written between January and March 1897, Ian Small posits that composition began as early as September 1896. See his introduction to *De Profundis; "Epistola: In Carcere et Vinculis,"* ed. Ian Small, vol. 2 of *The Complete Works of Oscar Wilde* (Oxford: Oxford University Press, 2005), 10.

33. Ibid., 13. Small also suggests that Wilde's prison manuscript might more properly be thought of as the synthesis of multiple documents, only one of which was strictly speaking a letter to Alfred Douglas.

34. *CL* 678.

35. Ibid.

36. Page 175 below. The other turning point, he writes, was his arrival at Oxford University in 1874.

37. *CL* 948, 950.

38. For a masterful account of Renan's influence on *De Profundis,* as Wilde's attempt to write a secular "gospel of his own," see Stephen Arata, "Oscar Wilde and Jesus Christ," in *Wilde Writings: Contextual Conditions,* ed. Joseph Bristow (Toronto: University of Toronto Press, 2003), 268. Wilde's thoughts about Christ in *De Profundis* also reflect his reading of the Greek New Testament, which he requested in July 1896 but which arrived five months later. See his comment: "Of late I have been studying the four prose-poems about Christ with some diligence. . . . [E]very morning, after I have cleaned my cell and polished my tins, I read a little of the Gospels, a dozen verses taken by chance anywhere. It is a delightful way of opening the day. . . . And while in reading the Gospels . . . I see this continual assertion of the imagination as the basis of all spiritual and material life, I see also that to Christ imagination was simply a form of Love" (pp. 215 and 217).

39. [Martin], "The Poet in Prison," 335.

40. R. B. Cunninghame Graham, "Vox Clamantis," signed rev. of *De Profundis* (1905), repr. in *Oscar Wilde: The Critical Heritage,* ed. Karl Beckson (London: Routledge and Kegan Paul, 1970), 256.

41. Gagnier, *Idylls of the Marketplace,* 193.

42. Byron, "Childe Harold's Pilgrimage," in *Byron,* ed. Jerome McGann (Oxford: Oxford University Press, 1986), Canto 4, ll. 1226–233, p. 187.

43. "Letters to Robert Ross on *De Profundis,*" in *Oscar Wilde: The Critical Heritage,* ed. Beckson, 243–44.

44. E. V. Lucas, unsigned rev. of *De Profundis* (1905), in *Oscar Wilde: The Critical Heritage,* ed. Beckson, 245.

45. Ibid., 247–48.

46. Max Beerbohm, "A Lord of Language," signed rev. of *De Profundis* (1905), rpt. in *Oscar Wilde: The Critical Heritage,* ed. Beckson, 249–50.

47. *CL* 666.

48. *CL* 780.

49. Small, introduction to *De Profundis; "Epistola: In Carcere et Vinculis,"* ed. Small, 9, 13.

50. *CL* 780.

51. *CL* 781.

52. *CL* 780, 782. Wilde named no fewer than seven individuals besides Douglas whom he wished to read copies of the manuscript in full or in part: Robert Ross, More Adey, Adela Schuster (whom Wilde identifies only as "the Lady of Wimbledon"), Frankie Forbes-Robertston, Eric Forbes-Robertson, Arthur Clifton, and Aleck Ross.

53. *CL* 782.

54. Small, Introduction to *De Profundis; "Epistola: In Carcere et Vinculis,"* ed. Small, 3.

55. The Prison Commission had refused permission for Wilde to send the manuscript by mail from prison, so he gave it to Robert Ross in person upon his arrival in Dieppe on 20 May 1897. Alfred Douglas first became aware of the manuscript's existence in 1912, when Arthur Ransome alluded to it in his book *Oscar Wilde: A Critical Study*. Thereafter the fate of the manuscript became a bone of bitter contention between Douglas and Ross, and Douglas sought legal redress on many occasions. In 1913 Douglas unsuccessfully sued Ransome for libel, whereupon *De Profundis* was read aloud in court and Ross testified that he had years earlier sent Douglas a typed copy of it. Douglas, who lost his case, admitted in court that Ross had sent him a typed copy along with an accompanying note but added that he had thrown it into the fire unread. See Laura Lee, *Oscar's Ghost: The Battle for Oscar Wilde's Legacy* (Stroud, UK: Amberley, 2017), 242–58. Subsequently, however, Douglas maintained that Ross had not sent him a copy and that the original manuscript belonged to himself by rights. In his 1929 autobiography, Douglas does allow that Ross sent him a letter containing extracts from remarks Wilde allegedly made about him in jail. But he says this letter arrived some time before Wilde's release, so it cannot have contained anything drawn directly from *De Profundis*—and that he tore it up in anger without reading it. See Douglas, *The Autobiography of Alfred Douglas* (London: Secker, 1929), 135.

56. See Lee, *Oscar's Ghost*, 9, 174ff.

57. *CL* 798.

58. *Children in Prison and Other Cruelties of Prison Life* (London: Murdoch, n.d.). According to a "Publisher's Note" serving as a foreword, this pamphlet appeared in February 1898, when the movement for prison reform that resulted in the 1898 Prisons Act was reaching its peak.

59. Shortly before his release, Wilde requested that he be sent a copy of a celebrated article "on prisons" by William D. Morrison, together with Du Cane's published reply, and a number of books written or edited by Morrison in his capacity as general editor of T. Fisher Unwin's Criminology Series, the first series of books devoted to criminology in English publishing. See CL 793. Wilde doesn't specify the title of the article by Morrison, but he probably meant "The Increase of Crime," *Nineteenth Century* 31 (1892): 950–57. Du

Cane's reply was "The Decrease of Crime," *Nineteenth Century* 33 (1893): 480–92.

60. *CL* 890.

61. *CL* 865; emphasis in original.

62. *CL* 1080.

63. *CL* 1063.

64. *CL* 1019.

65. *CL* 916, 992. By "out-Henleying Kipling," Wilde meant combining the grim realism of the poet William Ernest Henley—who had a real passion for what is horrible, ugly, or grotesque, Wilde once said—with the subject matter and form of Rudyard Kipling's "Danny Deever," from *Barrack-Room Ballads*.

66. *CL* 1011; unsigned rev. of *The Ballad of Reading Gaol, The Academy,* 26 February 1898, repr. in *Oscar Wilde: The Critical Heritage,* ed. Beckson, 212; *Yale Literary Magazine* 63, no. 9 (June 1898): 443.

67. Arthur Symons, signed rev. of *The Ballad of Reading Gaol, Saturday Review,* 12 March 1898, repr. in *Oscar Wilde: The Critical Heritage,* ed. Beckson, 221.

68. Ibid.

69. Henley, "De Profundis," unsigned rev. of *The Ballad of Reading Gaol, The Outlook,* 5 March 1898, rpt. in *Oscar Wilde: The Critical Heritage,* ed. Beckson, 214, 216.

70. *CL* 882.

A Note on the Texts

Oscar Wilde's prison writings are presented here in order of their composition, dates for which are given in the annotations. Wilde's July 1896 clemency petition was never intended for publication, so the text printed here is based on the original prison manuscript, now housed in the United Kingdom's National Archives and published in facsimile in 1997 by the United Kingdom's Public Record Office. Likewise, scholars question whether *De Profundis*—which remained untitled and unpublished in Wilde's lifetime—was ever meant for publication. To be sure, Wilde's literary executor Robert Ross oversaw a series of editions published under the title *De Profundis* in the decade or so after Wilde's death, but these were all incomplete, error-filled, and—with the significant exception of the extremely rare *Suppressed Portion of "De Profundis,"* published in New York in 1913 by Paul R. Reynolds in an edition of just fifteen copies—heavily redacted so as to disguise the fact that the text originated in a long letter to Lord Alfred Douglas. The authority on which Ross sanctioned these changes is questionable. Like the text of Wilde's clemency petition, the text of *De Profundis* given here is based on the original prison manuscript, composed in holograph on twenty folio sheets of what Wilde described as "loathsome" ruled blue prison notepaper, each embossed in blind on the front with the royal coat of arms and folded in two to make eighty pages in total. Since 1909 this manuscript has been housed in the British Library. Readers interested in studying it should consult *De Profundis: A Facsimile,* intro. Merlin Holland (London: British Library, 2000).

By contrast with the clemency petition and *De Profundis,* the texts of Wilde's two letters to the *Daily Chronicle* (neither of which survive in manuscript) and of *The Ballad of Reading Gaol* (which partially survives in manuscript, as well as in Wilde's corrected typescript and page proofs) are based on the earliest published versions. Wilde revised *The Ballad* meticulously in the weeks and months before its publication by Leonard Smithers in London in February 1898. The first edition sold out within days, was widely reviewed, and clearly bears the stamp of Wilde's personal authority. After distributing copies to friends and acquaintances, Wilde made a few further small changes for the second edition, the most significant of which are registered in the present edition's annotations.

A word is in order about my editorial handling and titling of *De Profundis*. Strict conditions were placed on Wilde's composition of the letter, which he was allowed to undertake in his cell during the last six months or so of his sentence as a special favor by the prison authorities. Reading Prison's governor, James O. Nelson, told his superiors that Wilde was allowed just one sheet of paper per day—that "each sheet was carefully numbered before being issued and withdrawn each evening at locking."[1] Although doubt has been cast on the truth of Nelson's assertion, Wilde's manuscript certainly registers what the scholar Regenia Gagnier calls "the material matrix of prison space and time—that is, confined, segmented space and timelessness."[2] Wilde himself describes his manuscript as "blotted in many places with tears, in some with the signs of passion or pain" (p. 265 below). His holograph script is in places scarred by self-erasure, corrections, and blots, crammed tightly into every inch of the cheap notepaper on which it is written. (Besides giving evidence of the constraints under which Wilde wrote, these markings also indicate that he revised the text meticulously, and Wilde's most interesting or revealing revisions are noted in my annotations.) While this makes his orthography and punctuation questionable at times, it has special implications for the letter's paragraphing, since Wilde could not afford the luxury of large line indentations and blank lines that writers with an abundance of paper possess. Where unfettered writers might incorporate paragraph breaks, for instance, he resorts on occasion to a string of ellipsis points. For this reason, while I have by and large followed Wilde's own spelling, capitalization, and punctuation insofar as they are decipherable, I have deleted ellipsis points and inserted paragraph breaks in many places, to make the text more readable and to make the sequencing of Wilde's ideas clearer. In a small handful of instances, moreover, where sense demands the insertion of additional punctuation, a missing letter, or in one case the missing word "I," I have inserted it, indicating such instances in the text with square brackets ("[ ]"). I have also made Wilde's use of quotation marks and italics more consistent.

Although Wilde died in 1900, it is only in the last sixty years that an edition like this has been possible. As explained in the Introduction, Wilde began *De Profundis* in late 1896 as a letter to his lover Lord Alfred Douglas, the youngest son of the Marquess of Queensberry. But his understanding of his text changed in the course of composition, and he never sent it to its addressee. On the day after his release, in May 1897, he gave the manuscript instead to his loyal friend and ex-lover Robert Ross, telling Ross that he wished him to be his literary executor and "to have complete control over my plays, books, and papers." To be sure, Wilde asked Ross to send the manuscript to Douglas after first having a typed copy made "on good paper such as is used for plays." Nonetheless he realized that the letter might one day restore honor to a name that had become "the shield and catspaw of the Queensberrys," and for this reason he gave Ross detailed instructions about passages "good and nice in intention" to be copied in typescript and sent to friends "interested to know something of what is happening to my soul." "Some day the truth will have to be known," he told Ross, "not necessarily in my lifetime or in Douglas's: but I am not prepared to sit in the grotesque pillory they put me into, for all time." Wilde even playfully gave his letter a title, telling Ross that it was "an Encyclical Letter, and as the Bulls of the Holy Father are named from their opening words, it may be spoken of as the *Epistola: In Carcere et Vinculis* [Letter: In Prison and in Chains]."[3]

But Ross did not send the manuscript to Douglas, and after the latter learned of its existence twelve years after Wilde's death, he (perhaps disingenuously) disputed Ross's claim that he had sent Douglas a typed copy instead.[4] As importantly, in 1905, five years after Wilde's death, Ross used Wilde's instructions about extracting passages "good and nice in intention" as a blueprint for the first edition, for which he chose the title *De Profundis,* meaning "from the depths" (from Psalm 130), rather than the one Wilde had playfully suggested. Ross knew that he could not publish the entire letter—that Douglas and the Queensberry family would immediately sue for defamation should he do so. For this reason, after publishing a further, slightly expanded edition in 1908 as well as sanctioning the publication in Germany of a still fuller selection from the manuscript,[5] Ross in 1909 donated the manuscript to the British Library with instructions that it remain sealed for fifty years. He knew that after this time span Douglas and others named in the manuscript would be dead.

Matters might have rested there had not Arthur Ransome vaguely alluded to the manuscript's existence and the personal recriminations it contained in his 1912 book *Oscar Wilde: A Critical Study.* Ransome's information had been supplied by Ross, and when Douglas unwisely sued Ransome for libel after reading this study, Ross arranged for the so-called "suppressed portion" of the manuscript to be read out loud in court, whereupon it was also widely quoted in the press. Douglas, understandably, lost his case and thereafter became deeply embittered about his treatment at the hands of both Ross and Wilde.[6]

The manuscript itself remained under lock and key until 1 January 1960, as Ross had requested. But in 1949, four years after Douglas's death and thirty-one years after Ross's, Wilde's youngest son, Vyvyan Holland, published what his publishers described as *De Profundis: The Complete Text.* Apart from the rare New York edition of 1913, Holland's was the first English-language edition to identify Douglas as the letter's addressee, to reproduce the bulk of Wilde's recriminations against him, and to allude to Wilde's own playfully suggested title: according to Holland's subtitle, his edition represented "the first complete and accurate version of 'Epistola: In Carcere et Vinculis' the last prose work in English of Oscar Wilde." It was used as a "base-text" for the controversial dual-text edition that Ian Small edited in 2005 under the title *De Profundis; "Epistola: In Carcere et Vinculis,"* in which Small reproduced Holland's text alongside Ross's shorter, expurgated text of 1905. Holland's 1949 edition was based not on the original manuscript, however, but on a now-lost typewritten transcription, overseen by Robert Ross after Wilde had left jail (one of a number of typewritten transcriptions that Ross authorized in the years around Wilde's death), and it is neither as complete nor as accurate as Holland's subtitle claims.

The incompleteness of Holland's text was revealed in 1962, two years after the manuscript was finally unsealed, when Rupert Hart-Davis published the first complete and accurate printed transcription of Wilde's letter in his compendious *Letters of Oscar Wilde.* Understandably perhaps, Hart-Davis treated *De Profundis* as one item of personal correspondence among many, although he carefully outlined the letter's fraught early history in a footnote. He left Wilde's letter untitled, heading it instead "To Lord Alfred Douglas." This remained the case in *The Complete Letters of Oscar Wilde,* the expanded edition of Wilde's correspondence that Hart-Davis edited jointly with Merlin Holland in 2000, where the few typographical errors that had crept into Hart-Davis's earlier transcription were silently corrected.[7]

But *De Profundis* is far more than a personal letter and is today widely viewed as one of its author's most important works. Despite the plethora of twentieth- and twenty-first-century editions, however, there exists no certainty that Wilde ever intended publishing *De Profundis*—and also a strong likelihood that parts of the letter were only ever meant by their author for the eyes of a very select group of friends. Wilde's joking comment that it is an "Encyclical letter" and "may be spoken of as the *Epistola: In Carcere et Vinculis*" was made in reference to the selections that he wanted Ross to send to friends "interested to know something of . . . my soul," in particular two "sweet women" whom he identified as Frankie

Forbes-Robertson and Adela Schuster: "It is a sort of message or letter I send them," he explained, "but of course it is a strict secret from the general world."[8] Given this aura of secrecy and selectiveness, as well as Wilde's tongue-in-cheek spirit, Wilde's own title cannot be seriously entertained as appropriate for the full manuscript reproduced here. Ross's chosen title, *De Profundis,* cannot be supported on strictly authorial grounds either. But it spawned a century of editions, all claiming to represent Wilde's work more fully and accurately than those that had come before, and I have drawn heavily from this tradition in my own editing and annotations. For this reason a decision has been made to retain Ross's title here. Wilde himself left the manuscript untitled, of course. But if a literary work consists of the aggregate of the texts by which it comes to be known, as editorial theorists propose,[9] we might say that *De Profundis* titles the *work* that is incarnated in the *text* of the letter reproduced in the present edition.

I owe a large debt to previous editors and commentators, particularly Ian Small, whose own meticulous research and commentary on *De Profundis,* frequently cited in my Introduction and annotations, remain invaluable; also to Merlin Holland, whose work on *De Profundis* has profoundly affected my own; to Rupert Hart-Davis, who was the first to edit and annotate the full manuscript text and from whose own annotations I have occasionally drawn; and to Karl Beckson and Bobby Fong, whose edition of Wilde's *Poems and Poems in Prose* should loom large on the shelf of any serious student of *The Ballad of Reading Gaol.*

NOTES

1. Nelson, facsimile of letter to the Prison Commission, 4 April 1897, in *Oscar Wilde, Trial and Punishment: 1895–1897* (London: Public Record Office, 1997).

2. Regenia Gagnier, *Idylls of the Marketplace: Oscar Wilde and the Victorian Public* (Palo Alto, CA: Stanford University Press, 1986), 179. For doubt about

the truth of Nelson's assertion, see Nicholas Frankel, *Oscar Wilde: The Unrepentant Years* (Cambridge, MA: Harvard University Press, 2017), 69–70.

3. *The Complete Letters of Oscar Wilde,* ed. Merlin Holland and Rupert Hart-Davis (New York: Henry Holt, 2000), 780–82.

4. During the Ransome trial, Ross testified that he had years previously sent Douglas a typescript of Wilde's letter. Although the latter conceded that Ross had indeed sent him a typescript containing remarks purportedly made by Wilde about him, Douglas later disputed that this was a transcript of *De Profundis.* See Ian Small, introduction to *De Profundis; "Epistola: In Carcere et Vinculis,"* ed. Ian Small, vol. 2 of *The Complete Works of Oscar Wilde* (Oxford: Oxford University Press, 2005), 16. Certainly if Ross sent him a typescript of *De Profundis* in 1897, Douglas failed to read it. As certainly, Douglas failed to recognize that the 1905 edition of *De Profundis* overseen by Ross—which Douglas reviewed in print for *The Motorist and Traveller*—was based on a letter to himself.

5. See Horst Schroeder, "The Importance of Reading Max," *The Wildean: A Journal of Oscar Wilde Studies* 28 (January 2006): 79–83.

6. See Laura Lee, *Oscar's Ghost: The Battle for Oscar Wilde's Legacy* (Stroud, UK: Amberley, 2017).

7. *The Complete Letters* introduced one or two transcription errors of its own, notably the omission of the sentence "We are doomed to be solitary while our sons still live" on p. 165 below. With Merlin Holland's generous assistance, these errors have been silently corrected in the present edition.

8. *The Complete Letters,* ed. Holland and Hart-Davis, 780.

9. See James McLaverty's answer to the question "If the Mona Lisa is in the Louvre, where is *Hamlet?,"* in his "The Mode of Existence of Literary Works of Art," *Studies in Bibliography* 37 (1984): 82–105; also Jerome McGann, "The Text, the Poem, and the Problem of Historical Method," in his *The Beauty of Inflections: Literary Investigations in Historical Method and Theory* (Oxford: Clarendon, 1986); and Peter Shillingsburg, "How Literary Works Exist," in his *Textuality and Knowledge* (University Park: Pennsylvania State University Press, 2017), 115–33.

* Composed on official paper headed "PETITION" in Reading Prison on
2 July 1896. The heading, address ("To the Right Honourable..."), and
opening phrase are part of the official language printed on the form itself,
but everything after "SHEWETH" was handwritten by Wilde. Victorian
prisoners were entitled to appeal to the home secretary, and remission of
part of a prisoner's sentence for good behavior was an accepted element of
the late-Victorian penal code: the 1898 Prisons Act formally authorized the
use of remission, and it proved to be an effective means of controlling
prisoner behavior. However, the chairman of the Prison Commission told
Frank Harris that Wilde couldn't possibly be granted a remission since
"good conduct meant, in prison parlance, absence of punishment, and
Oscar had been punished pretty often. Of course, his offenses were minor
offences... he was often talking, and he was often late in the morning; his
cell was not so well kept as it might be, and so forth.... [Y]et a certificate of
'good conduct' depended on such trifling observances" (Frank Harris,
Oscar Wilde [1916; repr., New York: Dorset, 1989], 203). Wilde's petition
would not have succeeded even had his behavior been perfect. Before 1898
remissions were granted only to prisoners serving sentences of more than
two years in one of the large government-run convict prisons, whereas
"people sentenced to imprisonment in a local prison... did not have the
inducement and advantage of a remission in sentence. A man or a woman
sentenced to two years imprisonment served the entire sentence, no
matter how good his or her conduct" (Sean McConville, "The Victorian
Prison: England 1865–1965," in *The Oxford History of the Prison*, ed. N. Morris
and D. J. Rothman [New York: Oxford University Press, 1995], 150). For the
distinction between "convict prisons" and "local prisons," see p. 306, n.17
below.

1. Wilde here shows his awareness of Richard Krafft-Ebing's important
book *Psychopathia Sexualis*, published in German in 1886 and first translated into English in 1892. Krafft-Ebing's work—which introduced the word
"homosexual" into the English language and became the leading medico-
legal textual authority on sexual pathology—had a profound influence on
the work of the British sexologists Havelock Ellis, John Addington Symonds,
and Edward Carpenter, the latter two of whom Wilde is known to have
read enthusiastically. Wilde is correct that France and Italy (where he was
to live after his release from prison) had decriminalized homosexual acts,

Clemency Petition to the Home Secretary*

2 July 1896

To the Right Honourable Her Majesty's Principal Secretary of State for the Home Department.

THE PETITION OF THE ABOVE-NAMED PRISONER HUMBLY SHEWETH that he does not desire to attempt to palliate in any way the terrible offences of which he was rightly found guilty, but to point out that such offences are forms of sexual madness and are recognised as such not merely by modern pathological science but by much modern legislation, notably in France, Austria, and Italy, where the laws affecting these misdemeanors have been repealed, on the ground that they are diseases to be cured by a physician, rather than crimes to be punished by a judge.[1] In the works of eminent men of science such as Lombroso and Nordau, to take merely two instances out of many, this is specially insisted on with reference to the intimate connection between madness and the literary and artistic temperament, Professor Nordau in his book on "Degenerescence" published in 1894 having devoted an entire chapter to the petitioner as a specially typical example of this fatal law.[2] The petitioner is now keenly conscious of the fact that while the three years preceding his arrest were from the intellectual point of view the most brilliant years of his life (four plays from his pen having been produced on the stage with immense success, and played not merely in England, America, and Australia, but in almost every European capital, and many books that excited much

the former as early as 1791, the latter as recently as 1889. The Austrian Penal Code of 1852 states that "A person is not punishable if because of a disturbed consciousness, a pathological disturbance of the mind, or a weak mind, he or she was, at the time of the deed, unable to understand the wrong of the deed or was unable to act upon this insight" (quoted in Robert D. Tobin, *Peripheral Desires: The German Discovery of Sex* [Philadelphia: University of Pennsylvania Press, 2015], 116). This meant that a psychiatric assessment became an important potential defense for those accused of criminal activity: "by being called upon to determine whether the pathological disturbance of mental activity was such that it precluded the free exercise of will, physicians came to be major arbiters of culpability, blameworthiness, and guilt in German and Austrian law in the nineteenth century—particularly in questions of sexuality" (Tobin, *Peripheral Desires*, 116).

Although Wilde describes his offenses as "diseases to be cured by a physician, rather than crimes to be punished by a judge," he would later say that "sins of the flesh are nothing. They are maladies for physicians to cure, *if they should be cured*" (p. 127 below; emphasis added), and also "the fact that I am . . . a pathological problem in the eyes of German scientists is only interesting to German scientists" (*CL* 1006).

2. Cesare Lombroso (1835–1909), Italian physician and criminologist, and Max Nordau (1849–1923), Austro-Hungarian physician and cultural critic. In *The Man of Genius* (1888; first English translation 1891) and *Degeneration* (1892; first French translation 1894; first English translation 1895), Lombroso and Nordau respectively drew connections between madness, or "moral insanity," and artistic genius. Nordau, for instance, writes that "the physician . . . recognises at a glance, in the *fin de siècle* disposition, in the tendencies of contemporary art and poetry, in the life and conduct of the men who write mystic, symbolic, and 'decadent' works, . . . two well-defined conditions of disease with which he is familiar" (*Degeneration*, trans. unknown [New York: Appleton, 1895], 15). Nordau—who dedicated *Degeneration* to Lombroso—attacked Wilde at length in order to demonstrate these assertions. Wilde probably read Nordau's work in French, since he refers to it by the title and publication date of the first French translation. See also p. 137 below, where Wilde cites Lombroso in support of the notion that "along with genius goes often a curious perversity of passion and desire."

interest at home and abroad having been published), still that during the entire time he was suffering from the most horrible form of erotomania,[3] which made him forget his wife and children, his high social position in London and Paris, his European distinction as an artist, the honour of his name and family, his very humanity itself, and left him the helpless prey of the most revolting passions, and of a gang of people who for their own profit ministered to them, and then drove him to his hideous ruin.

It is under the ceaseless apprehension lest this insanity, that displayed itself in monstrous sexual perversion before, may now extend to the entire nature and intellect, that the petitioner writes this appeal which he earnestly entreats may be at once considered. Horrible as all actual madness is, the terror of madness is no less appalling, and no less ruinous to the soul.[4]

For more than thirteen dreadful months now, the petitioner has been subject to the fearful system of solitary cellular confinement:[5] without human intercourse of any kind; without writing materials whose use might help to distract the mind: without suitable or sufficient books, so essential to any literary man, so vital for the preservation of mental balance: condemned to absolute silence: cut off from all knowledge of the external world and the movements of life: leading an existence composed of bitter degradations and terrible hardships, hideous in its recurring monotony of dreary task and sickening privation: the despair and misery of this lonely and wretched life having been intensified beyond words by the death of his mother, Lady Wilde,[6] to whom he was deeply attached, as well as by the contemplation of the ruin he has brought on his young wife and his two children.

By special permission the petitioner is allowed two books a week to read: but the prison library is extremely small and poor: it hardly contains a score of books suitable for an educated man: the books kindly added at the prisoner's request he has read and re-read till they have become almost meaningless to him:[7] he is practically left without anything to read: the world of ideas, as the actual world, is closed to him: he is

3. Melancholy or madness arising from passionate love (*Oxford English Dictionary*), classified in 1874 as "a species of insanity" and "a disease of the central nervous system, characterized by the existence of erotic desires without the power of accomplishing them" (W. H. Van Buren and E. L. Keyes, *A Practical Treatise on the Surgical Diseases of the Genito-urinary Organs, including Syphilis* [1874; repr., New York: Appleton, 1876], 464). In 1861 the French politician and physician Ulysse Trélat differentiated *erotomania*, as a psychological and emotional delusion, from *nympho-mania* and *satyromania*, "which arise from the reproductive organs and are a perversion of the genital instinct; they are exclusively about the pleasures of the flesh and lead to licentiousness and shameful behaviour. *Erotomania*, on the contrary, is love felt for someone real or imagined or for an inani-mate object, which is both pure, chaste and disinterested but also excessive and immoderate. In this mental disorder, the amorous ideas are fixed, dominant and often exclusive" (Trélat, *La Folie Lucide*, quoted in G. E. Berrios and N. Kennedy, "Erotomania: A Conceptual History," *History of Psychiatry* 13 [2002]: 391).

4. Wilde's fear of insanity was real, and cases of prisoners going insane were common in his day, as his letter on the case of Warder Martin (see p. 293 below) indicates. During a visit from Robert Ross and Robert Sherard in May 1896, Wilde cried the whole time and asked whether his "brain seemed all right" (Robert Ross, undated letter to More Adey [May 1896], in *Robert Ross, Friend of Friends*, ed. Margery Ross [London: Jonathan Cape, 1952], 40). Earlier, during his imprisonment at Pentonville and Wandsworth, the press had reported repeatedly that Wilde was going insane, whereupon an official inquiry was made into his mental health. Following receipt by the home secretary of Wilde's petition of July 1896, David Nicolson, the Lord Chancellor's Visitor in Lunacy, who had examined Wilde at Wandsworth the previous October, reasserted that "there is no indica-tion of insanity or approaching insanity" and that it was "hardly necessary to call in further medical assistance at present" (quoted in Ashley Robins, *Oscar Wilde: The Great Drama of His Life* [Brighton, UK: Sussex Academic, 2011], 60).

5. Wilde refers to the so-called separate system, introduced into Victorian prisons in the 1840s, mandating that prisoners each be confined in a

separate cell, where they were expected to remain silent and perform acts of hard labor, such as picking oakum or turning a crank, without contact or communication with other prisoners.

6. See p. 144, n.217 below. As Wilde writes in *De Profundis*, "My wife, at that time kind and gentle to me, rather than that I should hear the news from indifferent or alien lips, travelled, ill as she was, all the way from Genoa to England to break to me herself the tidings of so irreparable, so irredeemable a loss" (p. 147 below).

7. The special permission given Wilde to read two books per week was rendered useless by the limitations of Reading Prison's library. After visiting Wilde in Pentonville Prison in June 1895, the Liberal statesman Richard Haldane, Q.C., M.P., persuaded the Prison Commission to allow Wilde an allotment of some fifteen new books, including Augustine's *Confessions* and *De Civitate Dei*, Blaise Pascal's *Pensées*, John Henry Newman's *Apologia Pro Vita Sua* and *Grammar of Assent*, Theodor Mommsen's five-volume *History of Rome*, and multiple works by Walter Pater. No trace survives of the copies Haldane sent, but if these books accompanied Wilde to Reading Prison, they clearly numbered among those he had "read and re-read till they have become almost meaningless."

8. Wilde may be alluding here to a propensity to masturbate—considered by Victorians another form of sexual madness or depravity. In September 1895, the chaplain at Wandsworth, the sympathetic William D. Morrison, had written, "I fear from what I hear and see that perverse sexual practices are again getting the mastery over him." For more on Morrison and his claim of "perverse sexual practices," see Nicholas Frankel, *Oscar Wilde: The Unrepentant Years* (Cambridge, MA: Harvard University Press, 2017), 44–47.

deprived of everything that could soothe, distract, or heal a wounded and shaken mind: and horrible as all the physical privations of modern prison life are, they are as nothing compared to the entire privation of literature to one to whom Literature was once the first thing of life, the mode by which perfection could be realised, by which, and by which alone, the intellect could feel itself alive.

It is but natural that living in this silence, this solitude, this isolation from all human and humane influences, this tomb for those who are not yet dead, the petitioner should, day and night in every waking hour, be tortured by the fear of absolute and entire insanity. He is conscious that his mind, shut out artificially from all rational and intellectual interests, does nothing, and can do nothing, but brood on those forms of sexual perversity, those loathsome modes of erotomania, that have brought him from high place and noble distinction to the convict's cell and the common gaol. It is inevitable that it should do so. The mind is forced to think, and when it is deprived of the conditions necessary for healthy intellectual activity, such as books, writing materials, companionship, contact with the living world, and the like, it becomes, in the case of those who are suffering from sensual monomanias, the sure prey of morbid passions, and obscene fancies, and thoughts that defile, desecrate and destroy. Crimes may be forgotten or forgiven, but vices live on: they make their dwelling house in him who by horrible mischance or fate has become their victim: they are embedded in his flesh: they spread over him like a leprosy: they feed on him like a strange disease: at the end they become an essential part of the man: no remorse however poignant can drive them out: no tears however bitter can wash them away: and prison life, by its horrible isolation from all that could save a wretched soul, hands the victim over, like one bound hand and foot, to be possessed and polluted by the thoughts he most loathes and so cannot escape from.[8] For more than a year the petitioner's mind has borne this. It can bear it no longer. He is quite conscious of the approach of an insanity that will not be confined to one portion of the nature merely, but will extend over all alike, and his desire, his prayer is that his sentence may be remitted

now, so that he may be taken abroad by his friends and may put himself under medical care so that the sexual insanity from which he suffers may be cured. He knows only too well that his career as a dramatist and writer is ended, and his name blotted from the scroll of English Literature never to be replaced: that his children cannot bear that name again, and that an obscure life in some remote country is in store for him: he knows that, bankruptcy having come upon him, poverty of a most bitter kind awaits him, and that all the joy and beauty of existence is taken from him for ever: but at least in all his hopelessness he still clings to the hope that he will not have to pass directly from the common gaol to the common lunatic asylum. Dreadful as are the results of the prison system—a system so terrible that it hardens their hearts whose hearts it does not break, and brutalises those who have to carry it out no less than those who have to submit to it—yet at least amongst its aims is not the desire to wreck the human reason. Though it may not seek to make men better, yet it does not desire to drive them mad, and so, earnestly does the petitioner beg that he may be allowed to go forth while he has still some sanity left: while words have still a meaning, and books a message: while there is still some possibility that, by medical science and humane treatment, balance may be restored to a shaken mind and health given back to a nature that once knew purity: while there is still time to rid the temperament of a revolting madness and to make the soul, even for a brief space, clean. Most earnestly indeed does the petitioner beg the Home Secretary to take, if he so desires it, the opinion of any recognised medical authorities on what would be the inevitable result of solitary confinement in silence and isolation on one already suffering from sexual monomania of a terrible character.

The petitioner would also point out that while his bodily health is better in many respects here than it was at Wandsworth, where he was for two months in the hospital for absolute physical and mental collapse caused by hunger and insomnia, he has, since he has been in prison, almost entirely lost the hearing of his right ear through an abscess that has caused a perforation of the drum. The medical officer here has stated that

9. The date of the onset of Wilde's ear complaints is uncertain, but at some date before his imprisonment Wilde evidently consulted Sir William Dalby (1840–1918), an eminent U.K. otologist, presumably for a discharging right ear and incipient deafness. Dalby's assurance that with proper care there was no reason why Wilde should lose his hearing in the affected ear proved incorrect. The modern physicians Ashley Robins and Sean Sellars ("Oscar Wilde's Terminal Illness," *Lancet* 356 [2000]: 1841) contend that Wilde suffered from a cholesteatoma, a destructive form of chronic suppurative otitis media, requiring invasive surgery in the form of a radical mastoidectomy. By the time this surgery was eventually performed in October 1900, it was too late, and Wilde died one month later from meningoencephalitis as a result.

10. In his reaction to Wilde's allegations, the Reading Prison medical officer, Dr. Oliver Calley Maurice, reported, "It is perfectly true that he has a slight perforation of the drum of the right ear, but there is no evidence of mischief in the left, nor of any defect of vision" (quoted in Robins and Sellars, "Oscar Wilde's Terminal Illness," 1841). As Robins and Sellars write, Maurice "failed to comment on the discharge, the deafness, or on any treatment plan. It was a wholly unsatisfactory, almost contemptuous response to Wilde's grievances. . . . He did not institute the basic hygienic measures that might have brought some relief to his patient's discomfort and anguish. Little wonder that in a letter to the *Daily Chronicle* on prison reform (March 23, 1898) [see p. 373 below] Wilde stigmatised prison doctors as 'brutal in manner, coarse in temperament, and utterly indifferent to the health of the prisoners or their comfort.'" On 2 August 1896, on the recommendation of the prison Visiting Committee—and over the objection of Dr. Maurice—an external specialist, Dr. J. A. Price of Reading, was called in to evaluate Wilde's health. He recommended that the ear's discharge "may be improved by daily syringing . . . with dilute carbolic solution." This remedy at least kept the infection in abeyance, so much so that the following November, in a further unsuccessful appeal to the home secretary, Wilde could write that his ear, "that was in danger of total deafness, is now attended to daily."

he is unable to offer any assistance, and that the hearing must go entirely. The petitioner, however, feels sure that under the care of a specialist abroad his hearing might be preserved to him. He was assured by Sir William Dalby, the great aurist, that with proper care there was no reason at all why he should lose his hearing.[9] But though the abscess has been running now for the entire time of his imprisonment, and the hearing getting worse every week, nothing has been done in the way even of an attempted cure. The ear has been syringed on three occasions with plain water for the purpose of examination, that is all.[10] The petitioner is naturally apprehensive lest, as often happens, the other ear may be attacked in a similar way, and to the misery of a shattered and debilitated mind be added the horrors of complete deafness. His eyesight, of which like most men of letters he had always been obliged to take great care, has also suffered very much from the enforced living in a whitewashed cell with a flaring gas-jet at night: he is conscious of great weakness and pain in the nerves of the eyes, and objects even at a short distance become blurred. The bright daylight, when taking exercise in the prison-yard, often causes pain and distress to the optic nerve, and during the past four months the consciousness of failing eyesight has been a source of terrible anxiety, and should his imprisonment be continued, blindness and deafness may in all human probability be added to the certainty of increasing insanity and the wreck of the reason. There are other apprehensions of danger that the limitation of space does not allow the petitioner to enter on: his chief danger is that of madness, his chief terror that of madness, and his prayer that his long imprisonment may be considered with its attendant ruin a sufficient punishment, that the imprisonment may be ended now, and not uselessly or vindictively prolonged till insanity has claimed soul as well as body as its prey, and brought it to the same degradation and the same shame.

Oscar Wilde.

* *De Profundis*, meaning "from the depths" (after Psalm 130), remained unpublished and untitled in Wilde's lifetime. It was composed in holograph on "loathsome" ruled blue prison notepaper (*The Complete Letters of Oscar Wilde*, ed. Merlin Holland and Rupert Hart-Davis [New York: Henry Holt, 2000], 986, hereafter cited in annotations as *CL*) in Reading Prison at intervals between September 1896 and March 1897, toward the end of Wilde's prison sentence. It is addressed to Wilde's lover Lord Alfred Douglas, whose nickname "Bosie" (a contraction of "Boy-sie") was given him affectionately in childhood, and much of it concerns Douglas's character and behavior. It was given its present title in 1905, five years after Wilde's death, when Robert Ross published extracts, taking care to omit anything that referred to Douglas or his family, as well as anything that suggested the work's origins as a personal letter.

As related in greater detail in the Introduction, although *De Profundis* is addressed to Douglas, during the process of composition Wilde came to understand it as more than a letter merely. He meticulously revised the manuscript and also began making arrangements for it to be broadly disseminated, saying "some day the truth will have to be known" and "I am not prepared to sit in the grotesque pillory they put me into, for all time" (*CL* 780). Perhaps for this reason, Wilde never sent the letter to Douglas. Instead, upon release from jail in May 1897, he gave the manuscript to Robert Ross after first naming him his literary executor and ceding him "complete control over my plays, books, and papers" (*CL* 780). To be sure, so far as we know, Wilde did not positively instruct Ross to publish the letter; and he told Ross that, after having typewritten copies made, he should send the original manuscript to Douglas, adding that the letter was "the first time anyone has ever told him the truth about himself" and that it was one Douglas "thoroughly deserves" (*CL* 780). But Ross did not send the manuscript to Douglas, and Douglas—who only became aware of the manuscript's existence in 1912, when reading a reference to it in Arthur Ransome's book *Oscar Wilde: A Critical Study*—later wrote that Ross never sent him a copy either. For further details about the letter's composition and how Ross handled the manuscript, see "A Note on the Texts," pp. 33–39 above; also Laura Lee, *Oscar's Ghost: The Battle for Oscar Wilde's Legacy* (Stroud, UK: Amberley, 2017).

De Profundis[*]

H.M. Prison, Reading[1]

Dear Bosie,

After long and fruitless waiting I have determined to write to you myself, as much for your sake as for mine, as I would not like to think that I had passed through two long years of imprisonment without ever having received a single line from you, or any news or message even, except such as gave me pain.[2]

Our ill-fated and most lamentable friendship has ended in ruin and public infamy for me, yet the memory of our ancient affection is often with me, and the thought that loathing, bitterness and contempt should for ever take that place in my heart once held by love is very sad to me: and you yourself will, I think, feel in your heart that to write to me as I lie in the loneliness of prison-life is better than to publish my letters without my permission or to dedicate poems to me unasked,[3] though the world will know nothing of whatever words of grief or passion, of remorse or indifference you may choose to send as your answer or your appeal.

I have no doubt that in this letter in which I have to write of your life and of mine, of the past and of the future, of sweet things changed to bitterness and of bitter things that may be turned into joy, there will be much that will wound your vanity to the quick. If it prove so, read the letter over and over again till it kills your vanity. If you find in it something of which you feel that you are unjustly accused, remember that one should be thankful that there is any fault of which one can be unjustly accused.[4]

1. Wilde, a Royalist and admirer of Queen Victoria, inscribed "H.M. Prison" (meaning "Her Majesty's Prison," still the official designation for British prisons) directly adjacent to the Royal Coat of Arms embossed at the top-center of the first folio of prison notepaper. When writing to his lawyer shortly after completing *De Profundis*, Wilde described Reading Prison— where he had been imprisoned since November 1895—as "an address, which, however admirable from an ethical point of view, will not, I trust, be permanent" (*CL* 799).

2. Wilde's indictments of Douglas in *De Profundis* need to be approached with extreme caution; the pictures he draws of Douglas and their relation- ship are shaped by the bitterness of imprisonment. Following Wilde's arrest on 6 April 1895, while he remained imprisoned on remand in London's Holloway Prison awaiting trial, Douglas visited him daily in his cell, leading Wilde to remark that "every day someone whose name is Love comes to see me, and weeps so much through prison-bars that it is I who have to comfort him" (*CL* 644). But just before Wilde's first criminal trial opened on 26 April 1895—and at the urging of Wilde and his lawyers—Douglas fled to the Continent for fear that he would himself be prosecuted for the offenses of which Wilde was subsequently convicted. Douglas remained in exile for the entire course of Wilde's imprisonment, although he attempted to correspond early into Wilde's sentence. But Wilde was allowed to receive just one letter every quarter, an allocation given over initially to correspondence from his family. Wilde writes later in *De Profundis* that "it was a real grief to me when I had to let you know that I was obliged to reserve [my correspondence allowance] for family business" (see p. 131 below). In fact, Wilde told his wife four months into his sentence that he would kill Douglas if he ever saw him again, and Douglas had thereafter been led by Wilde's friends More Adey and Robert Ross to believe that Wilde wished to receive no letters from him.

3. In May 1896, during a prison visit from Robert Ross and Robert Sherard, Wilde was informed that Douglas intended to dedicate to Wilde his forthcoming first volume of poetry (*Poèmes / Poems* [Paris: Mercure de France, 1896]). On 30 May Wilde wrote to Ross telling him to prevent Douglas from doing this and also to secure the return of all letters and gifts he had sent Douglas, adding that "I will have nothing to do with him nor allow him to come near me" (*CL* 655). Ross immediately forwarded Wilde's

letter to Douglas. The original of Douglas's answer to Ross no longer
survives, but parts of it, dated 4 June 1896, were published years later in
connection with one of Douglas's many libel suits. Here Douglas writes, "I
have just got the terrible letter from Oscar. It has deprived me of all power
of thought and expression. . . . With regard to the letters, I cannot give them
up to anyone. Possession of these letters and the recollections they may
give me . . . prevent me from putting an end to a life which has now no
raison d'être. If Oscar asks me to kill myself, I will do so, and he shall have
the letters back when I am dead. . . . Morning and evening I have kissed
them and prayed over them" (quoted in Richard Ellmann, *Oscar Wilde*
[New York: Knopf, 1988], 501). Douglas's answer was probably transmitted
to Wilde by Ross's partner More Adey, a confidant of both Wilde and
Douglas, who visited Wilde in jail in August 1896, or else by Ross himself,
who visited Wilde in February 1897. However, it is likely that Douglas's
answer was distorted or misrepresented in the telling, since Adey and Ross
strove hard, both during and after Wilde's imprisonment, to deter any
further friendship between Wilde and Douglas and to effect Wilde's
reconciliation with his wife. Similarly, it seems likely that it was Adey or Ross
who told Wilde that Douglas had "gone complaining to his mother," since
Wilde had received no direct communication from Douglas. Douglas's first
book of poems (which Wilde praised highly after his release) appeared in
October 1896 without the dedication to Wilde. See also pp. 147–55 below.

Nine months before the fiasco over the poems' dedication, in August 1895,
Douglas wrote a passionate defense of Wilde, intended for publication in
the *Mercure de France.* Douglas hoped to show that their relationship was
based on "perfect love, more spiritual than sensual, a truly Platonic love, an
artist's love for a beautiful soul and a beautiful body," and he quoted
liberally from three of Wilde's love letters to him. As with the dedication of
Douglas's poems, Wilde was informed of this endeavor in advance and
managed to prevent it. The English original of Douglas's defense of Wilde
has not survived, but a version of it, based on a French translation, eventually appeared in English in Douglas, *Oscar Wilde: A Plea and a Reminiscence,*
intro. Casper Wintermans (Woubrugge, Holland: Avalon Press, 2002).

4. When instructing Robert Ross to send the manuscript of *De Profundis*
to Lord Alfred Douglas, Wilde remarked: "If it is unjust, he thoroughly
deserves injustice. Who indeed deserves it more than he who was always
so unjust to others?"

5. In a letter written to Ross in November 1896, Wilde closely echoes the present passage: "Do not let Alfred Douglas suppose that I am crediting him with unworthy motives. He really had no motives in his life at all. Motives are intellectual things. He had passions merely" (CL 671).

6. In a letter to More Adey, Wilde dated his relationship with Douglas from May 1892, although he was careful to add, "I hardly knew him at the time. I had known him eighteen months, but had only seen him four times in that space" (CL 795). If this dating is correct, Wilde first met Douglas in late 1890, when Douglas would have been barely twenty. See also Wilde's comment, later in De Profundis, "We have known each other now for more than four years. Half of the time we have been together: the other half I have had to spend in prison" (p. 119 below).

7. The opposition between romance and realism was commonplace in late-Victorian critical theory. Wilde's contemporary Robert Louis Stevenson writes that romance is "the poetry of circumstance" and that the great creative writer "shows us the realisation and the apotheosis of the day-dreams of common men" ("A Gossip on Romance" [1882], repr. in R. L. Stevenson on Fiction: An Anthology of Literary and Critical Essays, ed. Glenda Norquay [Edinburgh: Edinburgh University Press, 1999], 54, 56). Wilde's own contempt for what he called "the crude brutality of plain realism" (CL 436) runs through his writings.

8. "We are all in the gutter, but some of us are looking at the stars" (Wilde, Lady Windermere's Fan, ed. Ian Small [London: Ernest Benn, 1980], act 3, p. 64).

9. Wilde was asked to help extricate Douglas from a compromising situation. The details of the case are vague, but Douglas was probably being blackmailed over his relations with a local boy at Oxford. See Douglas Murray, Bosie: A Biography of Lord Alfred Douglas (New York: Hyperion, 2000), 33. Wilde later dates this "trouble" to July 1892.

10. "The wisdom of this world is foolishness with God" (1 Corinthians 3:19).

11. The Ancient Greek aphorism "know thyself" is one of the Delphic maxims, inscribed in the pronaos (forecourt) of the Temple of Apollo at Delphi, according to the Ancient Greek writer Pausanias. See Wilde's comment later in De Profundis (p. 227 below), "It is, of course, necessary, as

If there be in it one single passage that brings tears to your eyes, weep as we weep in prison where the day no less than the night is set apart for tears. It is the only thing that can save you. If you go complaining to your mother, as you did with reference to the scorn of you I displayed in my letter to Robbie, so that she may flatter and soothe you back into self-complacency or conceit, you will be completely lost. If you find one false excuse for yourself, you will soon find a hundred, and be just what you were before. Do you still say, as you said to Robbie in your answer, that I "attribute unworthy motives" to you? Ah! you had no motives in life. You had appetites merely. A motive is an intellectual aim.[5] That you were "very young" when our friendship began?[6] Your defect was not that you knew so little about life, but that you knew so much. The morning dawn of boyhood with its delicate bloom, its clear pure light, its joy of inno-cence and expectation you had left far behind. With very swift and running feet you had passed from Romance to Realism.[7] The gutter and the things that live in it had begun to fascinate you.[8] That was the origin of the trouble in which you sought my aid,[9] and I, so unwisely according to the wisdom of this world,[10] out of pity and kindness gave it to you. You must read this letter right through, though each word may become to you as the fire or knife of the surgeon that makes the delicate flesh burn or bleed. Remember that the fool in the eyes of the gods and the fool in the eyes of man are very different. One who is entirely ignorant of the modes of Art in its revolution or the moods of thought in its progress, of the pomp of the Latin line or the richer music of the vowelled Greek, of Tuscan sculpture or Elizabethan song may yet be full of the very sweetest wisdom. The real fool, such as the gods mock or mar, is he who does not know himself.[11] I was such a one too long. You have been such a one too long. Be so no more. Do not be afraid. The supreme vice is shallow-ness. Everything that is realised is right. Remember also that whatever is misery to you to read, is still greater misery to me to set down. To you the Unseen Powers have been very good. They have permitted you to see the strange and tragic shapes of Life as one sees shadows in a crystal. The head of Medusa that turns living men to stone, you have been the Greek oracle said, to know oneself." Wilde may be thinking too of Ralph Waldo Emerson's poem "ΓΝΩΘΙ ΣΕΑΥΤΟΝ" (Know Thyself):

> If thou canst bear
> Strong meat of simple truth
> If thou durst my words compare
> With what thou thinkest in the soul's free youth,
> Then take this fact unto thy soul,——
> God dwells in thee. . . .
>
> Clouded and shrouded there doth sit
> The Infinite
> Embosomed in a man;
> And thou art stranger to thy guest
> And know'st not what thou doth invest.
> The clouds that veil his light within
> Are thy thick woven webs of sin,
> Which his glory struggling through
> Darkens to thine evil hue.

(*Ralph Waldo Emerson: Collected Poems and Translations* [New York: Library of America, 1994], 337.)

12. According to ancient Greek myth, any man who looked into the face of the Gorgon Medusa would be turned to stone. She was finally vanquished by Perseus, who approached her sleeping form by viewing her reflected in his mirrored shield and was thus able to cut off her head.

13. This paragraph contains close verbal echoes of a letter that Wilde wrote to Robert Ross in November 1896, suggesting that it was composed around the same time. See CL 670–71.

14. Wilde wrote "I was" before substituting "I am."

15. Douglas found this indictment especially unjust. As Douglas later observed, Wilde wrote large parts of *A Woman of No Importance*, *An Ideal Husband*, and *The Importance of Being Earnest* in Douglas's company, just as he was to do with *The Ballad of Reading Gaol* in late 1897. Wilde's relationship with Douglas was a key inspiration for *The Importance of Being Earnest*, which makes sublimely farcical comedy out of Wilde's life in the

allowed to look at in a mirror merely.[12] You yourself have walked free among the flowers. From me the beautiful world of colour and motion has been taken away.

I will begin by telling you that I blame myself terribly.[13] As I sit here in this dark cell in convict clothes, a disgraced and ruined man, I blame myself. In the perturbed and fitful nights of anguish, in the long monotonous days of pain, it is myself I blame. I blame myself for allowing an unintellectual friendship, a friendship whose primary aim was not the creation and contemplation of beautiful things, to entirely dominate my life. From the very first there was too wide a gap between us. You had been idle at your school, worse than idle at your university. You did not realise that an artist, and especially such an artist as I am,[14] one, that is to say, the quality of whose work depends on the intensification of personality, requires for the development of his art the companionship of ideas, an intellectual atmosphere, quiet, peace, and solitude. You admired my work when it was finished: you enjoyed the brilliant successes of my first nights, and the brilliant banquets that followed them: you were proud, and quite naturally so, of being the intimate friend of an artist so distinguished: but you could not understand the conditions requisite for the production of artistic work. I am not speaking in phrases of rhetorical exaggeration but in terms of absolute truth to actual fact when I remind you that during the whole time we were together I never wrote one single line. Whether at Torquay, Goring, London, Florence or elsewhere, my life, as long as you were by my side, was entirely sterile and uncreative.[15] And with but few intervals you were, I regret to say, by my side always.

I remember, for instance, in September '93, to select merely one instance out of many, taking a set of chambers, purely in order to work undisturbed, as I had broken my contract with John Hare for whom I had promised to write a play, and who was pressing me on the subject.[16] During the first week you kept away. We had, not unnaturally indeed, differed on the question of the artistic value of your translation of *Salomé,* so you contented yourself with sending me foolish letters on the subject. In that week I wrote and completed in every detail, as it

period 1892–1894; indeed one of the male leads was named "Lord Alfred" in early drafts. Shortly after drafting *The Importance of Being Earnest*, in November 1894, Wilde jokingly proposed co-writing with Douglas a book titled *How to Live above One's Income: For the Use of the Sons of the Rich*.

16. From October 1893 until March 1894, Wilde rented rooms at 10 and 11 St. James's Place and went there daily to work. Most of *An Ideal Husband* was written there. Wilde had evidently committed himself to submitting the play to John Hare, actor-manager of the Garrick Theatre.

17. The Café Royal, in Regent Street, and the Berkeley Hotel, on the corner of Piccadilly and Berkeley Street.

18. London's oldest gentleman's club, located in Pall Mall.

19. The Savoy Hotel, in the Strand; and 16 (now 33) Tite Street, Chelsea, Wilde's family residence.

20. Willis's Rooms and Restaurant in King Street, St. James, where Wilde dined frequently. In late 1893 or early 1894, Wilde called Willis's a "lovely place" and remarked that "I go there daily," adding that "it has an excellent chef, and has the advantage of being terribly extravagant" (CL 579).

21. No record of this trip survives. But in early 1895 Wilde wired money to Douglas in Calais and insisted that, upon Douglas's return to England, "you will of course stay with me" (CL 633).

22. The Oxford temper, as Wilde defines it here, was a form of mental discipline inculcated by the liberal pedagogical regime of Benjamin Jowett, Mark Pattison, and the various college tutors teaching at Oxford under their influence in the latter half of the nineteenth century. It was associated especially with the Oxford Greats school, which Wilde called "the only sphere of thought where one can be, simultaneously, brilliant and unreasonable, speculative and well-informed, creative as well as critical" (CL 102).

23. John Gray (1866–1934) was a decadent poet who, by virtue of his youthful good looks and close friendship with Wilde, was in the early 1890s widely regarded as the real-life model for Wilde's Dorian Gray. In 1893 Gray renounced Wilde and decadence, and instead embraced Catholicism; he later became a Catholic priest. Pierre Louÿs (1870–1925) was a French novelist and poet with whom Wilde formed a close friendship in 1891.

was ultimately performed, the first act of *An Ideal Husband.* The second week you returned and my work practically had to be given up. I arrived at St James's Place every morning at 11.30, in order to have the opportunity of thinking and writing without the interruptions inseparable from my own household, quiet and peaceful as that household was. But the attempt was vain. At 12 o'clock you drove up, and stayed smoking cigarettes and chattering till 1.30, when I had to take you out to luncheon at the Café Royal or the Berkeley.[17] Luncheon with its *liqueurs* lasted usually till 3.30. For an hour you retired to White's.[18] At tea-time you appeared again, and stayed till it was time to dress for dinner. You dined with me either at the Savoy or at Tite Street.[19] We did not separate as a rule till after midnight, as supper at Willis's[20] had to wind up the entrancing day. That was my life for those three months, every single day, except during the four days when you went abroad. I then, of course, had to go over to Calais to fetch you back.[21] For one of my nature and temperament it was a position at once grotesque and tragic.

You surely must realise that now? You must see now that your incapacity of being alone: your nature so exigent in its persistent claim on the attention and time of others: your lack of any power of sustained intellectual concentration: the unfortunate accident—for I like to think it was no more—that you had not yet been able to acquire the "Oxford temper" in intellectual matters,[22] never, I mean, been one who could play gracefully with ideas but had arrived at violence of opinion merely:—that all these things, combined with the fact that your desires and interests were in Life not in Art, were as destructive to your own progress in culture as they were to my work as an artist? When I compare my friendship with you to my friendship with such still younger men as John Gray and Pierre Louÿs I feel ashamed.[23] My real life, my higher life was with them and such as they.

Of the appalling results of my friendship with you I don't speak at present. I am thinking merely of its quality while it lasted. It was intellectually degrading to me. You had the rudiments of an artistic temperament in its germ. But I met you either too late or too soon, I don't know

Louÿs assisted Wilde with the composition and publication of *Salomé* in French.

24. In November 1893, Wilde had written to Lady Queensberry: "Bosie is in a very bad state of health. . . . He does absolutely nothing, and is quite astray in life. . . . Why not try and make arrangements of some kind for him to go abroad for four or five months, to the Cromers in Egypt if that could be managed, where he would have new surroundings, proper friends, and a different atmosphere?" (*CL* 575). Douglas was indeed subsequently sent to Egypt for the winter, where he was a guest of the British consul-general, Lord Cromer, whose wife was a friend of Douglas's mother.

25. *A Florentine Tragedy* and *La Sainte Courtisane* are both erotic tragedies set in the distant past. Wilde finished neither of them, and only fragments survive today. The first, set in Renaissance Florence, was written in blank verse. The second, set in ancient Thebes, featured prose poetry reminiscent of *Salomé* and *The Song of Songs*.

26. See pp. 54–55, n.3 above.

27. Bracknell, in Berkshire, home to Lady Queensberry, Lord Alfred's mother.

28. Cromer, seaside town in Norfolk where Wilde vacationed and wrote much of *A Woman of No Importance* in the summer of 1892.

which. When you were away I was all right. The moment, in the early December of the year to which I have been alluding, I had succeeded in inducing your mother to send you out of England,[24] I collected again the torn and ravelled web of my imagination, got my life back into my own hands, and not merely finished the three remaining acts of *An Ideal Husband,* but conceived and had almost completed two other plays of a completely different type, the *Florentine Tragedy* and *La Sainte Courtisane,*[25] when suddenly, unbidden, unwelcome, and under circumstances fatal to my happiness you returned. The two works left then imperfect I was unable to take up again. The mood that created them I could never recover. You now, having yourself published a volume of verse,[26] will be able to recognise the truth of everything I have said here. Whether you can or not it remains as a hideous truth in the very heart of our friendship. While you were with me you were the absolute ruin of my Art, and in allowing you to stand persistently between Art and myself I give to myself shame and blame in the fullest degree. You couldn't know, you couldn't understand, you couldn't appreciate. I had no right to expect it of you at all. Your interests were merely in your meals and moods. Your desires were simply for amusements, for ordinary or less ordinary pleasures. They were what your temperament needed, or thought it needed for the moment. I should have forbidden you my house and my chambers except when I specially invited you. I blame myself without reserve for my weakness. It was merely weakness. One half hour with Art was always more to me than a cycle with you. Nothing really at any period of my life was ever of the smallest importance to me compared with Art. But in the case of an artist, weakness is nothing less than a crime, when it is a weakness that paralyses the imagination.

I blame myself again for having allowed you to bring me to utter and discreditable financial ruin. I remember one morning in the early October of '92 sitting in the yellowing woods at Bracknell[27] with your mother. At that time I knew very little of your real nature. I had stayed from a Saturday to Monday with you at Oxford. You had stayed with me at Cromer[28] for ten days and played golf. The conversation turned on you, and your

29. That is, as a "buttonhole," in the lapel of his jacket.

30. "I . . . / Flung roses, roses riotously with the throng, / . . . I cried for madder music and for stronger wine," wrote Wilde's good friend, the poet Ernest Dowson ("Non Sum Qualis Eram Bonae Sub Regno Cynarae," in *The Poetic Works of Ernest Christopher Dowson*, ed. Desmond Flower [London: Cassell and John Lane, 1934], 22). Dowson, who immortalized the phrase "days of wine and roses" ("Vitae summa brevis spem nos vetat incohare longam," in *The Poetic Works of Ernest Christopher Dowson*, ed. Flower, 2), proved to be a favorite companion of Wilde's in the days after the latter's release from prison; and in Dowson's company Wilde often spent and drank to excess, just as he had done with Douglas before his imprisonment. "His gorgeous spirits cheered me mightily," Dowson wrote of Wilde at this time: "I was amused by the unconscious contrast between his present talk about his changed position & his notions of economy & his practise, which is perversely extravagant" (quoted in Nicholas Frankel, *Oscar Wilde: The Unrepentant Years* [Cambridge, MA: Harvard University Press, 2017], 114). As Dowson suggests, Wilde was an inveterate eater and a heavy drinker; food and drink, as well as tobacco, were intertwined with Wilde's intellectual and sexual life; and he once asked rhetorically "who . . . in these degenerate days would hesitate between an ode and an omelette, a sonnet and a salmis?" ("Dinners and Dishes," *Pall Mall Gazette*, 7 March 1885, repr. in *Journalism: Part One*, vol. 6 of *The Complete Works of Oscar Wilde*, ed. John Stokes and Mark W. Turner [Oxford: Oxford University Press, 2013], 39). Wilde put much of himself into the character of Algernon Moncrieff, who eats and drinks throughout *The Importance of Being Earnest* and at one point remarks "I hate people who aren't serious about meals. It is so shallow of them" (*The Annotated Importance of Being Earnest*, ed. Nicholas Frankel [Cambridge, MA: Harvard University Press, 2015], 79).

31. Wilde and Douglas visited Algiers in January 1895. Wilde returned home on 3 February to attend final rehearsals of *The Importance of Being Earnest*. Douglas stayed on until 18 February.

32. Five thousand pounds was an immense amount of money, roughly equivalent to £460,000 or US$600,000 in 2018. It represents nearly half of Wilde's total earnings between 1891 and 1895, according to the estimate of

mother began to speak to me about your character. She told me of your two chief faults, your vanity, and your being, as she termed it, "all wrong about money." I have a distinct recollection of how I laughed. I had no idea that the first would bring me to prison, and the second to bankruptcy. I thought vanity a sort of graceful flower for a young man to wear;[29] as for extravagance—for I thought she meant no more than extravagance— the virtues of prudence and thrift were not in my own nature or my own race. But before our friendship was one month older I began to see what your mother really meant. Your insistence on a life of reckless profusion: your incessant demands for money: your claim that all your pleasures should be paid for by me whether I was with you or not: brought me after some time into serious monetary difficulties, and what made the extravagances to me at any rate so monotonously uninteresting, as your persistent grasp on my life grew stronger and stronger, was that the money was really spent on little more than the pleasures of eating, drinking, and the like. Now and then it is a joy to have one's table red with wine and roses,[30] but you outstripped all taste and temperance. You demanded without grace and received without thanks. You grew to think that you had a sort of right to live at my expense and in a profuse luxury to which you had never been accustomed, and which for that reason made your appetites all the more keen, and at the end if you lost money gambling in some Algiers Casino[31] you simply telegraphed next morning to me in London to lodge the amount of your losses to your account at your bank, and gave the matter no further thought of any kind.

When I tell you that between the autumn of 1892 and the date of my imprisonment I spent with you and on you more than £5000 in actual money,[32] irrespective of the bills I incurred, you will have some idea of the sort of life on which you insisted. Do you think I exaggerate?[33] My ordinary expenses with you for an ordinary day in London—for luncheon, dinner, supper, amusements, hansoms[34] and the rest of it—ranged from £12 to £20, and the week's expenses were naturally in proportion and ranged from £80 to £130.[35] For our three months at Goring my expenses (rent of course included) were £1340.[36] Step by step with the

Ian Small and Josephine Guy (*Oscar Wilde's Profession* [Oxford: Oxford University Press, 2000], 133).

33. Wilde is certainly exaggerating. At his bankruptcy hearing, it was determined that Wilde's total outlay (excluding solicitor's costs of £324) for the period from July 1893 to July 1895 was £5,818, "including expenses of self, wife, and two children" (Donald Mead, "Heading for Disaster: Oscar's Finances: Chapter Five, Bankruptcy," *The Wildean: A Journal of Oscar Wilde Studies* 46 [January 2015]: 92).

34. A private horse-drawn carriage for hire, akin to a modern taxi. In "The Model Millionaire," the impoverished Hughie Erskine gives away a sovereign even though "it means no hansoms for a fortnight."

35. This amount, £80 to £130, equates to roughly £5,000 to £8,000 or US$6,500 to US$10,500 in 2018. Wilde was a spendthrift long before he met Alfred Douglas and, as he just admitted, "the virtues of prudence and thrift were not in my own nature or my own race." While still an undergraduate at Oxford, in 1877, he was called before the Vice-Chancellor's Court on account of unpaid debts. Later, at the time of his marriage, he was £800 in debt; and shortly after this, he and his new bride were as much as £3,000 in debt, largely because of the extravagance with which they decorated their new home in fashionable Tite Street, Chelsea. As Wilde informed his friend, the actor-manager George Alexander, shortly before his arrest, "my life is so marred and maimed by extravagance. But I cannot live otherwise" (*CL* 633).

36. For Goring, see pp. 75 and 103 below.

37. Wilde was formally declared bankrupt on 19 November 1895, one week after his bankruptcy examination. Although present in the building, Wilde did not testify at an earlier hearing, on 24 September 1895, when the case was adjourned. For details of Wilde's bankruptcy, see Mead, "Heading for Disaster," 88–103.

38. "Rapine, avarice, expence, / This is idolatry; and these we adore: / Plain living and high thinking are no more" (William Wordsworth, "Written in London, September 1802"). From December 1896 onward, Wilde had a one-volume copy of Wordsworth's works in his cell.

Bankruptcy Receiver I had to go over every item of my life.[37] It was horrible. "Plain living and high thinking"[38] was, of course, an ideal you could not at that time have appreciated, but such extravagance was a disgrace to both of us. One of the most delightful dinners I remember ever having had is one Robbie[39] and I had together in a little Soho café, which cost about as many shillings as my dinners to you used to cost pounds. Out of my dinner with Robbie came the first and best of all my dialogues. Idea, title, treatment, mode, everything was struck out at a 3 franc 50 c. *table-d'hôte*.[40] Out of the reckless dinners with you nothing remains but the memory that too much was eaten and too much was drunk. And my yielding to your demands was bad for you. You know that now. It made you grasping often: at times not a little unscrupulous: ungracious always. There was on far too many occasions too little joy or privilege in being your host. You forgot—I will not say the formal courtesy of thanks, for formal courtesies will strain a close friendship—but simply the grace of sweet companionship, the charm of pleasant conversation, that τέρπνον κακόν as the Greeks called it,[41] and all those gentle humanities that make life lovely, and are an accompaniment to life as music might be, keeping things in tune and filling with melody the harsh or silent places. And though it may seem strange to you that one in the terrible position in which I am situated should find a difference between one disgrace and another, still I frankly admit that the folly of throwing away all this money on you, and letting you squander my fortune to your own hurt as well as to mine, gives to me and in my eyes a note of common profligacy to my Bankruptcy that makes me doubly ashamed of it. I was made for other things.

But most of all I blame myself for the entire ethical degradation I allowed you to bring on me. The basis of character is will-power, and my will-power became absolutely subject to yours. It sounds a grotesque thing to say, but it is none the less true. Those incessant scenes that seemed to be almost physically necessary to you, and in which your mind and body grew distorted and you became a thing as terrible to look at as to listen to: that dreadful mania you inherit from your father, the mania

39. The first of many mentions in *De Profundis* of Robert Baldwin Ross (1869–1918), Wilde's most loyal male lover, whom Wilde jokingly named "St. Robert of Phillimore" (Ross lived in London's Phillimore Gardens) on account of his "sweet companionship" (*CL* 859). For Wilde's delivery of *De Profundis* into Ross's hands and appointment of Ross as his literary executor, see "Note on the Texts," p. 35 above. For Wilde's intended dedication to Ross of *The Ballad of Reading Gaol*, see pp. 316–18, n.1 below. Ross's ashes are now interred in Wilde's grave at Père Lachaise Cemetery.

40. A fixed-price set menu costing three francs and fifty centimes, roughly equivalent to three shillings in Wilde's day. As Ian Small notes, that Wilde quotes the price charged by a café in London ("Soho") in French currency suggests some embroidery of the truth.

41. Wilde quotes the Greek for "delightful wickedness" from Euripides's *Hippolytus*, although the phrase τέρπνον κακόν should properly be accented τερπνὸν κακόν. As Ian Small observes (*De Profundis*; "Epistola: In Carcere et Vinculis," ed. Ian Small, vol. 2 of *The Complete Works of Oscar Wilde* [Oxford University Press, 2005], 208), there is irony in Wilde's citation, since the play concerns the destruction of Hippolytus by Phaedra's desire for him.

42. In his manuscript, Wilde originally wrote "all things" before substituting "your daily increasing demands."

43. "The history of women," says Lord Illingworth in *A Woman of No Importance*, "is the history of the worst form of tyranny.... The tyranny of the weak over the strong. It is the only tyranny that lasts" (*A Woman of No Importance*, ed. Ian Small, in *Two Society Comedies*, ed. Ian Small and Russell Jackson [London: Ernest Benn, 1983], act 3, p. 77).

44. Means of living.

for writing revolting and loathsome letters: your entire lack of any control over your emotions as displayed in your long resentful moods of sullen silence, no less than in the sudden fits of almost epileptic rage: all these things in reference to which one of my letters to you, left by you lying about at the Savoy or some other Hotel and so produced in Court by your father's counsel, contained an entreaty not devoid of pathos, had you at that time been able to recognise pathos either in its elements or its expression:—these, I say, were the origin and causes of my fatal yielding to you in your daily increasing demands.[42] You wore one out. It was the triumph of the smaller over the bigger nature. It was the case of that tyranny of the weak over the strong which somewhere in one of my plays I describe as being "the only tyranny that lasts."[43] And it was inevitable. In every relation of life with others one has to find some *moyen de vivre*.[44] In your case, one had either to give up to you or to give you up. There was no other alternative. Through deep if misplaced affection for you: through great pity for your defects of temper and temperament: through my own proverbial good-nature and Celtic laziness: through an artistic aversion to coarse scenes and ugly words: through that incapacity to bear resentment of any kind which at that time characterised me: through my dislike of seeing life made bitter and uncomely by what to me, with my eyes really fixed on other things, seemed to be mere trifles too petty for more than a moment's thought or interest;—through these reasons, simple as they may sound, I gave up to you always. As a natural result, your claims, your efforts at domination, your exactions grew more and more unreasonable. Your meanest motive, your lowest appetite, your most common passion, became to you laws by which the lives of others were to be guided always, and to which, if necessary, they were to be without scruple sacrificed. Knowing that by making a scene you could always have your way, it was but natural that you should proceed, almost unconsciously I have no doubt, to every excess of vulgar violence. At the end you did not know to what goal you were hurrying, or with what aim in view. Having made your own of my genius, my will-power, and my fortune, you required, in the blindness of an inexhaustible greed, my entire

45. This letter has not survived.

46. Slaughterhouse.

47. Walter Pater, *The Renaissance: Studies in Art and Poetry: The 1893 Text*, ed. Donald L. Hill (Berkeley: University of California Press, 1980), 189. Pater's *Renaissance*—which Wilde had first read while an undergraduate, and which he will refer to later as "that book which has had such a strange influence over my life"—was one of the first books to be issued to Wilde in prison. He received a copy at Wandsworth in August 1895 after the politician and prison reformer R. B. Haldane—one of Wilde's first prison visitors—persuaded the authorities to allow him a few books, and he took it with him to Reading three months later.

48. Wilde refers to Book II of Aristotle's *Ethics*, which he knew well from his undergraduate days at Oxford, in which Aristotle defines moral virtue as the product of "repeated acts of custom."

49. The warrant for Queensberry's arrest was issued on 1 March 1895. Eight days later, Wilde was present when Queensberry was committed for trial at Marlborough Street Magistrates Court. Wilde and Douglas left for Monte Carlo on 12 March, shortly after Wilde had told their close friend Ada Leverson: "For a week I go away with Bosie: then return to fight with panthers" (CL 635).

existence. You took it. At the one supremely and tragically critical moment of all my life, just before my lamentable step of beginning my absurd action, on the one side there was your father attacking me with hideous cards left at my club, on the other side there was you attacking me with no less loathsome letters. The letter I received from you on the morning of the day I let you take me down to the Police Court to apply for the ridiculous warrant for your father's arrest was one of the worst you ever wrote, and for the most shameful reason.[45] Between you both I lost my head. My judgment forsook me. Terror took its place. I saw no possible escape, I may say frankly, from either of you. Blindly I staggered as an ox into the shambles.[46] I had made a gigantic psychological error. I had always thought that my giving up to you in small things meant nothing: that when a great moment arrived I could reassert my will-power in its natural superiority. It was not so. At the great moment my will-power completely failed me. In life there is really no small or great thing. All things are of equal value and of equal size. My habit—due to indifference chiefly at first—of giving up to you in every thing had become insensibly a real part of my nature. Without my knowing it, it had stereotyped my temperament to one permanent and fatal mood. That is why, in the subtle epilogue to the first edition of his essays, Pater says that "Failure is to form habits."[47] When he said it the dull Oxford people thought the phrase a mere wilful inversion of the somewhat wearisome text of Aristotelian Ethics,[48] but there is a wonderful, a terrible truth hidden in it. I had allowed you to sap my strength of character, and to me the formation of a habit had proved to be not Failure merely but Ruin. Ethically you had been even still more destructive to me than you had been artistically.

The warrant once granted, your will of course directed everything. At a time when I should have been in London taking wise counsel, and calmly considering the hideous trap in which I had allowed myself to be caught—the booby-trap as your father calls it to the present day—you insisted on my taking you to Monte Carlo, of all revolting places on God's earth, that all day, and all night as well, you might gamble as long as the Casino remained open.[49] As for me—baccarat having no charms for

50. Such friends included Robert Ross, Frank Harris, and George Bernard Shaw, the latter two of whom implored Wilde, over lunch at the Café Royal, to drop his suit and go abroad. See Frank Harris, *Oscar Wilde: His Life and Confessions* (1916), repr. as *Oscar Wilde* (New York: Dorset, 1989), 116–17.

51. In Greek mythology, Clio, the daughter of Zeus and Mnemosyne, is the muse of history. Often depicted carrying a scroll or books, she is the "least serious" of the nine muses because the history she inspires is driven by "grotesqueness of effect."

52. Dedicated to God's service before birth by his mother Hannah (1 Samuel 1:11), the Infant Samuel, the embodiment of young masculine piety and innocence, was a popular subject in Victorian art.

53. In Dante's *Inferno*, which Wilde read intensively in Reading Prison for much of 1896, Malebolge, meaning "evil ditches," is the eighth and second-deepest circle (of nine) of hell. In Dante's vision of hell, different types of sin are punished in different circles, with the depth of the circle—and the sinner's placement within that circle—representative of the amount of punishment to be inflicted. Sinners consigned to the upper circles of hell are given relatively minor punishments, while sinners in the depths suffer far greater torments. Since it is the eighth of nine circles, Malebolge is one of the worst places in hell to be. Malebolge is itself subdivided into ten concentric ditches, trenches, or *bolgia*; in the worst of them ("the lowest mire"), Dante placed falsifiers, imposters, counterfeiters, and perjurors.

54. Gilles de Retz (1404–1440), a leader in the French army, and a companion-in-arms of Joan of Arc, was a prolific serial killer of children. He features prominently in Joris-Karl Huysmans's novel *Là-Bas*, which Wilde would have read on its appearance in 1891. The French aristocrat and writer the Marquis de Sade (1740–1814), from whom the words "sadism" and "sadist" are derived, put his libertine sexuality and lifestyle into his literary works, which combine philosophical discourse with sexual fantasies emphasizing violence, criminality, and blasphemy.

55. See Aeschylus, *Agamemnon*, in *Aeschylus II: Oresteia*, ed. and trans. Alan H. Sommerstein, Loeb Classical Library (Cambridge, MA: Harvard University Press, 2008), pp. 84–87, ll. 717–36.

me—I was left alone outside to myself. You refused to discuss even for
five minutes the position to which you and your father had brought me.
My business was merely to pay your Hotel expenses and your losses. The
slightest allusion to the ordeal awaiting me was regarded as a bore. A new
brand of champagne that was recommended to us had more interest for
you. . . . On our return to London those of my friends who really desired
my welfare implored me to retire abroad, and not to face an impossible
trial.[50] You imputed mean motives to them for giving such advice, and
cowardice to me for listening to it. You forced me to stay to brazen it out,
if possible, in the box by absurd and silly perjuries. At the end, I was of
course arrested and your father became the hero of the hour: more indeed than the hero of the hour merely: your family now ranks, strangely
enough, with the Immortals: for with that grotesqueness of effect that is
as it were a Gothic element in history, and makes Clio the least serious
of all the Muses,[51] your father will always live among the kind pure-
minded parents of Sunday-school literature, your place is with the Infant Samuel,[52] and in the lowest mire of Malebolge[53] I sit between Gilles
de Retz and the Marquis de Sade.[54]

Of course I should have got rid of you. I should have shaken you out
of my life as a man shakes from his raiment a thing that has stung him. In
the most wonderful of all his plays Aeschylus tells us of the great Lord
who brings up in his house the lion-cub, the λέοντος ἶνιν, and loves it
because it comes bright-eyed to his call and fawns on him for its food:

φαιδρωπὸς ποτὶ χεῖρα, σαίνων τε γαστρὸς ἀνάγκαις·[55]

and the thing grows up and shows the nature of its race, ἦθος τὸ πρόσθε
τοκήων, and destroys the lord and his house and all that he possesses. I
feel that I was such a one as he. But my fault was, not that I did not part
from you, but that I parted from you far too often. As far as I can make
out I ended my friendship with you every three months regularly, and
each time that I did so you managed by means of entreaties, telegrams,
letters, the interposition of your friends, the interposition of mine, and
the like to induce me to allow you back. When at the end of March '93

56. In a love letter inviting Douglas to visit him at Babbacombe Cliff, a large country house that Wilde rented near Torquay, in Devon, for three months in the winter of 1892–1893, Wilde writes that "those red rose-leaf lips of yours should have been made no less for music of song than for madness of kisses" and "your slim-gilt soul walks between passion and poetry.... Come here whenever you like. It is a lovely place—it only lacks you" (CL 544). In a second love letter to Douglas written over a month later, shortly after both of them had left Babbacombe Cliff, Wilde says, "I must see you soon—you are the divine thing I want—the thing of grace and genius.... Shall I come to Salisbury?... Why are you not here, my dear, my wonderful boy?" (CL 560). It certainly doesn't sound as if Wilde "had determined never to speak to you again, or to allow you under any circumstances to be with me."

57. Campbell Dodgson (1867–1948), a scholar of New College and former Winchester schoolmate of Douglas's, who tutored Douglas briefly in early February 1893 and journeyed with him to stay with Wilde at Babbacombe Cliff. Dodgson appears to have left Babbacombe Cliff some days or weeks before, not after, Douglas. For Wilde's description of life with Douglas at Babbacombe Cliff—which he said combined "the advantages of a public school with those of a private lunatic asylum"—see his amusing letter to Dodgson written shortly after the latter's departure (CL 555–56). For Dodgson's own description, see Letters of Oscar Wilde, ed. Rupert Hart-Davis (New York: Harcourt, Brace and World, 1962), appendix A, 867–68.

58. Magdalen College, the Oxford college of both Wilde and Douglas.

59. In March 1893, shortly after leaving Babbacombe Cliff, Wilde took rooms at London's Savoy Hotel for "about a month" (The Real Trial of Oscar Wilde, intro. and with commentary by Merlin Holland [New York: Harper Perennial, 2003], 111). Douglas stayed with Wilde for some of this time, and the Savoy sojourn provided particularly damaging evidence during Wilde's trials. Several young male sex workers visited Wilde in his hotel rooms, including the procurer Alfred Taylor and the prostitute Charles Parker, and during his trials several hotel workers, as well as Parker himself, testified against Wilde. Four of the seven counts of gross indecency on which Wilde was eventually found guilty concerned acts that took place at the Savoy during this period. See Joseph Bristow, Oscar Wilde on Trial: The Criminal

you left my house at Torquay I had determined never to speak to you again, or to allow you under any circumstances to be with me, so revolting had been the scene you had made the night before your departure.[56] You wrote and telegraphed from Bristol to beg me to forgive you and meet you. Your tutor,[57] who had stayed behind, told me that he thought that at times you were quite irresponsible for what you said and did, and that most, if not all of the men at Magdalen[58] were of the same opinion. I consented to meet you, and of course I forgave you. On the way up to town you begged me to take you to the Savoy. That was indeed a visit fatal to me.[59]

Three months later, in June, we are at Goring. Some of your Oxford friends come to stay from a Saturday to Monday. The morning of the day they went away you made a scene so dreadful, so distressing that I told you that we must part. I remember quite well, as we stood on the level croquet-ground with the pretty lawn all round us, pointing out to you that we were spoiling each other's lives, that you were absolutely ruining mine and that I evidently was not making you really happy, and that an irrevocable parting, a complete separation was the one wise philosophic thing to do. You went sullenly after luncheon, leaving one of your most offensive letters behind with the butler to be handed to me after your departure. Before three days had elapsed you were telegraphing from London to beg to be forgiven and allowed to return. I had taken the place to please you. I had engaged your own servants at your request.[60] I was always terribly sorry for the hideous temper to which you were really a prey. I was fond of you. So I let you come back and forgave you. Three months later still, in September, new scenes occurred, the occasion of them being my pointing out the schoolboy faults of your attempted translation of *Salomé*. You must by this time be a fair enough French scholar to know that the translation was as unworthy of you, as an ordinary Oxonian, as it was of the work it sought to render.[61] You did not of course know it then, and in one of the violent letters you wrote to me on the point you said that you were under "no intellectual obligation of any kind" to me. I remember that when I read that statement, I felt that it

Proceedings (New Haven, CT: Yale University Press, forthcoming); and
H. Montgomery Hyde, *The Trials of Oscar Wilde*, 2nd ed. (1962; repr.,
New York: Dover, 1973), 171–72, 193–94, and 236–38.

60. Wilde alludes to Walter Grainger, Douglas's manservant at Oxford,
whom Wilde engaged for two months in the summer of 1893 while renting
a small house at Goring-on-Thames, in Oxfordshire, ostensibly because his
own servant "went home to his parents under certain circumstances" (*The
Real Trial of Oscar Wilde*, 241–42). During Wilde's libel suit, Queensberry's
counsel, Edward Carson, imputed that Wilde slept with Grainger at Goring;
and according to Wilde himself, Grainger was to have been the principal
witness in Constance's abortive divorce suit against Wilde in 1897
(see *CL* 704).

61. Wilde's play *Salomé* was composed and first published in French, in
1891 and 1893, respectively. Wilde himself insisted that Douglas translate
the first English edition, which appeared in 1894 with illustrations by
Aubrey Beardsley, dedicated to "Lord Alfred Douglas, the translator of my
play." Wilde's indictment of the "schoolboy faults" of Douglas's translation
tainted the reputation of the first English edition for many years, and the
play has often been retranslated by others. But scholars now surmise that
Wilde himself had a hand in the first English translation and that he must
have been content enough with it to authorize its publication and honor
Douglas with the dedication. Douglas himself conceded in 1894 that he
and Wilde found it "impossible to agree about the translation of certain
passages, phrases, and words," while thirteen years later he wrote that
Wilde "revised the translation to the extent of taking out from it most of
the elements of original work on my part." For an overview of the issues
surrounding the first English translation, see Nicholas Frankel, review of
Salome: A Tragedy in One Act, trans. Joseph Donohue and illustr. Barry
Moser (Charlottesville: University of Virginia Press, 2011), *Journal of
Pre-Raphaelite Studies*, n.s., 22 (Spring 2013): 110–14.

62. *The Importance of Being Earnest* is subtitled "A Trivial Comedy for
Serious People."

63. The "one topic" was probably homosexual sex.

64. "terrible" was an afterthought, added to the manuscript in superscript.

was the one really true thing you had written to me in the whole course of our friendship. I saw that a less cultivated nature would really have suited you much better. I am not saying this in bitterness at all, but simply as a fact of companionship. Ultimately the bond of all companionship, whether in marriage or in friendship, is conversation, and conversation must have a common basis, and between two people of widely different culture the only common basis possible is the lowest level. The trivial in thought and action is charming. I had made it the keystone of a very brilliant philosophy expressed in plays and paradoxes.[62] But the froth and folly of our life grew often very wearisome to me: it was only in the mire that we met: and fascinating, terribly fascinating though the one topic round which your talk invariably centred[63] was, still at the end it became quite monotonous to me: I was often bored to death by it, and accepted it as I accepted your passion for going to music-halls, or your mania for absurd extravagances in eating and drinking, or any other of your to me less attractive characteristics, as a thing, that is to say, that one simply had to put up with, a part of the high price one paid for knowing you. When after leaving Goring I went to Dinard for a fortnight you were extremely angry with me for not taking you with me, and, before my departure there, made some very unpleasant scenes on the subject at the Albemarle Hotel, and sent me some equally unpleasant telegrams to a country house I was staying at for a few days. I told you, I remember, that I thought it was your duty to be with your own people for a little, as you had passed the whole season away from them. But in reality, to be perfectly frank with you, I could not under any circumstances have let you be with me. We had been together for nearly twelve weeks. I required rest and freedom from the terrible[64] strain of your companionship. It was necessary for me to be a little by myself. It was intellectually necessary. And so I confess I saw in your letter, from which I have quoted, a very good opportunity for ending the fatal friendship that had sprung up between us, and ending it without bitterness, as I had indeed tried to do on that bright June morning at Goring, three months before. It was however represented to me—I am

65. Wilde initially wrote "Robbie" [i.e., Robert Ross] before substituting "one of my own friends."

66. "unless one done by a poet" was an afterthought. The phrase it replaced is illegible and erased in the manuscript, though intriguingly it appears to begin "even by a poetic..."

67. "lightly" was an afterthought, added to the manuscript in superscript.

68. "more than usually" substituted for "quite" in the manuscript.

69. "family" substituted for "wife" in the manuscript.

bound to say candidly by one of my own friends,[65] to whom you had gone in your difficulty—that you would be much hurt, perhaps almost humiliated at having your work sent back to you like a schoolboy's exercise; that I was expecting far too much intellectually from you; and that, no matter what you wrote or did, you were absolutely and entirely devoted to me. I did not want to be the first to check or discourage you in your beginnings in literature: I knew quite well that no translation, unless one done by a poet,[66] could render the colour and cadence of my work in any adequate measure: devotion seemed to me, seems to me still, a wonderful thing, not to be lightly[67] thrown away: so I took the translation and you back. Exactly three months later, after a series of scenes culminating in one more than usually[68] revolting, when you came one Monday evening to my rooms accompanied by two of your friends, I found myself actually flying abroad next morning to escape from you, giving my family[69] some absurd reason for my sudden departure, and leaving a false address with my servant for fear you might follow me by the next train. And I remember that afternoon, as I was in the railway-carriage whirling up to Paris, thinking in what an impossible, terrible, utterly wrong state my life had got into, when I, a man of worldwide reputation, was actually forced to run away from England, in order to try and get rid of a friendship that was entirely destructive of everything fine in me either from the intellectual or ethical point of view: the person from whom I was flying, being no terrible creature sprung from sewer or mire into modern life with whom I had entangled my days, but you yourself, a young man of my own social rank and position, who had been at my own college at Oxford, and was an incessant guest at my house. The usual telegrams of entreaty and remorse followed: I disregarded them. Finally you threatened that unless I consented to meet you, you would under no circumstances consent to proceed to Egypt. I had myself, with your knowledge and concurrence, begged your mother to send you to Egypt away from England, as you were wrecking your life in London. I knew that if you did not go it would be a terrible disappointment to her, and for her sake I did meet

70. "under the influence of great emotion, which even you cannot have forgotten" added to the manuscript as an afterthought.

71. "sadly and seriously trying to make up my mind" was an afterthought, replacing "wondering" in the manuscript.

72. "fairest of spirits." The Latin phrase is frequently found in Classical epitaphs.

73. The biblical Philistines were a warlike people who came into conflict with the children of Israel a full millennium before Christ. In Wilde's day, however, "Philistines" referred euphemistically to the unenlightened and materialistic wealthy classes of England (see also n.406 below). Wilde will later say that the Philistine is he "who upholds and aids the heavy, cumbrous, blind mechanical forces of Society, and who does not recognise the dynamic force when he meets it either in a man or a movement" and that Philistinism is "that side of man's nature that is not illumined by the imagination" (pp. 239 and 223 below).

74. See p. 56, n.9 above.

75. Wilde refers to a trip Douglas made with Robert Ross to Bruges in October 1893. In a letter written to his brother during the trip, Douglas explained that he had gone to Bruges because "Ross, one of my greatest friends, has got into a scrape connected with some people out here" (quoted in Neil McKenna, *The Secret Life of Oscar Wilde* [New York: Basic Books, 2005], 267). In fact the "scrape" was more serious than Douglas makes it sound—and Douglas was involved just as deeply as Ross. Evidence had come to light that both Ross and Douglas had seduced and had sex with pupils at an English boys' boarding school in Bruges administered by a relative of Wilde's friend the Cambridge don Oscar Browning. In the aftermath of Douglas's and Ross's trip, a settlement was reached and the affair was kept out of the courts. For details of the affair, see McKenna, *The Secret Life of Oscar Wilde*, 263–68; and Ellmann, *Oscar Wilde*, 406–7.

you, and under the influence of great emotion, which even you cannot have forgotten,[70] I forgave the past; though I said nothing at all about the future.

On my return to London next day I remember sitting in my room and sadly and seriously trying to make up my mind[71] whether or not you really were what you seemed to me to be, so full of terrible defects, so utterly ruinous both to yourself and to others, so fatal a one to know even or to be with. For a whole week I thought about it, and wondered if after all I was not unjust and mistaken in my estimate of you. At the end of the week a letter from your mother is handed in. It expressed to the full every feeling I myself had about you. In it she spoke of your blind exaggerated vanity which made you despise your home, and treat your elder brother—that *candidissima anima*[72]—"as a Philistine":[73] of your temper which made her afraid to speak to you about your life, the life she felt, she knew you were leading: about your conduct in money matters, so distressing to her in more ways than one: of the degeneration and change that had taken place in you. She saw, of course, that heredity had burdened you with a terrible legacy, and frankly admitted it, admitted it with terror: he is "the one of my children who has inherited the fatal Douglas temperament," she wrote of you. At the end she stated that she felt bound to declare that your friendship with me, in her opinion, had so intensified your vanity that it had become the source of all your faults, and earnestly begged me not to meet you abroad. I wrote to her at once, in reply, and told her that I agreed entirely with every word she had said. I added much more. I went as far as I could possibly go. I told her that the origin of our friendship was you in your undergraduate days at Oxford coming to beg me to help you in very serious trouble of a very particular character.[74] I told her that your life had been continually in the same manner troubled. The reason of your going to Belgium you had placed to the fault of your companion in that journey,[75] and your mother had reproached me with having introduced you to him. I replaced the fault on the right shoulders, on yours. I assured her at the end that I had not the smallest intention of meeting you abroad, and begged her to try

76. "I read them, and tore them up" added to the manuscript as an afterthought. Wilde's statement that he took "not the smallest notice" of Douglas's communications from Egypt is contradicted by a letter written toward the end of December 1893, while Douglas was in Cairo, in which Wilde thanks Douglas for writing and tells him, "Our love has . . . come out rose-crowned as of old. Let us always be infinitely dear to each other, as indeed we have been always. . . . I think of you daily, and am always devotedly yours" (CL 577–78).

77. "and I gladly devoted myself to the Art whose progress I had allowed you to interrupt" added to the manuscript as an afterthought.

78. "so as to prevent your returning to England" added to the manuscript as an afterthought.

to keep you there, either as an honorary *attaché,* if that were possible, or to learn modern languages, if it were not, or for any reason she chose, at least during two or three years, and for your sake as well as for mine.

In the meantime you are writing to me by every post from Egypt. I took not the smallest notice of any of your communications. I read them, and tore them up.[76] I had quite settled to have no more to do with you. My mind was made up, and I gladly devoted myself to the Art whose progress I had allowed you to interrupt.[77] At the end of three months, your mother with that unfortunate weakness of will that characterises her, and that in the tragedy of my life has been an element no less fatal than your father's violence, actually writes to me herself—I have no doubt, of course, at your instigation—tells me that you are extremely anxious to hear from me, and in order that I should have no excuse for not communicating with you, sends me your address in Athens, which, of course, I knew perfectly well. I confess I was absolutely astounded at her letter. I could not understand how, after what she had written to me in December, and what I in answer had written to her, she could in any way try to repair or to renew my unfortunate friendship with you. I acknowledged her letter, of course, and again urged her to try and get you connected with some Embassy abroad, so as to prevent your returning to England,[78] but I did not write to you, or take any more notice of your telegrams than I did before your mother had written to me. Finally you actually telegraphed to my wife begging her to use her influence with me to get me to write to you. Our friendship had always been a source of distress to her: not merely because she had never liked you personally, but because she saw how your continual companionship altered me and not for the better: still, just as she had always been most gracious and hospitable to you, so she could not bear the idea of my being in any way unkind—for so it seemed to her—to any of my friends. She thought, knew indeed that it was a thing alien to my character. At her request I did communicate with you. I remember the wording of my telegram quite well. I said that time healed every wound but that for many months to come I would neither write to you nor see you. You started without

79. "the family has always been noted for an eccentricity which has led to some strange romances, to some extremely dramatic episodes, and to a large number of episodes" (Obituary of Percy Douglas, 10th Marquess of Queensberry, August 1920, quoted in Linda Stratmann, *The Marquess of Queensberry: Wilde's Nemesis* [New Haven, CT: Yale University Press, 2013], vi).

80. "ugly" added to the manuscript as an afterthought.

81. "one last interview" was an afterthought, substituted for "one interview at any rate" in the manuscript.

82. Café Restaurant Voisin, at 261 Rue Saint-Honoré, ruled by the celebrated chef Alexandre Étienne Choron (1837–1924); and Café Paillard, at 38 Boulevard des Italiens. At the former, whose immense wine cellars were said to be the largest of any restaurant in the world, "none but the rich dare sit at the tables," while the latter, according to C. R. Graham, was "distinguished not for its size and splendid furnishings but because it is the resort of a class that has no proper appreciation of money and very little of propriety" ("Midnight in the Swell Cafés," in his *Roses and Thorns of Paris and London* [New York: Western W. Wilson, 1897], 56–57).

83. "unfeigned" and "gentle and penitent" were added to this clause, in superscript, as afterthoughts.

84. Shortly after their reunion in Paris at the end of March 1894, Wilde wrote to Douglas, "I miss you so much. The gay, gilt and gracious lad has gone away." Three months later still, in July of 1894, Wilde wrote Douglas one of the most eloquent love letters he ever composed, saying: "I want to see you. . . . I can't live without you. You are so dear, so wonderful. I think of you all day long and miss your grace, your boyish beauty, the bright sword-play of your wit, the delicate fancy of your genius. . . . Your lovely life goes always hand in hand with mine. . . . I have no words for how I love you" (*CL* 594).

85. On 1 April 1894, after joining Wilde and Douglas at lunch at the Café Royal, Queensberry wrote to Douglas, "Your intimacy with this man Wilde . . . must either cease or I will disown you. . . . I now hear on good authority, but this may be false, that his wife is petitioning to divorce him for sodomy and other crimes. . . . If I thought the actual thing was true, . . . I should be quite justified in shooting him at sight" (quoted in Ellmann, *Oscar Wilde*, 417–18). Two days later, Queensberry told Douglas, "If I catch

delay for Paris, sending me passionate telegrams on the road to beg me
to see you once, at any rate. I declined. You arrived in Paris late on a
Saturday night, and found a brief letter from me waiting for you at your
Hotel stating that I would not see you. Next morning I receive in Tite
Street a telegram of some ten or eleven pages in length from you. You
stated in it that no matter what you had done to me you could not believe that I would absolutely decline to see you: you reminded me that
for the sake of seeing me even for one hour you had travelled six days
and nights across Europe without stopping once on the way: you made
what I must admit was a most pathetic appeal, and ended with what
seemed to me a threat of suicide, and one not thinly veiled. You had yourself often told me how many of your race there had been who had
stained their hands in their own blood; your uncle certainly, your grand-
father possibly; many others in the mad, bad line from which you
come.[79] Pity, my old affection for you, regard for your mother to whom
your death under such dreadful circumstances would have been a blow
almost too great for her to bear, the horror of the idea that so young a
life, and one that amidst all its ugly[80] faults had still promise of beauty
in it, should come to so revolting an end, mere humanity itself—all
these, if excuses be necessary, must serve as my excuse for consenting
to accord you one last interview.[81] When I arrived in Paris, your tears,
breaking out again and again all through the evening, and falling over
your cheeks like rain as we sat, at dinner first at Voisin's, at supper at
Paillard's[82] afterwards: the unfeigned joy you evinced at seeing me,
holding my hand whenever you could, as though you were a gentle and
penitent child:[83] your contrition, so simple and sincere, at the moment:
made me consent to renew our friendship.[84] Two days after we had returned to London, your father saw you having luncheon with me at the
Café Royal, joined my table, drank of my wine, and that afternoon,
through a letter addressed to you, began his first attack on me.[85]

It may be strange, but I had once again, I will not say the chance, but
the duty of separating from you forced on me. I need hardly remind you
that I refer to your conduct to me at Brighton from October 10th to 13th,

you again with that man I will make a public scandal in a way you little dream of" (quoted in Ellmann, *Oscar Wilde*, 418).

86. Wilde and Douglas stayed at Brighton's Hotel Metropole (not the Grand Hotel, as Wilde mistakenly says below) from 4 to 7 October 1894 (not the 10th to 13th).

87. "profligacy" added to the manuscript as an afterthought.

88. "in Art" and "the treatment of" added to the manuscript as an afterthought.

89. Wilde arrived in Worthing—"a seaside resort," as Jack explains to Lady Bracknell in Act 1 of *The Importance*—on or shortly before 10 August 1894, a day or two after his wife and children. Wilde intended to compose *The Importance of Being Earnest* there, but he also looked forward to a vacation with his family. Before he left London, Wilde invited Douglas to come too, writing, "When you come to Worthing . . . all things will be done for your honour and joy. . . . You may find the meals, etc, tedious. But you will come, won't you ?" (*CL* 598). Douglas arrived on or around 14 August and stayed for three weeks. Shortly after Douglas's departure, Wilde wrote, "Dear dear boy, you are more to me than any one . . . has any idea; you are the atmosphere of beauty through which I see life . . . the incarnation of all lovely things. . . . I think of you night and day" (*CL* 602). Clearly missing Douglas, he asked some days later, "Could you meet me at Newhaven on the 15th? Dieppe is very amusing and bright. Or would you come down here first?" signing his letter, "ever devotedly yours" (*CL* 607). Constance and the children left on 12 September to prepare for the children's return to school. Douglas's second visit to Worthing, probably a short one, was also the result of a direct invitation. It took place a day or two after Constance's departure, or else shortly after he had joined Wilde on a four-day trip to Dieppe. For precise details, see Antony Edmonds, *Oscar Wilde's Scandalous Summer: The 1894 Worthing Holiday and the Aftermath* (Stroud, UK: Amberley, 2015), 65–119.

90. What Douglas "actually proposed" was originally something different in the manuscript: "stay in my house" is a substitution, added in super-script, but what it replaced is now illegible.

91. "I had no option in the matter" added to the manuscript as an afterthought.

1894.[86] Three years ago is a long time for you to go back. But we who live in prison, and in whose lives there is no event but sorrow, have to measure time by throbs of pain, and the record of bitter moments. We have nothing else to think of. Suffering—curious as it may sound to you—is the means by which we exist, because it is the only means by which we become conscious of existing; and the remembrance of suffering in the past is necessary to us as the warrant, the evidence of our continued identity. Between myself and the memory of joy lies a gulf no less deep than that between myself and joy in its actuality. Had our life together been as the world fancied it to be, one simply of pleasure, profligacy[87] and laughter, I would not be able to recall a single passage in it. It is because it was full of moments and days tragic, bitter, sinister in their warnings, dull or dreadful in their monotonous scenes and unseemly violences, that I can see or hear each separate incident in its detail, can indeed see or hear little else. So much in this place do men live by pain that my friendship with you, in the way through which I am forced to remember it, appears to me always as a prelude consonant with those varying modes of anguish which each day I have to realise; nay more, to necessitate them even; as though my life, whatever it had seemed to myself and to others, had all the while been a real Symphony of Sorrow, passing through its rhythmically-linked movements to its certain resolution, with that inevitableness that in Art characterises the treatment of every great theme.[88]

I spoke of your conduct to me on three successive days, three years ago, did I not? I was trying to finish my last play at Worthing by myself. The two visits you had paid to me had ended.[89] You suddenly appeared a third time bringing with you a companion whom you actually proposed should stay in my house.[90] I (you must admit now quite properly) absolutely declined. I entertained you, of course; I had no option in the matter:[91] but elsewhere, and not in my own home. The next day, a Monday, your companion returned to the duties of his profession, and you stayed with me. Bored with Worthing, and still more, I have no doubt, with my fruitless efforts to concentrate my attention on my play, the only thing that really interested me at the moment, you insist on being taken

92. Wilde's manuscript revisions of this sentence give interesting insight into his effort to represent Douglas as interfering with his art: "fruitless" and "the only thing that really interested me at the moment" were afterthoughts, added in superscript, while "attention" was a substitution for "interest."

93. "whatever you may think" added to the manuscript as an afterthought.

94. On 5 October 1894, Wilde wrote from the Hotel Metropole to Ada Leverson: "My friend is not allowed to go out today. I sit by his side and read him passages from his own life" (CL 618). On the following day he added: "Much better, temperature gone down, is to be allowed chicken to the sound of flutes at 7.30" (CL 618).

95. At 26 King's Road, Brighton, from 8–18 October 1894. See *The Real Trial of Oscar Wilde*, 66, n.118.

96. "calmly" added to the manuscript as an afterthought.

to the Grand Hotel, at Brighton.[92] The night we arrive you fall ill with
that dreadful low fever that is foolishly called the influenza, your second, if
not third attack. I need not remind you how I waited on you, and tended
you, not merely with every luxury of fruit, flowers, presents, books, and
the like that money can procure, but with that affection, tenderness and
love that, whatever you may think,[93] is not to be procured for money.[94]
Except for an hour's walk in the morning, an hour's drive in the afternoon[,] I never left the Hotel. I got special grapes from London for
you, as you did not care for those the Hotel supplied, invented things to
please you, remained either with you or in the room next to yours, sat
with you every evening to quiet or amuse you. After four or five days
you recover, and I take lodgings[95] in order to try and finish my play. You,
of course, accompany me. The morning after the day on which we were
installed I feel extremely ill. You have to go to London on business, but
promise to return in the afternoon. In London you meet a friend, and do
not come back to Brighton till late the next day, by which time I am in a
terrible fever, and the Doctor finds I have caught the influenza from you.
Nothing could have been more uncomfortable for anyone ill than the
lodgings turn out to be. My sitting-room is on the first floor, my bedroom on the third. There is no manservant to wait on one, not even
anyone to send out on a message, or to get what the Doctor orders. But
you are there. I feel no alarm. The next two days you leave me entirely
alone without care, without attendance, without anything. It was not a
question of grapes, flowers, and charming gifts: it was a question of mere
necessaries: I could not even get the milk the doctor had ordered for me:
lemonade was pronounced an impossibility: and when I begged you to
procure me a book at the bookseller's, or if they had not got whatever I
had fixed on to choose something else, you never even take the trouble
to go there. And when I was left all day without anything to read in
consequence, you calmly[96] tell me that you bought me the book and that
they promised to send it down, a statement which I found out by chance
afterwards to have been entirely untrue from beginning to end. All the
while you are of course living at my expense, driving about, dining at

Frans Masereel, woodcut illustration for Oscar Wilde, *The Ballad of Reading Gaol* (Munich: Drei Masken Verlages, 1923).

the Grand Hotel, and indeed only appearing in my room for money. On the Saturday night, you having left me completely unattended and alone since the morning, I asked you to come back after dinner, and sit with me for a little. With irritable voice and ungracious manner you promise to do so. I wait till eleven o'clock and you never appear. I then left a note for you in your room just reminding you of the promise you had made me, and how you had kept it. At three in the morning, unable to sleep, and tortured with thirst, I made my way, in the dark and cold, down to the sitting-room in the hopes of finding some water there. I found *you*. You fell on me with every hideous word an intemperate mood, an undisciplined and untutored nature could suggest. By the terrible alchemy of egotism you converted your remorse into rage. You accused me of selfishness in expecting you to be with me when I was ill; of standing between you and your amusements; of trying to deprive you of your pleasures. You told me, and I know it was quite true, that you had come back at midnight simply in order to change your dress-clothes, and go out again to where you hoped new pleasures were waiting for you, but that by leaving for you a letter in which I had reminded you that you had neglected me the whole day and the whole evening, I had really robbed you of your desire for more enjoyments, and diminished your actual capacity for fresh delights. I went back upstairs in disgust, and remained sleepless till dawn, nor till long after dawn was I able to get anything to quench the thirst of the fever that was on me. At eleven o'clock you came into my room. In the previous scene I could not help observing that by my letter I had, at any rate, checked you in a night of more than usual excess. In the morning you were quite yourself. I waited naturally to hear what excuses you had to make, and in what way you were going to ask for the forgiveness that you knew in your heart was invariably waiting for you, no matter what you did; your absolute trust that I would always forgive you being the thing in you that I always really liked the best, perhaps the best thing in you to like. So far from doing that, you began to repeat the same scene with renewed emphasis and more violent assertion. I told you at length to leave the room: you pretended

97. "state of absolute nervous prostration, as well as in a" was an afterthought, added to the manuscript in superscript.

98. An important indicator of Wilde's faulty memory: in 1894 his birthday fell on a Tuesday.

99. "But I was entirely deceived. I had underrated you" added to the manuscript as an afterthought.

to do so, but when I lifted up my head from the pillow in which I had buried it, you were still there, and with brutality of laughter and hysteria of rage you moved suddenly towards me. A sense of horror came over me, for what exact reason I could not make out; but I got out of my bed at once, and bare-footed and just as I was, made my way down the two flights of stairs to the sitting-room, which I did not leave till the owner of the lodgings—whom I had rung for—had assured me that you had left my bedroom, and promised to remain within call, in case of necessity. After an interval of an hour, during which time the doctor had come and found me, of course, in a state of absolute nervous prostration, as well as in a worse condition of fever than I had been at the outset,[97] you returned silently, for money: took what you could find on the dressing-table and mantelpiece, and left the house with your luggage. Need I tell you what I thought of you during the two wretched lonely days of illness that followed? Is it necessary for me to state that I saw clearly that it would be a dishonour to myself to continue even an acquaintance with such a one as you had showed yourself to be? That I recognised that the ultimate moment had come, and recognised it as being really a great relief? And that I knew that for the future my Art and Life would be freer and better and more beautiful in every possible way? Ill as I was, I felt at ease. The fact that the separation was irrevocable gave me peace.

By Tuesday the fever had left me, and for the first time I dined downstairs. Wednesday was my birthday.[98] Amongst the telegrams and communications on my table was a letter in your handwriting. I opened it with a sense of sadness over me. I knew that the time had gone by when a pretty phrase, an expression of affection, a word of sorrow would make me take you back. But I was entirely deceived. I had underrated you.[99] The letter you sent to me on my birthday was an elaborate repetition of the two scenes, set cunningly and carefully down in black and white! You mocked me with common jests. Your one satisfaction in the whole affair was, you said, that you retired to the Grand Hotel, and entered your luncheon to my account before you left for Town. You congratulated me on my

100. Wilde will later specify that the restaurant where Douglas's "ridicu-lous pistol" went off was the Berkeley Hotel (p. 115 below).

101. Queensberry's threatening visit to Wilde in Tite Street took place on 30 June 1894.

102. Wilde was incarcerated in a cell by himself in five different prisons: Holloway Prison while on remand (6 April–7 May 1895); Newgate Prison immediately following conviction (25–27 May 1895); Pentonville Prison (27 May–4 July 1895 and again 18–19 May 1897); Wandsworth Prison (4 July–20 November 1895); and Reading Prison (20 November 1895–18 May 1897).

prudence in leaving my sickbed, on my sudden flight downstairs. "It was an ugly moment for you," you said, "uglier than you imagine." Ah! I felt it but too well. What it had really meant I did not know: whether you had with you the pistol you had bought to try and frighten your father with, and that, thinking it to be unloaded, you had once fired off in a public restaurant in my company:[100] whether your hand was moving towards a common dinner-knife that by chance was lying on the table between us: whether, forgetting in your rage your low stature and inferior strength, you had thought of some specially personal insult, or attack even, as I lay ill there: I could not tell. I do not know to the present moment. All I know is that a feeling of utter horror had come over me, and that I had felt that unless I left the room at once, and got away, you would have done, or tried to do something that would have been, even to you, a source of lifelong shame. Only once before in my life had I experienced such a feeling of horror at any human being. It was when in my library at Tite Street, waving his small hands in the air in epileptic fury, your father, with his bully, or his friend, between us, had stood uttering every foul word his foul mind could think of, and screaming the loathsome threats he afterwards with such cunning carried out.[101] In the latter case he, of course, was the one who had to leave the room first. I drove him out. In your case I went. It was not the first time I had been obliged to save you from yourself.

You concluded your letter by saying: "When you are not on your pedestal you are not interesting. The next time you are ill I will go away at once." Ah! what coarseness of fibre does that reveal! What an entire lack of imagination! How callous, how common had the temperament by that time become! "When you are not on your pedestal you are not interesting. The next time you are ill I will go away at once." How often have those words come back to me in the wretched solitary cell of the various prisons I have been sent to.[102] I have said them to myself over and over again, and seen in them, I hope unjustly, some of the secret of your strange silence. For you to write thus to me, when the very illness and fever from which I was suffering I had caught from tending you, was of course

103. "and shamed" added as an afterthought.

104. Sir George Henry Lewis (1833–1911), the most respected society lawyer of his day. "When one professional gentleman is traduced by another in print," reported *The Era* on 16 December 1893, "the injured party goes off at once to Mr. George Lewis" (quoted in Henry James, *A Life in Letters*, ed. Philip Horne [Harmondsworth: Penguin, 1999], 263). Wilde called him "Brilliant. Formidable. A man of the world. Concerned in every great case in England. Oh, he knows all about us—and forgives us all" (quoted in *CL* 134, n.4). Wilde will shortly write, "When I was deprived of his advice and help and regard I was deprived of the one great safeguard of my life." Unfortunately for Wilde, Lewis was retained by Douglas's father in the libel case that led to Wilde's downfall.

105. It was widely believed that Douglas's elder brother, Francis Douglas, Viscount Drumlanrig, committed suicide when his gun discharged on 18 October 1894, possibly because he expected public revelation of his alleged affair with Lord Rosebery. Alfred Douglas came to believe this too, although as Douglas Murray observes, "there is no proof that Drumlanrig was having an affair with Rosebery," "all the accounts point to an accident," and "the truth will almost certainly never be known" (Murray, *Bosie*, 68). See also p. 112, n.140 below.

106. Latin phrase meaning "tears for things," deriving from the *Aeneid* (1:462).

revolting in its coarseness and crudity; but for any human being in the whole world to write thus to another would be a sin for which there is no pardon, were there any sin for which there is none.

I confess that when I had finished your letter I felt almost polluted, as if by associating with one of such a nature I had soiled and shamed[103] my life irretrievably. I had, it is true, done so, but I was not to learn how fully till just six months later on in life. I settled with myself to go back to London on the Friday, and see Sir George Lewis[104] personally and request him to write to your father to state that I had determined never under any circumstances to allow you to enter my house, to sit at my board, to talk to me, walk with me, or anywhere and at any time to be my companion at all. This done I would have written to you just to inform you of the course of action I had adopted; the reasons you would inevitably have realised for yourself. I had everything arranged on Thursday night, when on Friday morning, as I was sitting at breakfast before starting, I happened to open the newspaper and saw in it a telegram stating that your elder brother, the real head of the family, the heir to the title, the pillar of the house, had been found dead in a ditch with his gun lying discharged beside him. The horror of the circumstances of the tragedy, now known to have been an accident,[105] but then stained with a darker suggestion; the pathos of the sudden death of one so loved by all who knew him, and almost on the eve, as it were, of his marriage; my idea of what your own sorrow would, or should be; my consciousness of the misery awaiting your mother at the loss of the one to whom she clung for comfort and joy in life, and who, as she told me once herself, had from the very day of his birth never caused her to shed a single tear; my consciousness of your own isolation, both your other brothers being out of Europe, and you consequently the only one to whom your mother and sister could look not merely for companionship in their sorrow, but also for those dreary responsibilities of dreadful detail that Death always brings with it; the mere sense of the *lacrimae rerum*,[106] of the tears of which the world is made, and of the sadness of all human things; . . . out of the confluence of these thoughts and emotions crowding into my brain came infinite pity

107. Wilde originally wrote "told" before replacing it with "invited, nay entreated" and then deleting "nay entreated."

108. "now be weeping" substituted for "be now" in the manuscript.

109. "for pleasure or" was an afterthought, added to the manuscript in superscript.

for you and your family. My own griefs and bitternesses against you I forgot. What you had been to me in my sickness, I could not be to you in your bereavement. I telegraphed at once to you my deepest sympathy, and in the letter that followed invited[107] you to come to my house as soon as you were able. I felt that to abandon you at that particular moment, and formally through a solicitor, would have been too terrible for you.

On your return to town from the actual scene of the tragedy to which you had been summoned, you came at once to me very sweetly and very simply, in your suit of woe, and with your eyes dim with tears. You sought consolation and help, as a child might seek it. I opened to you my house, my home, my heart. I made your sorrow mine also, that you might have help in bearing it. Never, even by one word, did I allude to your conduct towards me, to the revolting scenes, and the revolting letter. Your grief, which was real, seemed to me to bring you nearer to me than you had ever been. The flowers you took from me to put on your brother's grave were to be a symbol not merely of the beauty of his life, but of the beauty that in all lives lies dormant and may be brought to light. . . . The Gods are strange. It is not of our vices only they make instruments to scourge us. They bring us to ruin through what in us is good, gentle, humane, loving. But for my pity and affection for you and yours, I would not now be weeping[108] in this terrible place.

Of course I discern in all our relations, not Destiny merely, but Doom: Doom that walks always swiftly, because she goes to the shedding of blood. Through your father you come of a race, marriage with whom is horrible, friendship fatal, and that lays violent hands either on its own life or on the lives of others. In every little circumstance in which the ways of our lives met; in every point of great, or seemingly trivial import in which you came to me for pleasure or for help;[109] in the small chances, the slight accidents that look, in their relation to life, to be no more than the dust that dances in a beam, or the leaf that flutters from a tree, Ruin followed, like the echo of a bitter cry, or the shadow that hunts with the beast of prey. Our friendship really begins with your begging me in a most pathetic and charming letter to assist you in a position appalling to

110. "a young man at Oxford" substituted for "an undergraduate" in the manuscript. For the "Oxford temper," see p. 60, n.22 above. For the nature of Douglas's "appalling position," see p. 56, n.9 above.

111. In Ancient Greek myth, Hylas was the favorite companion of Heracles (the Roman Hercules); Hyacinth was a beautiful youth and lover of the god Apollo, also much admired by the West Wind, Zephyr; Narcisse is the French name for the beautiful Greek youth Narcissus, beloved by youths of both sexes, who died of infatuation with his own image; Jonquil, based on the jonquil or *Narcissus jonquilla*, a species of daffodil, is a figure of Wilde's own invention, almost certainly meant to call Narcissus to mind.

112. Plato's *Symposium*, written in the form of a dramatic dialogue between Socrates (Plato's teacher) and six young male interlocutors, is a philosophical inquiry into the nature and genesis of love. In Wilde's day, it was widely viewed as an apologia for love between men.

113. "wit or culture" substituted for "feeling" in the manuscript; "either university" refers to Oxford and Cambridge.

114. Alfred Wood, a young clerk and one-time lover of both Wilde and Douglas. Upon finding love letters from Wilde in an old suit of clothes given to him by Douglas, Wood, in concert with the blackmailers William Allen and Robert Henry Cliburn, sent copies of the most revealing letter to the actor-manager Herbert Beerbohm Tree, among others, in an attempt to blackmail Wilde. See *The Real Trial of Oscar Wilde*, 50–55, 118–34.

115. "had to pay a huge sum of money" substituted for "been blackmailed" in the manuscript.

116. "That is the result of writing you a charming letter" added to the manuscript as an afterthought.

117. "I am forced to take everything you have done on my own shoulders and answer for it" added to the manuscript as an afterthought.

anyone, doubly so to a young man at Oxford:[110] I do so, and ultimately through your using my name as your friend with Sir George Lewis, I began to lose his esteem and friendship, a friendship of fifteen years standing. When I was deprived of his advice and help and regard I was deprived of the one great safeguard of my life. You send me a very nice poem, of the undergraduate school of verse, for my approval: I reply by a letter of fantastic literary conceits: I compare you to Hylas, or Hyacinth, Jonquil or Narcisse,[111] or someone whom the great god of Poetry favoured, and honoured with his love. The letter is like a passage from one of Shakespeare's sonnets, transposed to a minor key. It can only be understood by those who have read the *Symposium* of Plato,[112] or caught the spirit of a certain grave mood made beautiful for us in Greek marbles. It was—let me say frankly—the sort of letter I would, in a happy if wilful moment, have written to any graceful young man of either University who had sent me a poem of his own making, certain that he would have sufficient wit or culture[113] to interpret rightly its fantastic phrases. Look at the history of that letter! It passes from you into the hands of a loathsome companion:[114] from him to a gang of blackmailers: copies of it are sent about London to my friends, and to the manager of the theatre where my work is being performed: every construction but the right one is put on it: society is thrilled with the absurd rumours that I have had to pay a huge sum of money[115] for having written an infamous letter to you: this forms the basis of your father's worst attack: I produce the original letter myself in Court to show what it really is: it is denounced by your father's counsel as a revolting and insidious attempt to corrupt Innocence: ultimately it forms part of a criminal charge: the Crown takes it up: the Judge sums up on it with little learning and much morality: I go to prison for it at last. That is the result of writing you a charming letter.[116] While I am staying with you at Salisbury you are terribly alarmed at a threatening communication from a former companion of yours: you beg me to see the writer and help you: I do so: the result is Ruin to me. I am forced to take everything you have done on my own shoulders and answer for it.[117] When, having failed to take your degree, you have

118. Wilde's "Phrases and Philosophies for the Use of the Young" appeared on 1 December 1894 as the lead item in the first and only number of *The Chameleon*, edited by John Francis Bloxam, "an undergraduate of strange beauty" (*CL* 625). It is doubtful that "Phrases and Philosophies" was originally destined for *The Saturday Review* since that paper had already published Wilde's "A Few Maxims for the Instruction of the Over-educated," a similar page of paradoxes, the previous month. Shortly after this, Wilde wrote to Ada Leverson that her "exquisite" aphorisms "must appear in the second number of *The Chameleon*" (*CL* 625).

119. Wilde is referring to Bloxam's story "The Priest and the Acolyte" and to Douglas's poem "Two Loves," which ends, "I am the Love that dare not speak its name." Both of these texts about male same-sex love originally appeared alongside Wilde's "Phrases and Philosophies" in *The Chameleon*, and Wilde was pressed in court about their "indecencies."

120. "and 'the Love that dares not tell its name'" added to the manuscript as an afterthought. Asked in court to explain "the Love that dare not speak its name," Wilde replied:

> "The Love that dare not speak its name" in this century is such a great affection of an elder for a younger man as there was between David and Jonathan, such as Plato made the very basis of his philosophy, and such as you find in the sonnets of Michelangelo and Shakespeare. It is that deep, spiritual affection that is as pure as it is perfect. It dictates and pervades great works of art like those of Shakespeare and Michelangelo, and those two letters of mine, such as they are. It is in this century misunderstood, so much misunderstood that it may be described as the "Love that dare not speak its name," and on account of it I am placed where I am now. It is beautiful, it is fine, it is the noblest form of affection. There is nothing unnatural about it. It is intellectual, and it repeatedly exists between an elder and a younger man, when the elder man has intellect, and the younger man has all the joy, hope and glamour of life before him. That it should be so the world does not understand. The world mocks at it and sometimes puts one in the pillory for it. (Quoted in Hyde, *The Trials of Oscar Wilde*, 201.)

121. Although the sale of Wilde's possessions and household effects on 24 April 1895 is sometimes described mistakenly as "forced by Queensberry,

to go down from Oxford, you telegraph to me in London to beg me to come to you: I do so at once: you ask me to take you to Goring, as you did not like, under the circumstances, to go home: at Goring you see a house that charms you: I take it for you: the result from every point of view is Ruin to me. One day you come to me and ask me, as a personal favour to you, to write something for an Oxford undergraduate magazine, about to be started by some friend of yours, whom I had never heard of in all my life, and knew nothing at all about. To please you—what did I not do always to please you?—I send him a page of paradoxes destined originally for the *Saturday Review.*[118] A few months later I find myself standing in the dock of the Old Bailey on account of the character of the magazine. It forms part of the Crown charge against me. I am called upon to defend your friend's prose and your own verse.[119] The former I cannot palliate; the latter I, loyal to the bitter extreme, to your youthful literature as to your youthful life, do very strongly defend, and will not hear of your being a writer of indecencies. But I go to prison, all the same, for your friend's undergraduate magazine, and 'the Love that dares not tell its name.'[120] At Christmas I give you a "very pretty present," as you described it in your letter of thanks, on which I knew you had set your heart, worth some £40 or £50 at most. When the crash of my life comes, and I am ruined, the bailiff who seizes my library, and has it sold, does so to pay for the "very pretty present." It was for that the execution was put into my house.[121] At the ultimate and terrible moment when I am taunted, and spurred-on by your taunts, to take an action against your father and have him arrested, the last straw to which I clutch in my wretched efforts to escape is the terrible expense. I tell the Solicitor in your presence that I have no funds, that I cannot possibly afford the appalling costs, that I have no money at my disposal. What I said was, as you know, perfectly true. On that fatal Friday instead of being in Humphreys's office[122] weakly consenting to my own ruin, I would have been happy and free in France, away from you and your father, unconscious of his loathsome card, and indifferent to your letters, if I had been able to leave the Avondale Hotel. But the Hotel people absolutely refused to

who demanded payment of his £600 costs" (Ellmann, *Oscar Wilde*, 459), it was initiated by other creditors to whom Wilde had been long indebted. According to one newspaper at the time, the sale was occasioned by "three writs representing somewhere about £400.... [T]he creditors enforcing the proceedings claimed principally for cigarettes and cigarette cases" (*The Morning,* 25 April 1895, quoted in *The Oscar Wilde File*, comp. Jonathan Goodman [London: Allison and Busby, 1989], 100); and Wilde himself will later tell Douglas "I cannot leave the jeweller out of pocket for the presents I gave you" (p. 279 below). Presumably *The Morning* refers to the writs originally served on Wilde in or by late February 1895, when he complained that "rumours of [his] prosperity [had] reached the commercial classes" (*CL* 633). However, according to Donald Mead, the sale was occasioned principally by the actions of Wilde's landlord, who distrained for unpaid rent ("Oscar's Finances: The Pillage of the House Beautiful," *The Wildean: A Journal of Oscar Wilde Studies* 47 [July 2015]: 39).

122. Charles Octavius Humphreys (1828–1902), Wilde's lawyer throughout his three trials. Wilde and Douglas met with him on Friday, 1 March 1895.

123. "of yours" was an afterthought, added in superscript to the manuscript. This companion was almost certainly Ernest Scarfe, named in Queensberry's plea of justification as "committing acts of gross indecency and immorality" with Wilde, with whom Wilde admitted in court to having been at the Avondale Hotel at 68a Piccadilly in February 1895 (*The Real Trial of Oscar Wilde*, 200). Although Douglas had first met Scarfe "at a skating rink" (*The Real Trial of Oscar Wilde*, 198), Scarfe had been introduced to Wilde by the procurer Alfred Taylor (see *The Real Trial of Oscar Wilde*, 197).

124. To obtain a warrant for Queensberry's arrest on the charge of criminal libel.

125. Wilde will say later in the text that he had been served by Queensberry's lawyers with a writ for "a paltry £700, the amount of their taxed costs" (p. 133 below). Queensberry's bankruptcy petition against Wilde claimed £677 "in respect of law costs in connexion with legal proceedings instituted by the debtor" (*The Oscar Wilde File*, comp. Goodman, 138). The sum of £677 represented the "meagre balance" because Wilde's own legal costs had been far greater.

allow me to go. You had been staying with me for ten days: indeed you had ultimately, to my great and, you will admit, rightful indignation, brought a companion of yours[123] to stay with me also: my bill for the ten days was nearly £140. The proprietor said he could not allow my luggage to be removed from the Hotel till I had paid the account in full. That is what kept me in London. Had it not been for the Hotel bill I would have gone to Paris on Thursday morning.

When I told the Solicitor I had no money to face the gigantic expense, you interposed at once. You said that your own family would be only too delighted to pay all the necessary costs: that your father had been an incubus to them all: that they had often discussed the possibility of getting him put into a lunatic asylum so as to keep him out of the way: that he was a daily source of annoyance and distress to your mother and to everyone else: that if I would only come forward to have him shut up I would be regarded by the family as their champion and their benefactor: and that your mother's rich relations themselves would look on it as a real delight to be allowed to pay all costs and expenses that might be incurred in any such effort. The Solicitor closed at once, and I was hurried to the Police Court.[124] I had no excuse left for not going. I was forced into it. Of course your family don't pay the costs, and when I am made bankrupt, it is by your father, and *for* the costs—the meagre balance of them—some £700.[125] At the present moment my wife, estranged from me over the important question of whether I should have £3 or £3.10[126] a week to live on, is preparing a divorce suit, for which, of course, entirely new evidence and an entirely new trial, to be followed perhaps by more serious proceedings, will be necessary. I, naturally, know nothing of the details. I merely know the name of the witness on whose evidence my wife's solicitors rely. It is your own Oxford servant, whom at your special request I took into my service for our summer at Goring.[127]

But, indeed, I need not go on further with more instances of the strange Doom you seem to have brought on me in all things big or little. It makes me feel sometimes as if you yourself had been merely a puppet worked by some secret and unseen hand to bring terrible events to a

126. Three pounds and ten shillings.

127. In the early months of 1897, Wilde's estranged wife, Constance, was willing to provide Wilde with an allowance of £150 per year (he was holding out for £200 per year) as well as considering instituting divorce proceedings. Since Constance could not legally divorce Wilde on the grounds of his conviction for gross indecency, a divorce action would have been successful only if Constance managed to prove in court that Wilde had committed the more serious crime of sodomy. To this end, she had solicited Douglas's manservant, Walter Grainger (whom, according to Queensberry's Plea of Justification, Wilde "did solicit and incite...to commit sodomy"), to serve as a witness in possible divorce proceedings. In the end, Constance did not pursue the divorce, and it was with considerable relief that, in April 1897, Wilde accepted her terms, including an allowance of £150 per year, for legal separation.

128. Five years earlier, Wilde had felt differently. When likening actors to "moving puppets," he had said they had "many advantages.... They never argue. They have no views about art. They have no private lives.... They are admirably docile, and have no personalities at all" (*CL* 519–20).

129. "great affection" substituted for "devotion to me" in the manuscript; also "wonderful" added to "appreciation" as an afterthought.

130. "to you it seemed so" substituted for "it was" in the manuscript.

131. Lady Queensberry, Lord Alfred's mother, possessed a house in Cathedral Close, Salisbury, in Wiltshire. Douglas commemorated the place in his 1893 sonnet "In Sarum Close" (*Sarum* was the Roman name for modern-day Salisbury, with its famous Gothic cathedral), in which he writes:

> I thought to cool my burning hands
> In this calm twilight of gray Gothic things:
> But Love has laughed, and, spreading swifter wings
> Than my poor pinions, once again with bands
> Of silken strength my fainting heart commands,
> And once again he plays on passionate strings.

(Caspar Wintermans, *Alfred Douglas: A Poet's Life and His Finest Work* [London: Peter Owen, 2007], 212.)

terrible issue. But puppets themselves have passions.[128] They will bring a new plot into what they are presenting, and twist the ordered issue of vicissitude to suit some whim or appetite of their own. To be entirely free, and at the same time entirely dominated by law, is the eternal paradox of human life that we realise at every moment; and this, I often think, is the only explanation possible of your nature, if indeed for the profound and terrible mysteries of a human soul there is any explanation at all, except one that makes the mystery more marvellous still.

Of course you had your illusions, lived in them indeed, and through their shifting mists and coloured veils saw all things changed. You thought, I remember quite well, that your devoting yourself to me, to the entire exclusion of your family and family life, was a proof of your wonderful appreciation of me, and your great affection.[129] No doubt to you it seemed so.[130] But recollect that with me was luxury, high living, unlimited pleasure, money without stint. Your family life bored you. The "cold cheap wine of Salisbury,"[131] to use a phrase of your own making, was distasteful to you. On my side, and along with my intellectual attractions, were the fleshpots of Egypt.[132] When you could not find me to be with, the companions whom you chose as substitutes were not flattering.

You thought again that in sending a lawyer's letter to your father to say that, rather than sever your eternal friendship with me, you would give up the allowance of £250 a year which, with I believe deductions for your Oxford debts, he was then making you, you were realising the very chivalry of friendship, touching the noblest note of self-denial. But your surrender of your little allowance did not mean that you were ready to give up even one of your most superfluous luxuries, or most unnecessary extravagances. On the contrary. Your appetite for luxurious living was never so keen. My expenses for eight days in Paris for myself, you, and your Italian servant were nearly £150: Paillard alone absorbing £85.[133] At the rate at which you wished to live, your entire income for a whole year, if you had taken your meals alone, and been especially economical in your selection of the cheaper form of pleasures, would hardly have lasted you for three weeks. The fact that in what was merely a pretence

132. Now, as in Wilde's day, *fleshpots of Egypt* evokes high-living, self-indulgence, and loose sexuality. In the Bible, however, the phrase connotes cauldrons of plentiful meat, for which the starving Israelites were nostalgic following their exodus from Egypt.

133. For Paillard, see p. 84, n.82 above.

134. "what was merely a pretence of" substituted for "your" in the manuscript.

135. Lady Queensberry, born Sybil Montgomery (1845–1935), divorced the Marquess of Queensbury in 1887 after twenty-one years of marriage. The "terrible wrongs and sufferings" to which Wilde alludes include infidelities, rages, and even a suggestion by the Marquess that she should share their home with his mistress. According to Lord Alfred Douglas, Queensberry wrote his wife abusive letters during his long absences from home, and he once turned her and the rest of his family out of the house, without notice, in order that he might host a party of his friends, including his mistress. See Frank Harris and Lord Alfred Douglas, *A New Preface to "The Life and Confessions of Oscar Wilde"* (London: Fortune Press, 1925), 22.

136. "You should have taken him as your model" added to the manuscript as an afterthought.

of[134] bravado you had surrendered your allowance, such as it was, gave you at last a plausible reason for your claim to live at my expense, or what you thought a plausible reason: and on many occasions you seriously availed yourself of it, and gave the very fullest expression to it: and the continued drain, principally of course on me, but also to a certain extent, I know, on your mother, was never so distressing, because in my case at any rate, never so completely unaccompanied by the smallest word of thanks, or sense of limit.

You thought again that in attacking your own father with dreadful letters, abusive telegrams, and insulting postcards you were really fighting your mother's battles, coming forward as her champion, and avenging the no doubt terrible wrongs and sufferings of her married life.[135] It was quite an illusion on your part; one of your worst indeed. The way for you to have avenged your mother's wrongs on your father, if you considered it part of a son's duty to do so, was by being a better son to your mother than you had been: by not making her afraid to speak to you on serious things: by not signing bills the payment of which devolved on her: by being gentler to her, and not bringing sorrow into her days. Your brother Francis made great amends to her for what she had suffered, by his sweetness and goodness to her through the brief years of his flower-like life. You should have taken him as your model.[136] You were wrong even in fancying that it would have been an absolute delight and joy to your mother if you *had* managed through me to get your father put into prison. I feel sure you were wrong. And if you want to know what a woman really feels when her husband, and the father of her children, is in prison dress, in a prison cell, write to my wife and ask her. She will tell you.

I also had my illusions. I thought life was going to be a brilliant comedy, and that you were to be one of many graceful figures in it. I found it to be a revolting and repellent tragedy, and that the sinister occasion of the great catastrophe, sinister in its concentration of aim and intensity of narrowed will-power, was yourself, stripped of that mask of joy and pleasure by which you, no less than I, had been deceived and led astray.

137. "twitch and" added to the manuscript as an afterthought.

138. "the street or river down which we passed," added to the manuscript as an afterthought.

You can now understand—can you not?—a little of what I am suffering. Some paper, the *Pall Mall Gazette* I think, describing the dress-rehearsal of one of my plays, spoke of you as following me about like my shadow: the memory of our friendship is the shadow that walks with me here: that seems never to leave me: that wakes me up at night to tell me the same story over and over till its wearisome iteration makes all sleep abandon me till dawn: at dawn it begins again: it follows me into the prison-yard and makes me talk to myself as I tramp round: each detail that accompanied each dreadful moment I am forced to recall: there is nothing that happened in those ill-starred years that I cannot recreate in that chamber of the brain which is set apart for grief or for despair: every strained note of your voice, every twitch and[137] gesture of your nervous hands, every bitter word, every poisonous phrase comes back to me: I remember the street or river down which we passed,[138] the wall or woodland that surrounded us, at what figure on the dial stood the hands of the clock, which way went the wings of the wind, the shape and colour of the moon.

There is, I know, one answer to all that I have said to you, and that is that you loved me: that all through those two and a half years during which the Fates were weaving into one scarlet pattern the threads of our divided lives you really loved me. Yes: I know you did. No matter what your conduct to me was, I always felt that at heart you really did love me. Though I saw quite clearly that my position in the world of Art, the interest my personality had always excited, my money, the luxury in which I lived, the thousand and one things that went to make up a life so charmingly, so wonderfully improbable as mine was, were, each and all of them, elements that fascinated you and made you cling to me: yet besides all this there was something more, some strange attraction for you: you loved me far better than you loved anybody else. But you, like myself, have had a terrible tragedy in your life, though one of an entirely opposite character to mine. Do you want to learn what it was? It was this. In you Hate was always stronger than Love. Your hatred of your father was of such stature that it entirely outstripped, o'erthrew, and overshadowed your

139. "my" was an afterthought, added to the manuscript in superscript. At first Wilde wrote simply "you gambled with money."

140. Lord Alfred's older brother, Francis Douglas, Viscount Drumlanrig, was private secretary to Britain's foreign secretary (and later prime minister), Lord Rosebery, from 1892 until his sudden violent death in 1894 (see p. 96, n.105 above). In June 1893, as a result of Rosebery's patronage, Drumlanrig was given a seat in the House of Lords as a preliminary to becoming a lord-in-waiting to Queen Victoria. The Marquess of Queensberry, already suspecting a homosexual relationship between his oldest son and his patron, was incensed by this promotion, which he took as a personal slight (Queensberry himself possessed no automatic right to sit in the House of Lords, and he consequently felt that his son had been promoted over his head). In August 1893 Queensberry pursued Rosebery to the German spa resort of Bad Homburg, where he had retreated for his health, in order to provoke a physical confrontation. A confrontation was only averted through the personal intervention of the Prince of Wales.

love of me. There was no struggle between them at all, or but little; of such dimensions was your Hatred and of such monstrous growth. You did not realise that there is no room for both passions in the same soul. They cannot live together in that fair carven house. Love is fed by the imagination, by which we become wiser than we know, better than we feel, nobler than we are: by which we can see Life as a whole: by which, and by which alone, we can understand others in their real as in their ideal relations. Only what is fine, and finely conceived, can feed Love. But anything will feed Hate. There was not a glass of champagne you drank, not a rich dish you ate of in all those years that did not feed your Hate and make it fat. So to gratify it, you gambled with my life, as you gambled with my[139] money, carelessly, recklessly, indifferent to the consequence. If you lost, the loss would not, you fancied, be yours. If you won, yours, you knew, would be the exultation, and the advantages of victory.

Hate blinds people. You were not aware of that. Love can read the writing on the remotest star, but Hate so blinded you that you could see no further than the narrow, walled-in, and already lust-withered garden of your common desires. Your terrible lack of imagination, the one really fatal defect of your character, was entirely the result of the Hate that lived in you. Subtly, silently, and in secret, Hate gnawed at your nature, as the lichen bites at the root of some sallow plant, till you grew to see nothing but the most meagre interests and the most petty aims. That faculty in you which Love would have fostered, Hate poisoned and paralysed. When your father first began to attack me it was as your private friend, and in a private letter to you. As soon as I had read the letter, with its obscene threats and coarse violences, I saw at once that a terrible danger was looming on the horizon of my troubled days: I told you I would not be the catspaw between you both in your ancient hatred of each other: that I in London was naturally much bigger game for him than a Secretary for Foreign Affairs at Homburg:[140] that it would be unfair to me to place me even for a moment in such a position: and that I had something better to do with my life than to have scenes with a man drunken,

141. Degraded, or having come down in the world.

142. "Hate blinded you" added to the manuscript as an afterthought.

143. On 2 April 1894, following his father's threat the previous day to disown him if he didn't cease his relations with Wilde, Douglas sent his father an insulting telegram saying, "What a funny little man you are" (quoted in Ellmann, *Oscar Wilde*, 418).

144. Originally this sentence began with "The result of . . ." "From pert telegrams to priggish lawyers' letters was a natural progress, and" was added to the manuscript as an afterthought.

145. Wilde added this sentence to the manuscript as an afterthought.

146. "Your father is on the rampage again," Wilde wrote to Douglas in August 1894. "[He has] been to Café Royal to enquire for us, with threats, etc. I think now it would have been better for me to have him bound over to keep the peace, but what a scandal! Still, it is intolerable to be dogged by a maniac" (*CL* 598).

147. "Hate blinded you" added to the manuscript as an afterthought.

déclassé,[141] and half-witted as he was. You could not be made to see this. Hate blinded you.[142] You insisted that the quarrel had really nothing to do with me: that you would not allow your father to dictate to you in your private friendships: that it would be most unfair of me to interfere. You had already, before you saw me on the subject, sent your father a foolish and vulgar telegram, as your answer.[143] That of course committed you to a foolish and vulgar course of action to follow. The fatal errors of life are not due to man's being unreasonable: an unreasonable moment may be one's finest moment. They are due to man's being logical. There is a wide difference. That telegram conditioned the whole of your subsequent relations with your father, and consequently the whole of my life. And the grotesque thing about it is that it was a telegram of which the commonest street-boy would have been ashamed. From pert telegrams to priggish lawyers' letters was a natural progress, and the result of your lawyer's letters to your father was, of course, to urge him on still further.[144] You left him no option but to go on. You forced it on him as a point of honour, or of dishonour rather, that your appeal should have the more effect.[145] So the next time he attacks me, no longer in a private letter and as your private friend, but in public and as a public man. I have to expel him from my house. He goes from Restaurant to Restaurant looking for me, in order to insult me before the whole world,[146] and in such a manner that if I retaliated I would be ruined, and if I did not retaliate I would be ruined also. *Then* surely was the time when *you* should have come forward, and said that you would not expose me to such hideous attacks, such infamous persecution, on your account, but would, readily and at once, resign any claim you had to my friendship? You feel that now, I suppose. But it never even occurred to you then. Hate blinded you.[147] All you could think of (besides of course writing to him insulting letters and telegrams) was to buy a ridiculous pistol that goes off in the Berkeley, under circumstances that create a worse scandal than ever came to *your* ears. Indeed the idea of your being the object of a terrible quarrel between your father and a man of my position seemed to delight you. It, I suppose very naturally, pleased your vanity, and flattered your self-importance.

148. This sentence and the previous two, from "That your father" to "safe delighted you," were added to the manuscript as an afterthought.

149. The postcard, introduced in the 1870s, was not only cheaper to mail than a letter, but also blurred the border between private and public speech, meaning that the message it contained might legally be considered defamatory or libelous. Douglas's exploitation of the postcard's "immense possibilities" foreshadows his father's use of his private calling card—with the phrase "For Oscar Wilde, posing somdomite" [sic] hastily scrawled on it—as a means of luring Wilde into a libel suit that Queensberry knew Wilde could not win. Queensberry's card—Exhibit A in the disastrous libel trial that led to Wilde's prosecution—is reproduced in facsimile in *Oscar Wilde: Trial and Punishment 1895–1897* (London: Public Record Office, 1997); also in *The Real Trial of Oscar Wilde*, xiv; and in *The Picture of Dorian Gray: An Annotated Uncensored Edition*, ed. Nicholas Frankel (Cambridge, MA: Harvard University Press, 2011), 16.

150. This sentence added as an afterthought. Wilde means that Queensberry was acting according to traits that were hereditary.

151. As Wilde relates, Queensberry was only narrowly prevented from entering the St. James's Theatre on the opening night of *The Importance of Being Earnest*, 14 February 1895, where he planned to denounce Wilde in front of the audience.

That your father might have had your body, which did not interest me, and left me your soul, which did not interest him, would have been to you a distressing solution of the question. You scented the chance of a public scandal and flew to it. The prospect of a battle in which you would be safe delighted you.[148] I never remember you in higher spirits than you were for the rest of that season. Your only disappointment seemed to be that nothing actually happened, and that no further meeting or fracas had taken place between us. You consoled yourself by sending him telegrams of such a character that at last the wretched man wrote to you and said that he had given orders to his servants that no telegram was to be brought to him under any pretence whatsoever. That did not daunt you. You saw the immense opportunities afforded by the open postcard, and availed yourself of them to the full.[149] You hounded him on in the chase still more. I do not suppose he would ever really have given it up. Family instincts were strong in him. His hatred of you was just as persistent as your hatred of him, and I was the stalking-horse for both of you, and a mode of attack as well as a mode of shelter. His very passion for notoriety was not merely individual but racial.[150] Still, if his interest had flagged for a moment your letters and postcards would soon have quickened it to its ancient flame. They did so. And he naturally went on further still. Having assailed me as a private gentleman and in private, as a public man and in public, he ultimately determines to make his final and great attack on me as an artist, and in the place where my Art is being represented.[151] He secures by fraud a seat for the first night of one of my plays, and contrives a plot to interrupt the performance, to make a foul speech about me to the audience, to insult my actors, to throw offensive or indecent missiles at me when I am called before the curtain at the close, utterly in some hideous way to ruin me through my work. By the merest chance, in the brief and accidental sincerity of a more than usually intoxicated mood, he boasts of his intention before others. Information is given to the police, and he is kept out of the theatre. You had your chance then. Then was your opportunity. Don't you realise now that you should have seen it, and come forward and said that you would not have my Art, at any

152. Wilde is quoting directly from the previous folio sheet of the manuscript (see p. 113 above). The quotation's accuracy indicates that he had access to the previous sheet when quoting it here.

153. French plural noun meaning "sayings" or "refrains."

154. Wilde's libel proceedings against Queensberry began on 3 April at London's Central Criminal Court. Wilde withdrew his suit on 5 April after his case had collapsed under the weight of evidence brought against him in Queensberry's defense. On the same date a warrant was issued for Wilde's arrest.

155. See p. 342, n.50 below.

rate, ruined for your sake? You knew what my Art was to me, the great primal note by which I had revealed, first myself to myself, and then myself to the world; the real passion of my life; the love to which all other loves were as marsh-water to red wine, or the glow-worm of the marsh to the magic mirror of the moon. Don't you understand now that your lack of imagination was the one really fatal defect of your character? What you had to do was quite simple, and quite clear before you, but Hate had blinded you, and you could see nothing. I could not apologise to your father for his having insulted me and persecuted me in the most loathsome manner for nearly nine months. I could not get rid of you out of my life. I had tried it again and again. I had gone so far as actually leaving England and going abroad in the hope of escaping from you. It had all been of no use. You were the only person who could have done anything. The key of the situation rested entirely with yourself. It was the one great opportunity you had of making some slight return to me for all the love and affection and kindness and generosity and care I had shown you. Had you appreciated me even at a tenth of my value as an artist you would have done so. But Hate blinded you. The faculty "by which, and by which alone, we can understand others in their real as in their ideal relations"[152] was dead in you. You thought simply of how to get your father into prison. To see him "in the dock." as you used to say: that was your one idea. The phrase became one of the many *scies*[153] of your daily conversation. One heard it at every meal. Well, you had your desire gratified. Hate granted you every single thing you wished for. It was an indulgent Master to you. It is so, indeed, to all who serve it. For two days you sat on a high seat with the Sheriffs, and feasted your eyes with the spectacle of your father standing in the dock of the Central Criminal Court. And on the third day I took his place.[154] What had occurred? In your hideous game of hate together, you had both thrown dice for my soul,[155] and you happened to have lost. That was all.

You see that I have to write your life to you, and you have to realise it. We have known each other now for more than four years. Half of the time we have been together: the other half I have had to spend in prison

156. For the commencement of Wilde's relationship with Douglas, see p. 56, n.6 above.

157. "if indeed it ever reaches you" added to the manuscript as an afterthought.

158. Sexual relations between men were not a crime in France and Italy, and like many English homosexuals, Douglas fled to the Continent shortly after Wilde's arrest (and at Wilde's urging) in order to avoid possible legal prosecution at home. Wilde himself was to spend the rest of his life in France and Italy upon release, including three months in late 1897 when he shared a house with Douglas at Naples. See Frankel, *Oscar Wilde: The Unrepentant Years*, esp. chaps. 3–9.

159. "with shame" added to the manuscript as an afterthought.

160. The phrases "the supreme vice is shallowness" and "whatever is realised is right" are repeated throughout *De Profundis*, like recurrent refrains, although in this instance they were added as an afterthought. By contrast, Wilde had once written that "only the shallow know themselves" and that "nothing that actually occurs is of the smallest importance" ("Phrases and Philosophies for the Use of the Young" [1894], repr. in *The Artist as Critic: Critical Writings of Oscar Wilde*, ed. Richard Ellmann [New York: Random House, 1969], 433–34).

161. Wilde spent the night of his arrest, 5 April 1895, in a cell at Bow Street Police Station, where he "slept little, and for more than half the night paraded his cell" (*The Oscar Wilde File*, comp. Goodman, 85). The following day, after being formally charged with "gross indecency" under the Criminal Law Amendment Act of 1885, he was refused bail and transferred to Holloway Prison ("The House of Detention"), in North London, where he was held on remand until 7 May 1895, five days after his first criminal trial had ended in a hung jury.

162. While imprisoned on remand in Holloway in April 1895, Wilde wrote, "Nothing but Alfred Douglas's daily visits quicken me into life.... I care less when I think that he is thinking of me. I think of nothing else" (*CL* 644–45).

163. "blow" substituted for "tragedy" in the manuscript.

as the result of our friendship.[156] Where you will receive this letter, if indeed it ever reaches you,[157] I don't know. Rome, Naples, Paris, Venice, some beautiful city on sea or river, I have no doubt, holds you.[158] You are surrounded, if not with all the useless luxury you had with me, at any rate with everything that is pleasurable to eye, ear, and taste. Life is quite lovely to you. And yet, if you are wise, and wish to find Life much lovelier still, and in a different manner, you will let the reading of this terrible letter—for such I know it is—prove to you as important a crisis and turning point of your life as the writing of it is to me. Your pale face used to flush easily with wine or pleasure. If, as you read what is here written, it from time to time becomes scorched, as though by a furnace-blast, with shame,[159] it will be all the better for you. The supreme vice is shallowness. Whatever is realised is right.[160]

I have now got as far as the House of Detention, have I not? After a night passed in the Police Cells I am sent there in the van.[161] You were most attentive and kind. Almost every afternoon, if not actually every afternoon till you go abroad, you took the trouble to drive up to Holloway to see me.[162] You also wrote very sweet and nice letters. But that it was not your father but you who had put me into prison, that from beginning to end you were the responsible person, that it was through you, for you, and by you that I was there, never for one instant dawned upon you. Even the spectacle of me behind the bars of a wooden cage could not quicken that dead unimaginative nature. You had the sympathy and the sentimentality of the spectator of a rather pathetic play. That you were the true author of the hideous tragedy did not occur to you. I saw that you realised nothing of what you had done. I did not desire to be the one to tell you what your own heart should have told you, what it indeed would have told you if you had not let Hate harden it and make it insensate. Everything must come to one out of one's own nature. There is no use in telling a person a thing that they don't feel and can't understand. If I write to you now as I do it is because your own silence and conduct during my long imprisonment have made it necessary. Besides, as things had turned out, the blow[163] had fallen upon me alone. That was a source

164. "That was a source of pleasure to me" added to the manuscript as an afterthought.

165. Wilde refers here to a letter that appeared in *The Star* on 20 April 1895, shortly after Wilde had been refused bail, in which Douglas, by his own description, "raise[d his] voice against the chorus of the pack of those... hounding Mr. Oscar Wilde to his ruin" and complained that, by virtue of the wide and disparaging press coverage, Wilde's case "has been almost hopelessly prejudiced in the eyes of the public from whom the jury who must try his case will be drawn" (*CL* 711–12, n.1). The phrases Wilde attributes to Douglas do not appear in the letter and in fact grossly simplify, even mischaracterize, Douglas's warnings about mob justice.

166. In June 1895 Douglas wrote long letters to *The Review of Reviews* and *Truth*. The latter printed an excerpt from Douglas's letter, in which Douglas deplored the cruelty and prejudice with which Wilde had been treated, while defending himself against *Truth's* charge of cowardice. The excerpt is reproduced in *CL* 712, n.1. Douglas's letter to *The Review of Reviews* (which H. Montgomery Hyde calls "a spirited defence of homosexual conduct"), unpublished in Douglas's lifetime, is reproduced in full in Hyde, *The Trials of Oscar Wilde*, 342–44.

167. "and that the feeling was thoroughly reciprocated" added to the manuscript as an afterthought.

168. As described above (p. 102, n.121), the bailiff's sale of Wilde's household effects on 24 April 1895 was brought about by the actions of Wilde's landlord and others to whom Wilde owed money. The proceedings that led to Wilde's bankruptcy, however, did not begin till 21 June 1895, when the Marquess of Queensberry, in an effort to recover his legal costs, filed a petition in Bankruptcy Court requesting that a receiving order be made against Wilde. The order was not formally made out till 25 July 1895. Wilde's first bankruptcy hearing did not take place till September 1895, and his bankruptcy was not formally completed until November 1895. See Mead, "Heading for Disaster," 89.

169. "the home where you had so often dined" substituted for "the house" in the manuscript.

of pleasure to me.[164] I was content for many reasons to suffer, though there was always to my eyes, as I watched you, something not a little contemptible in your complete and wilful blindness. I remember your producing with absolute pride a letter you had published in one of the halfpenny newspapers about me. It was a very prudent, temperate, indeed commonplace production. You appealed to the "English sense of fair play," or something very dreary of that kind, on behalf of "a man who was down."[165] It was the sort of letter you might have written had a painful charge been brought against some respectable person with whom personally you had been quite unacquainted. But you thought it a wonderful letter. You looked on it as a proof of almost quixotic chivalry. I am aware that you wrote other letters to other newspapers that they did not publish. But then they were simply to say that you hated your father.[166] Nobody cared if you did or not. Hate, you have yet to learn, is, intellectually considered, the Eternal Negation. Considered from the point of view of the emotions it is a form of Atrophy, and kills everything but itself. To write to the papers to say that one hates someone else is as if one were to write to the papers to say that one had some secret and shameful malady: the fact that the man you hated was your own father, and that the feeling was thoroughly reciprocated,[167] did not make your Hate noble or fine in any way. If it showed anything it was simply that it was an hereditary disease.

I remember again, when an execution was put into my house, and my books and furniture were seized and advertised to be sold, and Bankruptcy was impending, I naturally wrote to tell you about it.[168] I did not mention that it was to pay for some gifts of mine to you that the bailiffs had entered the home where you had so often dined.[169] I thought, rightly or wrongly, that such news might pain you a little. I merely told you the bare facts. I thought it proper that you should know them. You wrote back from Boulogne in a strain of almost lyrical exultation. You said that you knew your father was "hard up for money," and had been obliged to raise £1500 for the expenses of the trial, and that my going bankrupt was really a "splendid score" off him, as he would not then be able to get any of his

170. "my Whistler drawings" and "my Simeon Solomons" added as afterthoughts. Wilde is referring here to works by the artists Edward Burne-Jones (1833–98), James McNeill Whistler (1834–1903), Adolphe Monticelli (1824–86), and Simeon Solomon (1840–1905). For details of the bailiffs' sale, see Mead, "Oscar's Finances."

171. "its wonderful array of college and school prizes" added to the manuscript as an afterthought.

172. The Orleans was a gentleman's club, now defunct, housed in King Street, St. James. Twenty thousand pounds equates to about £1.8 million, or US$2.8 million in 2018.

173. Wilde was formally declared bankrupt on 19 November 1895, one week after his bankruptcy examination. The event was reported in *The Times* and other newspapers.

costs out of me! Do you realise now what Hate blinding a person is? Do you recognise now that when I described it as an Atrophy destructive of everything but itself, I was scientifically describing a real psychological fact? That all my charming things were to be sold: my Burne-Jones drawings: my Whistler drawings: my Monticelli: my Simeon Solomons:[170] my china: my Library with its collection of presentation volumes from almost every poet of my time, from Hugo to Whitman, from Swinburne to Mallarmé, from Morris to Verlaine; with its beautifully bound editions of my father's and mother's works; its wonderful array of college and school prizes,[171] its *éditions de luxe,* and the like; was absolutely nothing to you. You said it was a great bore: that was all. What you really saw in it was the possibility that your father might ultimately lose a few hundred pounds, and that paltry consideration filled you with ecstatic joy. As for the costs of the trial, you may be interested to know that your father openly said in the Orleans Club that if it had cost him £20,000[172] he would have considered the money thoroughly well spent, he had extracted such enjoyment, and delight, and triumph out of it all. The fact that he was able not merely to put me into prison for two years, but to take me out for an afternoon and make me a public bankrupt[173] was an extra-refinement of pleasure that he had not expected. It was the crowning-point of my humiliation, and of his complete and perfect victory. Had your father had no claim for his costs on me, you, I know perfectly well, would, as far as words go, at any rate have been most sympathetic about the entire loss of my library, a loss irreparable to a man of letters, the one of all my material losses the most distressing to me. You might even, remembering the sums of money I had lavishly spent on you and how you had lived on me for years, have taken the trouble to buy in some of my books for me. The best all went for less than £150: about as much as I would spend on you in an ordinary week. But the mean small pleasure of thinking that your father was going to be a few pence out of pocket made you forget all about trying to make me a little return, so slight, so easy, so inexpensive, so obvious, and so enormously welcome to me, had you brought it

174. Frederick Atkins, a young bookmaker and blackmailer who accompanied Wilde to Paris in November 1892 and with whom, according to Queensberry's Plea of Justification, Wilde allegedly committed acts of sodomy and gross indecency. Called up as a principal witness against Wilde in the first criminal trial, Atkins was dismissed from the dock for perjury. See *The Real Trial of Oscar Wilde*, 182–96 and 381, n.173; also Hyde, *The Trials*, 184–88 and 191–93.

175. For Wilde's description of the offenses for which he was imprisoned as "forms of sexual madness and . . . diseases to be cured by a physician, rather than crimes to be punished by a judge," see p. 41 above.

about. Am I right in saying that Hate blinds people? Do you see it now? If you don't, try to see it.

How clearly I saw it then, as now, I need not tell you. But I said to myself "At all costs I must keep Love in my heart. If I go into prison without Love what will become of my Soul?" The letters I wrote to you at that time from Holloway were my efforts to keep Love as the dominant note of my own nature. I could if I had chosen have torn you to pieces with bitter reproaches. I could have rent you with maledictions. I could have held up a mirror to you, and shown you such an image of yourself that you would not have recognised it as your own till you found it mimicking back your gestures of horror, and then you would have known whose shape it was, and hated it and yourself for ever. More than that indeed. The sins of another were being placed to my account. Had I so chosen, I could on either trial have saved myself at his expense, not from shame indeed but from imprisonment. Had I cared to show that the Crown witnesses—the three most important—had been carefully coached by your father and his Solicitors, not in reticences merely, but in assertions, in the absolute transference, deliberate, plotted, and rehearsed, of the actions and doings of someone else on to me, I could have had each one of them dismissed from the box by the Judge, more summarily than even wretched perjured Atkins was.[174] I could have walked out of Court with my tongue in my cheek, and my hands in my pockets, a free man. The strongest pressure was put upon me to do so. I was earnestly advised, begged, entreated to do so by people whose sole interest was my welfare, and the welfare of my house. But I refused. I did not choose to do so. I have never regretted my decision for a single moment, even in the most bitter periods of my imprisonment. Such a course of action would have been beneath me. Sins of the flesh are nothing. They are maladies for physicians to cure, if they should be cured.[175] Sins of the soul alone are shameful. To have secured my acquittal by such means would have been a life-long torture to me. But do you really think that you were worthy of the love I was showing you then, or that for a single moment I thought you were? Do you really think that at any period in

176. "Hatred and Vanity and Greed" added to the manuscript as an afterthought.

177. "three" substituted for "two" in the manuscript.

178. Although this important sentence ends with a question mark, Wilde begins it as a statement.

Jean-Gabriel Daragnès, wood-engraved illustration for *Ballade de La Geôle de Reading, par C.3.3.*, trans. Henry-D. Davray (Paris: Léon Pichon, 1918).

our friendship you were worthy of the love I showed you, or that for a single moment I thought you were? I knew you were not. But Love does not traffic in a marketplace, nor use a huckster's scales. Its joy, like the joy of the intellect, is to feel itself alive. The aim of Love is to love: no more, and no less. You were my enemy: such an enemy as no man ever had. I had given you my life, and to gratify the lowest and most contempt-ible of all human passions, Hatred and Vanity and Greed,[176] you had thrown it away. In less than three[177] years you had entirely ruined me from every point of view. For my own sake there was nothing for me to do but to love you. I knew, if I allowed myself to hate you that in the dry desert of existence over which I had to travel, and am travelling still, every rock would lose its shadow, every palm tree be withered, every well of water prove poisoned at its source. Are you beginning now to understand a little? Is your imagination wakening from the long lethargy in which it has lain? You know already what Hate is. Is it beginning to dawn on you what Love is, and what is the nature of Love? It is not too late for you to learn, though to teach it to you I may have had to go to a convict's cell?[178]

179. "And a certain man drew a bow at a venture, and smote the King of Israel between the joints of his harness" (1 Kings 22:34).

180. "forced myself to believe" substituted for "felt" in the manuscript.

181. Cyril Holland (born Cyril Wilde, 1885–1915), Wilde's oldest son. Wilde makes no mention here of his younger son, Vyvyan (1886–1967), who would later author several books about his father.

182. Wilde added "the entire chrysolite of" as an afterthought. As Ian Small observes (De Profundis; "Epistola: In Carcere et Vinculis," ed. Small, 233), the phrase is adapted from Shakespeare's Othello, V, ii: "If heaven would make me such another world / Of one entire and perfect chrysolite / I'd not have sold her for it."

183. Robert Harborough Sherard (1861–1943), one of Wilde's staunchest friends and later his first biographer.

184. Avant-garde French literary review closely associated with the Symbolist movement. Wilde's Ballad of Reading Gaol would later be reviewed—and still later, translated—in the Mercure de France, and Wilde would in 1898 become friendly with the magazine's editor, Alfred Vallette, and his collaborator (and wife), the novelist Rachilde, as well as with their close associate Henry-D. Davray, who reviewed and translated English works for the magazine. For Sherard's account of this incident, see his Oscar Wilde: The Story of An Unhappy Friendship (1905; repr., London: Greening, 1909), 204–6.

After my terrible sentence, when the prison-dress was on me, and the prison-house closed, I sat amidst the ruins of my wonderful life, crushed by anguish, bewildered with terror, dazed through pain. But I would not hate you. Every day I said to myself, "I must keep Love in my heart today, else how shall I live through the day." I reminded myself that you meant no evil, to me at any rate: I set myself to think that you had but drawn a bow at a venture, and that the arrow had pierced a King between the joints of the harness.[179] To have weighed you against the smallest of my sorrows, the meanest of my losses, would have been, I felt, unfair. I determined I would regard you as one suffering too. I forced myself to believe[180] that at last the scales had fallen from your long-blinded eyes. I used to fancy, and with pain, what your horror must have been when you contemplated your terrible handiwork. There were times, even in those dark days, the darkest of all my life, when I actually longed to console you. So sure was I that at last you had realised what you had done. It did not occur to me then that you could have the supreme vice, shallowness. Indeed, it was a real grief to me when I had to let you know that I was obliged to reserve for family business my first opportunity of receiving a letter: but my brother-in-law had written to me to say that if I would only write once to my wife she would, for my own sake and for our children's sake, take no action for divorce. I felt my duty was to do so. Setting aside other reasons, I could not bear the idea of being separated from Cyril,[181] that beautiful, loving, loveable child of mine, my friend of all friends, my companion beyond all companions, one single hair of whose little golden head should have been dearer and of more value to me than, I will not merely say you from top to toe, but the entire chrysolite of the whole world:[182] was so indeed to me always, though I failed to understand it till too late.

Two weeks after your application, I get news of you. Robert Sherard,[183] that bravest and most chivalrous of all brilliant beings, comes to see me, and amongst other things tells me that in that ridiculous *Mercure de France*,[184] with its absurd affectation of being the true centre of literary corruption, you are about to publish an article on me with specimens of

185. The sequence of events was rather different than Wilde remembers it. A law clerk representing the Marquess of Queensberry served Wilde with a bankruptcy order when he was imprisoned in Pentonville Prison, in late June or early July 1895 (according to J. Robert Maguire, the order was served on 2 July). But the visit during which Robert Sherard informed Wilde of Douglas's plan to publish a defense in the *Mercure de France* did not take place till late September 1895, over two months after Wilde had been transferred to Wandsworth Prison.

186. "less than half" substituted for "about half" in the manuscript.

187. "Fleur-de-Lys" was one of Wilde's pet nicknames for Douglas: on 3 May 1895, Wilde wrote sadly from Holloway prison, "I have had no letter as yet today from Fleur-de-Lys" (*CL* 648). According to Douglas, when Wilde later resided on the northern French coast, he suggested that Douglas take the pseudonym "Le Chevalier Fleur-de-Lys" in order to meet Wilde clandestinely (*Autobiography*, 151). Douglas might have confused Fleur-de-Lys with another French nickname suggested by Wilde, since on 15 June 1897 Wilde told Douglas "your name is to be Jonquil du Vallon" (*CL* 898).

my letters. He asks me if it really was by my wish. I was greatly taken aback, and much annoyed, and gave orders that the thing was to be stopped at once. You had left my letters lying about for blackmailing companions to steal, for Hotel servants to pilfer, for housemaids to sell. That was simply your careless want of appreciation of what I had written to you. But that you should seriously propose to publish selections from the balance was almost incredible to me. And which of my letters were they? I could get no information. That was my first news of you. It displeased me.

The second piece of news followed shortly afterwards. Your father's solicitors had appeared in the prison, and served me personally with a Bankruptcy notice, for a paltry £700, the amount of their taxed costs. I was adjudged a public insolvent, and ordered to be produced in Court.[185] I felt most strongly, and feel still, and will revert to the subject again, that these costs should have been paid by your family. You had taken personally on yourself the responsibility of stating that your family would do so. It was that which had made the Solicitor take up the case in the way he did. You were absolutely responsible. Even irrespective of your engagement on your family's behalf you should have felt that as you had brought the whole ruin on me, the least that could have been done was to spare me the additional ignominy of bankruptcy for an absolutely contemptible sum of money, less than half[186] of what I spent on you in three brief summer months at Goring. Of that, however, no more here. I did through the Solicitor's clerk, I fully admit, receive a message from you on the subject, or at any rate in connection with the occasion. The day he came to receive my depositions and statements, he leant across the table—the prison warder being present—and having consulted a piece of paper which he pulled from his pocket, said to me in a low voice, "Prince Fleur-de-Lys wishes to be remembered to you."[187] I stared at him. He repeated the message again. I did not know what he meant. "The gentleman is abroad at present," he added mysteriously. It all flashed across me, and I remember that, for the first and last time in my entire prison-life, I laughed. In that laugh was all the scorn of all the world.

188. Wilde's greatest play, *The Importance of Being Earnest*, is subtitled "A Trivial Comedy for Serious People." Its leading man, Algernon Moncrieff, originally named "Lord Alfred" in draft texts, is a dandy into whom Wilde put more of himself than of Douglas. See *The Annotated Importance of Being Earnest*, ed. Frankel, 26–32.

189. To ornament.

190. Wilde would later proudly wear his Reading Prison cell number "C. 3. 3."—cell block C, landing 3, cell 3—as an author's signature on the title-page of the first edition of *The Ballad of Reading Gaol*.

191. But see Wilde's comment later in *De Profundis*, p. 287, when anticipating a fresh meeting with Douglas upon release, "you will have to change your name. The little title of which you were so vain . . . you will have to surrender, if you wish to see *me*."

192. Following a fall in which he hurt his ear (see Harris, *Oscar Wilde*, 196), Wilde spent roughly six weeks in the infirmary at Wandsworth Prison, up until 20 November 1895, the day of his transfer to Reading Prison.

193. Wilde's account of being asked by Douglas directly, in October 1895 via the Governor of Wandsworth Prison, for permission to publish Wilde's letters suggests that Sherard had either reneged on or failed in his promise the previous month to prevent their publication. But Sherard says that he acted immediately and effectively to make sure that Douglas's article was withdrawn (*Oscar Wilde: The Story of an Unhappy Friendship*, 204–5), and he even reprints a letter from Douglas himself, written in immediate reply to Sherard, in which he agreed to withdraw his article and noted that "no possible good can be done by worrying Oscar" further about the matter (206).

Prince Fleur-de-Lys! I saw—and subsequent events showed me that I rightly saw—that nothing that had happened had made you realise a single thing. You were in your own eyes still the graceful prince of a trivial comedy,[188] not the sombre figure of a tragic show. All that had occurred was but as a feather for the cap that gilds a narrow head, a flower to pink[189] the doublet that hides a heart that Hate, and Hate alone, can warm, that Love, and Love alone, finds cold. Prince Fleur-de-Lys! You were, no doubt, quite right to communicate with me under an assumed name. I myself, at that time, had no name at all. In the great prison where I was then incarcerated I was merely the figure and letter of a little cell in a long gallery, one of a thousand lifeless numbers, as of a thousand lifeless lives.[190] But surely there were many real names in real history which would have suited you much better, and by which I would have had no difficulty at all in recognising you at once? I did not look for you behind the spangles of a tinsel vizard only suitable for an amusing masquerade. Ah! had your soul been, as for its own perfection even it should have been, wounded with sorrow, bowed with remorse, and humble with grief, such was not the disguise it would have chosen beneath whose shadow to seek entrance to the House of Pain! The great things of life are what they seem to be, and for that reason, strange as it may sound to you, are often difficult to interpret. But the little things of life are symbols. We receive our bitter lessons most easily through them. Your seemingly casual choice of a feigned name was, and will remain, symbolic. It reveals you.[191]

Six weeks later a third piece of news arrives. I am called out of the Hospital Ward, where I was lying wretchedly ill,[192] to receive a special message from you through the Governor of the Prison. He reads me out a letter you had addressed to him in which you stated that you proposed to publish an article "on the case of Mr. Oscar Wilde," in the *Mercure de France* ("a magazine," you added for some extraordinary reason, "corresponding to our English *Fortnightly Review*") and were anxious to obtain my permission to publish extracts and selections from . . . what letters?[193] The letters I had written to you from Holloway Prison! The letters that should have been to you things sacred and secret beyond

194. A member or follower of the Decadent Movement.

195. French term, equating roughly to the English "hack journalist" or "pamphleteer."

196. The Latin Quarter, the Parisian neighborhood on the Left Bank of the Seine, still associated with bohemians and artists. Wilde himself resided there for nearly the last three years of his life.

197. Wilde is quoting from his own "Sonnet. On the Recent Sale by Auction of Keats' Love Letters." Wilde laments that a writer's private life should become public knowledge and acquire a monetary value, but ironically Wilde himself purchased some of Keats's love letters at auction. Wilde's personal identification with Keats runs through much of his early writing.

198. Street urchin.

199. For Lombroso, the Italian criminologist and physician whose theories on the psychological and genetic roots of criminality, widely current in the 1890s, quickly veered into broader disquisitions on the psychological roots of cultural "degeneracy," see p. 42, n.2 above.

200. The eminent French dramatic critic Henri Bauër (1851–1915), the son of Alexander Dumas, published a powerful article in the *Echo de Paris* on 3 June 1895 attacking the barbarity of Wilde's sentence, in which he called the Marquess of Queensberry *"type de brute sportive malfaisante, mauvais mari, méchant père"* (an evil-doing, sport-playing, brutish type, a bad husband, and a wicked father) (*CL* 653).

201. Wilde is possibly referring to a letter of 29 April 1895 in which he had told Douglas, "Those who know not what love is will write, I know, if fate is against us, that I have had a bad influence upon your life. If they do that, you shall write, you shall say in your turn, that it is not so. Our love was always beautiful and noble, and if I have been the butt of a terrible tragedy, it is because the nature of that love has not been understood" (*CL* 646–47).

202. "on account of my relations with the witnesses on my trial" substi-tuted in the manuscript for "for having had [*two illegible words*] with Charlie Parker." Similarly, in the next sentence, "people of that kind" substituted for "Charlie Parker." Charlie Parker, one of the young men with whom Wilde was

anything in the whole world! These actually were the letters you proposed to publish for the jaded *décadent*[194] to wonder at, for the greedy *feuilletoniste*[195] to chronicle, for the little lions of the *Quartier Latin*[196] to gape and mouth at! Had there been nothing in your own heart to cry out against so vulgar a sacrilege you might at least have remembered the sonnet he wrote who saw with such sorrow and scorn the letters of John Keats sold by public auction in London and have understood at last the real meaning of my lines

> I think they love not Art
> Who break the crystal of a poet's heart
> That small and sickly eyes may glare or gloat.[197]

For what was your article to show? That I had been too fond of you? The Paris *gamin*[198] was quite aware of the fact. They all read the newspapers, and most of them write for them. That I was a man of genius? The French understood that, and the peculiar quality of my genius, much better than you did, or could have been expected to do. That along with genius goes often a curious perversity of passion and desire? Admirable: but the subject belongs to Lombroso[199] rather than to you. Besides, the pathological phenomenon in question is also found amongst those who have not genius. That in your war of hate with your father I was at once shield and weapon to each of you? Nay more, that in that hideous hunt for my life, that took place when the war was over, he never could have reached me had not your nets been already about my feet? Quite true: but I am told that Henri Bauër had already done it extremely well.[200] Besides, to corroborate his view, had such been your intention, you did not require to publish my letters; at any rate those written from Holloway Prison.

Will you say, in answer to my questions, that in one of my Holloway letters I had myself asked you to try, as far as you were able, to set me a little right with some small portion of the world? Certainly, I did so.[201] Remember how and why I am here, at this very moment. Do you think I am here on account of my relations with the witnesses on my trial?[202]

found to have committed acts of gross indecency—and who almost
certainly blackmailed Wilde on account of it—was the prosecution's chief
witness in Wilde's second trial. See also p. 74, n.59 above.

203. "real or supposed" added to the manuscript as an afterthought.

204. That is, for having Queensberry charged with criminal libel.

205. Wilde unsuccessfully petitioned the home secretary on 2 July 1896
and on 10 November 1896 for a curtailment of his sentence. For the earlier
of these petitions, see pp. 41–51 above.

206. But see p. 123 above, where Wilde acknowledges the letter Douglas
wrote in his defense to *The Star* and adds, "I am aware that you wrote . . .
letters to . . . newspapers that they did not publish." As well as publicly
defending Wilde's conduct and "vices," Douglas had petitioned Queen
Victoria to stay Wilde's sentence, calling attention to the falsity of his
father's claim to have been motivated by love for his youngest son and also
to how maliciously Queensberry had persecuted Wilde and himself in the
run-up to the disastrous libel trial. Douglas had also vainly tried to organize
petitions on Wilde's behalf to be signed by eminent men of letters in
France and England. In the unpublished defense of Wilde that he had
written for the *Mercure de France* in 1895, he states that his relationship
with Wilde "was love, real love—. . . completely pure but extremely
passionate . . . perfect love, more spiritual than sensual, a truly Platonic
love." In a controversial article written for *La Revue Blanche* in 1896,
Douglas had defiantly proclaimed: "I couldn't be prouder to have been
loved by a great poet."

207. "quoted" substituted for "accepted" in the manuscript, where Wilde
also added the next clause, from "the preacher has taken" to "for his barren
theme," when revising.

My relations, real or supposed,[203] with people of that kind were matters of no interest to either the Government or Society. They knew nothing of them, and cared less. I am here for having tried to put your father into prison.[204] My attempt failed of course. My own counsel threw up their briefs. Your father completely turned the tables on me, and had *me* in prison, has me there still. That is why there is contempt felt for me. That is why people despise me. That is why I have to serve out every day, every hour, every minute of my dreadful imprisonment. That is why my petitions have been refused.[205]

You were the only person who, and without in any way exposing yourself to scorn or danger or blame, could have given another colour to the whole affair: have put the matter in a different light: have shown to a certain degree how things really stood.[206] I would not of course have expected, nor indeed wished you to have stated how and for what purpose you had sought my assistance in your trouble at Oxford: or how, and for what purpose, if you had a purpose at all, you had practically never left my side for nearly three years. My incessant attempts to break off a friendship that was so ruinous to me as an artist, as a man of position, as a member of society even, need not have been chronicled with the accuracy with which they have been set down here. Nor would I have desired you to have described the scenes you used to make with such almost monotonous recurrence: nor to have reprinted your wonderful series of telegrams to me with their strange mixture of romance and finance; nor to have quoted from your letters the more revolting or heartless passages, as I have been forced to do. Still, I thought it would have been good, as well for you as for me, if you had made some protest against your father's version of our friendship, one no less grotesque than venomous, and as absurd in its reference to you as it was dishonouring in its reference to me. That version has now actually passed into serious history: it is quoted,[207] believed, and chronicled: the preacher has taken it for his text, and the moralist for his barren theme: and I who appealed to all the ages have had to accept my verdict from one who is an ape and a buffoon. I have said, and with some bitterness, I admit, in this letter that such

208. The second English edition of *De Profundis* (1908) began at this point, starting with "my place would be between Gilles de Retz and the Marquis de Sade," although it omitted much of the rest of the manuscript, including the entire next paragraph.

209. That is, Retz and de Sade. See p. 72, n.54 above.

210. Principal characters in *The History of Sandford and Merton* (1783), by Thomas Day, a pious children's fable popular in the nineteenth century.

211. In his March 1893 letter, Wilde had in fact written: "I cannot listen to your curved lips saying hideous things to me—don't do it—you break my heart—I'd sooner be rented all day, than have you bitter, unjust, and horrid" (*CL* 559–60). To spare Wilde embarrassment, Edward Carson, Queensberry's counsel, had omitted the phrase "I'd sooner be rented all day" when reading Wilde's letter out loud in court. See *The Real Trial of Oscar Wilde*, 108–10. Among active homosexuals in the 1890s, "renting" meant obtaining money from a person, often through blackmail, as a result of providing homosexual favors, although "renter" was also sometimes used merely as slang for *male prostitute*. In the manuscript of *De Profundis*, "renter" was an afterthought for "brute."

was the irony of things that your father would live to be the hero of a Sunday-school tract: that you would rank with the Infant Samuel: and that my place would be between Gilles de Retz and the Marquis de Sade.[208] I dare say it is best so. I have no desire to complain. One of the many lessons that one learns in prison is that things are what they are, and will be what they will be. Nor have I any doubt but that the leper of mediaevalism, and the author of *Justine*,[209] will prove better company than Sandford and Merton.[210]

But at the time I wrote to you I felt that for both our sakes it would be a good thing, a proper thing, a right thing *not* to accept the account your father had put forward through his counsel for the edification of a Philistine world, and that is why I asked you to think out and write something that would be nearer the truth. It would at least have been better for you than scribbling to the French papers about the domestic life of your parents. What did the French care whether or not your parents had led a happy domestic life? One cannot conceive a subject more entirely uninteresting to them. What did interest them was how an artist of my distinction, one who by the school and movement of which he was the incarnation had exercised a marked influence on the direction of French thought, could, having led such a life, have brought such an action. Had you proposed for your article to publish the letters, endless I fear in number, in which I had spoken to you of the ruin you were bringing on my life, of the madness of moods of rage that you were allowing to master you to your own hurt as well as to mine, and of my desire, nay, my determination to end a friendship so fatal to me in every way, I could have understood it, though I would not have allowed such letters to be published: when your father's counsel desiring to catch me in a contradiction suddenly produced in Court a letter of mine, written to you in March '93, in which I stated that, rather than endure a repetition of the hideous scenes you seemed to take such a terrible pleasure in making, I would readily consent to be "blackmailed by every renter in London," it was a very real grief to me that that side of my friendship with you should incidentally be revealed to the common gaze:[211] but that you should

212. This is the second time Wilde has quoted this phrase verbatim from earlier in the manuscript. Wilde's self-quotation here was originally longer, but after beginning with "by which one can see Life as a whole" (as on p. 113 above), Wilde deleted some of this self-quotation. See also p. 118, n.152 above.

213. "Vanity had barred up the windows" added to the manuscript as an afterthought.

214. "All this" refers to Douglas's proposal to publish Wilde's love letters and the anguish it caused Wilde, not the use made of incriminating letters during Wilde's trials over six months previously. This sentence was clearly written in early 1897.

215. The first edition of *De Profundis* (1905) began at this point, although Ross, its editor, redacted and altered much of what follows. Among many other changes, Ross inserted "very" into the present sentence, so that the opening sentence read, "Suffering is one very long moment." For the full text of the first edition, see *De Profundis; "Epistola: In Carcere et Vinculis,"* ed. Small, 159–93.

have been so slow to see, so lacking in all sensitiveness, and so dull in apprehension of what is rare, delicate and beautiful, as to propose yourself to publish the letters in which, and through which, I was trying to keep alive the very spirit and soul of Love, that it might dwell in my body through the long years of that body's humiliation—this was, and still is to me, a source of the very deepest pain, the most poignant disappointment. Why you did so, I fear I know but too well. If Hate blinded your eyes, Vanity sewed your eyelids together with threads of iron. The faculty "by which, and by which alone, one can understand others in their real as in their ideal relations,"[212] your narrow egotism had blunted, and long disuse had made of no avail. The imagination was as much in prison as I was. Vanity had barred up the windows,[213] and the name of the warder was Hate.

All this took place in the early part of November of the year before last.[214] A great river of life flows between you and a date so distant. Hardly, if at all, can you see across so wide a waste. But to me it seems to have occurred, I will not say yesterday, but today. Suffering is one long moment.[215] We cannot divide it by seasons. We can only record its moods, and chronicle their return. With us time itself does not progress. It revolves. It seems to circle round one centre of pain. The paralysing immobility of a life, every circumstance of which is regulated after an unchangeable pattern, so that we eat and drink and walk and lie down and pray, or kneel at least for prayer, according to the inflexible laws of an iron formula: this immobile quality, that makes each dreadful day in the very minutest detail like its brother, seems to communicate itself to those external forces the very essence of whose existence is ceaseless change. Of seed-time or harvest, of the reapers bending over the corn, or the grape-gatherers threading through the vines, of the grass in the orchard made white with broken blossoms, or strewn with fallen fruit, we know nothing, and can know nothing. For us there is only one season, the season of Sorrow. The very sun and moon seem taken from us. Outside, the day may be blue and gold, but the light that creeps down through the thickly-muffled glass of the small iron-barred window beneath which one sits is grey and niggard. It is always twilight in one's cell, as it is always midnight

216. "A week later" substituted in the manuscript for "On the 15th of November." Wilde was transferred from Wandsworth to Reading Prison on 20 November 1895.

217. On 3 February 1896.

218. Wilde is comparing himself to Virgil, whom Tennyson had once described as a "lord of language … / All the chosen coin of fancy / flashing out from many a golden phrase" ("To Virgil," ll. 5–8 in *Tennyson's Poetry*, ed. Robert W. Hill Jr. [New York: Norton, 1971], 455).

John Vassos, photolithographic illustration for Oscar Wilde, *The Ballad of Reading Gaol* (New York: E. P. Dutton & Co., Inc., 1928).

in one's heart. And in the sphere of Thought, no less than in the sphere of Time, motion is no more. The thing that you personally have long ago forgotten, or can easily forget, is happening to me now, and will happen to me again tomorrow. Remember this, and you will be able to understand a little of why I am writing to you, and in this manner writing.

A week later, I am transferred here.[216] Three more months go over and my mother dies.[217] You knew, none better, how deeply I loved and honoured her. Her death was so terrible to me that I, once a lord of language,[218] have no words in which to express my anguish and my

219. "incommunicable" added to the manuscript as an afterthought.

220. Wilde's parents were among Ireland's leading intellectuals. His father Sir William Wilde (1815–1876) was a leading eye and ear surgeon as well as a highly skilled amateur archaeologist, folklorist, and demographer. When still a young man, Wilde's father founded St. Mark's Opthalmic Hospital, the most advanced eye and ear hospital in Ireland, and he pioneered a number of modern medical procedures. In 1863 he was made Surgeon Oculist to Queen Victoria in Ireland, and he was knighted in 1864, partly for his work as Assistant Commissioner of the Irish Census for 1851 and 1861. Along with a medical textbook on aural surgery still regarded as classic in its field, he authored numerous books on Irish history, antiquities, and legends. Wilde's mother, Lady Wilde, born Jane Elgee (1821–1896), who was awarded a Civil List pension in 1890, was no less accomplished: even before Wilde's birth, she had achieved repute as an Irish nationalist poet, writing under the pen name "Speranza," and as a translator of French and German literature. Over the course of her life she authored many books of poetry and social criticism, as well as further translations and collections of Irish mythology.

221. Constance's visit took place on 19 February 1896 by special arrangement with the prison commissioners. Constance had long suffered bouts of what she termed "rheumatism" or "neuralgia" and had been regularly bedridden. In late-December 1895 she underwent painful surgery at a clinic near her home in Genoa, Italy, in the belief that her sufferings had a gynecological or genitourinary foundation. The surgery involved a long hospitalization, although by mid-January 1896 Constance was confident "that her dreadful aches and pains had been substantially improved" (Franny Moyle, *Constance: The Tragic and Scandalous Life of Mrs. Oscar Wilde* [London: John Murray, 2011], 286). In fact, her sufferings grew worse, and she would in 1898 die of complications arising from further gynecological surgery. Her sufferings are now understood to be symptoms of degenerative multiple sclerosis, which remained undiagnosed in her own lifetime. See Ashley H. Robins and Merlin Holland, "The Enigmatic Illness and Death of Constance, Wife of Oscar Wilde," *The Lancet* 385, no. 9962 (3–9 January 2015): 21–22.

222. "Speak not of them, but look and pass them by" (Dante, *Inferno*, trans. H. F. Cary, Canto III, line 49). Wilde received an Italian-language edition of

shame: never, even in the most perfect days of my development as an artist, could [I] have had words fit to bear so august a burden, or to move with sufficient stateliness of music through the purple pageant of my incommunicable[219] woe. She and my father had bequeathed me a name they had made noble and honoured not merely in Literature, Art, Archaeology and Science, but in the public history of my own country in its evolution as a nation.[220] I had disgraced that name eternally. I had made it a low byword among low people. I had dragged it through the very mire. I had given it to brutes that they might make it brutal, and to fools that they might turn it into a synonym for folly. What I suffered then, and still suffer, is not for pen to write or paper to record. My wife, at that time kind and gentle to me, rather than that I should hear the news from indifferent or alien lips, travelled, ill as she was,[221] all the way from Genoa to England to break to me herself the tidings of so irreparable, so irredeemable a loss. Messages of sympathy reached me from all who had still affection for me. Even people who had not known me personally, hearing what a new sorrow had come into my broken life, wrote to ask that some expression of their condolence should be conveyed to me. You alone stood aloof, sent me no message, and wrote me no letter. Of such actions, it is best to say what Virgil says to Dante of those whose lives have been barren in noble impulse and shallow of intention: *"Non ragioniam di lor, ma guarda e passa."*[222]

Three more months go over. The calendar of my daily conduct and labour that hangs on the outside of my cell-door, with my name and sentence written upon it, tells me that it is May-time. My friends come to see me again.[223] I enquire, as I always do, after you. I am told that you are in your villa at Naples,[224] and are bringing out a volume of poems. At the close of the interview it is mentioned casually that you are dedicating them to me. The tidings seemed to give me a sort of nausea of life. I said nothing, but silently went back to my cell with contempt and scorn in my heart. How could you dream of dedicating a volume of poems to me without first asking my permission?[225] Dream, do I say? How could you dare to do such a thing? Will you give as your answer that in the days of

Dante's *Divina Commedia* in January 1896. Six months later, he successfully petitioned for a prose translation, and four months later still he told Robert Ross that "I read Dante, and make excerpts and notes for the pleasure of using a pen and ink" (*CL* 669).

223. In late May 1896, Robert Ross—who had first visited Wilde three months earlier, accompanied by Ernest Leverson—visited Wilde in prison accompanied by Robert Sherard. Ross left a detailed, moving account of this visit. See *Robert Ross: Friend of Friends*, ed. Margery Ross (London: Jonathan Cape, 1952), 39–43.

224. In August 1895, Douglas leased a small villa, the Villa Tarnasse, at Sorrento, near Naples.

225. Wilde's annoyance at not being forewarned of Douglas's dedication recalls that of his friend Rennell Rodd fourteen years earlier, when Wilde himself, in the process of overseeing publication of the first American edition of Rodd's poems, incorporated (without forewarning Rodd) as a dedication an inscription that Rodd had written into Wilde's personal copy of the first English edition: "To Oscar Wilde—'Heart's Brother'—These Few Songs and many Songs to Come" (see Ellmann, *Oscar Wilde*, 199). Like Wilde fourteen years later, Rodd wrote trying to prevent the dedication's publication, but in Rodd's case it was too late. It is relevant too that one year before his imprisonment, Wilde incorporated into the first English edition of *Salomé* a dedication reading "To My Friend Lord Alfred Douglas, the Translator of My Play."

226. "If youth only knew it" added to the manuscript as an afterthought.

227. When a student at Oxford University, Wilde had asked, "Is all human sorrow as meaningless as sea sickness?" (*Oscar Wilde's Oxford Notebooks: A Portrait of Mind in the Making*, ed. Philip E. Smith II and Michael S. Helfand [Oxford: Oxford University Press, 1989], 164). But on visiting Wilde in prison early in his sentence and enjoining him to write again, Wilde's visitor R. B. Haldane reminded Wilde that he had now "got a great subject," and Wilde will shortly write "there are times when Sorrow seems to me to be the only truth. . . . [O]ut of Sorrow have the worlds been built, and at the birth of a child or a star there is pain." Ian Small suggests that Wilde's new preoccupation with sorrow "could have been prompted by contemporary

my greatness and fame I had consented to receive the dedication of your early work? Certainly, I did so; just as I would have accepted the homage of any other young man beginning the difficult and beautiful art of literature. All homage is delightful to an artist, and doubly sweet when youth brings it. Laurel and bay leaf wither when aged hands pluck them. Only youth has a right to crown an artist. That is the real privilege of being young, if youth only knew it.[226] But the days of abasement and infamy are different from those of greatness and of fame. You have yet to learn that Prosperity, Pleasure and Success may be rough of grain and common in fibre, but that Sorrow is the most sensitive of all created things. There is nothing that stirs in the whole world of Thought or motion to which Sorrow does not vibrate in terrible if exquisite pulsation.[227] The thin beaten-out leaf of tremulous gold that chronicles the direction of forces that the eye cannot see[228] is in comparison coarse. It is a wound that bleeds when any hand but that of Love touches it and even then must bleed again, though not for pain. You could write to the Governor of Wandsworth Prison to ask my permission to publish my letters in the *Mercure de France,* "corresponding to our English *Fortnightly Review.*" Why not have written to the Governor of the Prison at Reading to ask my permission to dedicate your poems to me, whatever fantastic description you may have chosen to give of them? Was it because in the one case the magazine in question had been prohibited by me from publishing letters the legal copyright of which, as you are of course perfectly well aware, was and is vested entirely in me, and in the other you thought that you could enjoy the wilfulness of your own way without my knowing anything about it till it was too late to interfere? The mere fact that I was a man disgraced, ruined, and in prison should have made you, if you desired to write my name on the fore-page of your work, beg it of me as a favour, an honour, a privilege. That is the way in which one should approach those who are in distress and[229] sit in shame.

Where there is Sorrow there is holy ground. Some day you will realise what that means. You will know nothing of life till you do. Robbie, and natures like his, can realise it. When I was brought down from my

discussions of the topic in Spinoza's work, particularly by Matthew Arnold in *Essays in Criticism* and by Pater in *Imaginary Portraits*" (*De Profundis*; "*Epistola: In Carcere et Vinculis*," ed. Small, 215).

228. Rupert Hart-Davis suggests this is a reference to the Gold-Leaf Electroscope, used to detect charges of static electricity (*Letters of Oscar Wilde*, ed. Hart-Davis, 459, n.1). A more likely reference is the weathervane, which was often covered with thin gold-leaf so as to maintain brightness and prevent corrosion.

229. "are in distress and" added to the manuscript as an afterthought.

230. Wilde's initial appearance at Bankruptcy Court, in Carey Street, took place on 24 September 1895, although at this hearing his bankruptcy examination was adjourned for another seven weeks.

231. This sentence is replete with biblical echoes, as Ian Small observes (*De Profundis*; "*Epistola: In Carcere et Vinculis*," ed. Small, 239): "dust and ashes" echoes Genesis 18:27 ("I am nothing but dust and ashes") as well as Milton's *Paradise Lost*, in which satanic serpents, greedily reaching for forbidden fruit, "chew dust and bitter ashes"; "wells of pity" echoes Isaiah 12:3 ("wells of salvation"); and "desert blossom like a rose" echoes Isaiah 35:1 ("the desert shall rejoice, and blossom as the rose").

232. Altered in the manuscript from "Though it would perhaps have pleased me to have been asked."

233. Both Oxford locations. The former, a large meadow behind Magdalen College, is invoked in Wilde's early poem "Magdalen Walks." Cumnor, a village and parish to the west of Oxford, notable for its hills more than its fields, was made famous in Matthew Arnold's poem "The Scholar-Gypsy" and is invoked in Wilde's early poem "The Burden of Itys."

prison to the Court of Bankruptcy between two policemen,[230] Robbie waited in the long dreary corridor, that before the whole crowd, whom an action so sweet and simple hushed into silence, he might gravely raise his hat to me, as handcuffed and with bowed head I passed him by. Men have gone to heaven for smaller things than that. It was in this spirit, and with this mode of love that the saints knelt down to wash the feet of the poor, or stooped to kiss the leper on the cheek. I have never said one single word to him about what he did. I do not know to the present moment whether he is aware that I was even conscious of his action. It is not a thing for which one can render formal thanks in formal words. I store it in the treasury-house of my heart. I keep it there as a secret debt that I am glad to think I can never possibly repay. It is embalmed and kept sweet by the myrrh and cassia of many tears. When Wisdom has been profitless to me, and Philosophy barren, and the proverbs and phrases of those who have sought to give me consolation as dust and ashes in my mouth, the memory of that little lowly silent act of Love has unsealed for me all the wells of pity, made the desert blossom like a rose, and brought me out of the bitterness of lonely exile into harmony with the wounded, broken and great heart of the world.[231] When you are able to understand not merely how beautiful Robbie's action was, but why it meant so much to me, and always will mean so much, then, perhaps, you will realise how and in what spirit you should have approached me for permission to dedicate to me your verses.

It is only right to state that in any case I would not have accepted the dedication. Though, possibly, it would under other circumstances have pleased me to have been asked,[232] I would have refused the request for *your* sake, irrespective of any feelings of my own. The first volume of poems that in the very springtime of his manhood a young man sends forth to the world should be like a blossom or flower of spring, like the white thorn in the meadow at Magdalen, or the cowslips in the Cumnor fields.[233] It should not be burdened by the weight of a terrible, a revolting tragedy, a terrible, a revolting scandal. If I had allowed my name to serve as herald to the book it would have been a grave artistic error. It would

234. In Classical idyllic and pastoral poetry, Sicily and Arcadia are associated with rustic innocence. For Wilde's idealization of Sicily (which he visited in late 1897 and again in 1900) as "a pastoral Arcadia that evoked images of abundance and sensuous splendor," see Frankel, *Oscar Wilde: The Unrepentant Years*, 164–65.

235. In Greek mythology, Nemesis is the goddess of vengeance.

have brought a wrong atmosphere round the whole work, and in modern art atmosphere counts for so much. Modern life is complex and relative. Those are its two distinguishing notes. To render the first we require atmosphere with its subtlety of *nuances,* of suggestion, of strange perspectives: as for the second we require background. That is why sculpture has ceased to be a representative art; and why music *is* a representative art; and why Literature is, and has been, and always will remain the supreme representative art. Your little book should have brought with it Sicilian and Arcadian airs,[234] not the pestilent foulness of the criminal dock or the close breath of the convict cell. Nor would such a dedication as you proposed have been merely an error of taste in Art; it would from other points of view have been entirely unseemly. It would have looked like a continuance of your conduct before and after my arrest. It would have given people the impression of being an attempt at foolish bravado: an example of that kind of courage that is sold cheap and bought cheap in the streets of shame. As far as our friendship is concerned Nemesis has crushed us both like flies.[235] The dedication of verses to me when I was in prison would have seemed a sort of silly effort at smart repartee, an accomplishment on which in your old days of dreadful letter-writing—days never, I sincerely hope for your sake, to return—you used openly to pride yourself and about which it was your joy to boast. It would not have produced the serious, the beautiful effect which I trust—I believe indeed—you had intended. Had you consulted me, I would have advised you to delay the publication of your verses for a little; or, if that proved displeasing to you, to publish anonymously at first, and then when you had won lovers by your song—the only sort of lovers really worth the winning—you might have turned round and said to the world "These flowers that you admire are of my sowing, and now I offer them to one whom you regard as a pariah and an outcast, as my tribute to what I love and reverence and admire in him." But you chose the wrong method and the wrong moment. There is a tact in love, and a tact in literature. You were not sensitive to either.

236. In a letter to Ross dated 30 May 1896 (see p. 54, n.3 above), Wilde had advised: "In writing to Douglas, you had better quote [this] letter fully and frankly, so that he should have no loophole of escape. Indeed he cannot possibly refuse. He has ruined my life—that should content him" (CL 655).

237. "like the soul of Branca d'Oria in Dante" added to the manuscript as an afterthought. In Dante's *Inferno*, Branca d'Oria, a Ghibelline contemporary of Dante's who murdered his own father-in-law after inviting him to dinner, "in soul already in Cocytus bathes" even though "not dead as yet, / [He] eats, and drinks, and sleeps, and puts on clothes." In Greek mythology, Cocytus is a river that flows into Hades, or Hell.

238. See pp. 54–55, n.3 above.

I have spoken to you at length on this point in order that you should grasp its full bearings, and understand why I wrote at once to Robbie in terms of such scorn and contempt of you, and absolutely prohibited the dedication, and desired that the words I had written of you should be copied out carefully and sent to you.[236] I felt that at last the time had come when you should be made to see, to recognise, to realise a little of what you had done. Blindness may be carried so far that it becomes grotesque, and an unimaginative nature, if something be not done to rouse it, will become petrified into absolute insensibility, so that while the body may eat, and drink, and have its pleasures, the soul, whose house it is, may, like the soul of Branca d'Oria in Dante,[237] be dead absolutely. My letter seems to have arrived not a moment too soon. It fell on you, as far as I can judge, like a thunderbolt. You describe yourself, in your answer to Robbie, as being "deprived of all power of thought and expression."[238] Indeed, apparently, you can think of nothing better than to write to your mother to complain. Of course, she, with that blindness to your real good that has been her ill-starred fortune and yours, gives you every comfort she can think of, and lulls you back, I suppose, into your former unhappy, unworthy condition; while as far as I am concerned, she lets my friends know that she is "very much annoyed" at the severity of my remarks about you. Indeed it is not merely to my friends that she conveys her sentiments of annoyance, but also to those—a very much larger number, I need hardly remind you—who are not my friends: and I am informed now, and through channels very kindly-disposed to you and yours, that in consequence of this a great deal of the sympathy that, by reason of my distinguished genius and terrible sufferings, had been gradually but surely growing up for me, has been entirely taken away. People say "Ah! he first tried to get the kind father put into prison and failed: now he turns round and blames the innocent son for his failure. How right we were to despise him! How worthy of contempt he is!" It seems to me that, when my name is mentioned in your mother's presence, if she has no word of sorrow or regret for her share—no slight one—in the ruin of my house, it would be more seemly if she remained

239. Very little is known about Edwin Levy, although a number of scholars tentatively suggest he was a moneylender whom Wilde had known since at least 1882. See *CL* 156, n.1.

240. Alfred Taylor (1862–?), a purported brothelkeeper and procurer of young men for Wilde and other homosexual clients, was tried alongside Wilde in the first of Wilde's criminal trials, which ended in a hung jury. Although Taylor was tried separately from Wilde at their second criminal trial, Taylor's conviction four days before Wilde's likely swayed the case against the latter. After Wilde was also found guilty on all but one charge, Taylor was sentenced alongside Wilde and to the same term.

241. According to Douglas, he did not write because he had been led by Robert Ross to believe that a letter from him would be unwelcome to Wilde. As already noted, in early June 1896 Ross had shown Douglas the letter in which Wilde states: "I will have nothing to do with him nor allow him to come near me" (see p. 54, n.3 above). Well before this, according to Douglas, when he first proposed risking a return to England expressly to visit Wilde in prison, he had been "very much upset" when Ross told him "that he had just come from Wilde and that, as his correspondence and visitors were strictly limited, he desired that I should neither write to him nor visit him" (quoted in Rupert Croft-Cooke, *Bosie: Lord Alfred Douglas, His Friends and Enemies* [Indianapolis: Bobbs-Merrill, 1963], 141). In 1913, when pressed why he did not write to Wilde in prison, Douglas testified in court, "I was particularly told that he did not want me to write to him, because it would be detrimental to him if I wrote him" (quoted in Wintermans, *Alfred Douglas: A Poet's Life and His Finest Work*, 188, n.22). As Douglas later wrote, Wilde "either did not know, or pretended not to know, that Ross had given me most positive instructions, purporting to come from Wilde himself, that I was on no account to write to him or to attempt to visit him" (Lord Alfred Douglas, "The Wilde Myth" [1916], unpublished page proofs, p. 114, Lord Alfred Douglas Collection, 1.7 Harry Ransom Center, University of Texas at Austin).

silent. And as for you—don't you think now that, instead of writing to *her* to complain, it would have been better for you, in every way, to have written to *me* directly, and to have had the courage to say to me whatever you had or fancied you had to say? It is nearly a year ago now since I wrote that letter. You cannot have remained during that entire time "deprived of all power of thought and expression." Why did you not write to me? You saw by my letter how deeply wounded, how outraged I was by your whole conduct. More than that; you saw your entire friendship with me set before you, at last, in its true light, and by a mode not to be mistaken. Often in old days I had told you that you were ruining my life. You had always laughed. When Edwin Levy[239] at the very beginning of our friendship, seeing your manner of putting me forward to bear the brunt, and annoyance, and expense even of that unfortunate Oxford mishap of yours, if we must so term it, in reference to which his advice and help had been sought, warned me for the space of a whole hour against knowing you, you laughed, as at Bracknell I described to you my long and impressive interview with him. When I told you how even that unfortunate young man who ultimately stood beside me in the Dock[240] had warned me more than once that you would prove far more fatal in bringing me to utter destruction than any even of the common lads whom I was foolish enough to know, you laughed, though not with such sense of amusement. When my more prudent or less well-disposed friends either warned me or left me, on account of my friendship with you, you laughed with scorn. You laughed immoderately when, on the occasion of your father writing his first abusive letter to you about me, I told you that I knew I would be the mere catspaw of your dreadful quarrel and come to some evil between you. But every single thing has happened as I had said it would happen, as far as the result goes. You had no excuse for not seeing how all things had come to pass. Why did you not write to me? Was it cowardice? Was it callousness? What was it? The fact that I was outraged with you, and had expressed my sense of outrage, was all the more reason for writing.[241] If you thought my letter just, you should have written. If you thought it in the smallest point unjust, you should

242. "The contents of a bag or wallet; a bundle, ... Chiefly *fig.*, esp. of news; *spec.* a long letter full of news" (*Oxford English Dictionary*, hereafter OED).

243. A *causerie intime* (lit. "intimate conversation") is a short, informal, frequently witty essay in the columns of a French newspaper.

244. "the supreme arbiter to some" added to the manuscript as an afterthought

245. "of appetite without distinction, desire without limit" added to the manuscript as an afterthought.

246. Alfred Austin (1835–1913), minor poet controversially made Poet Laureate in 1896; George S. Street (1867–1936), humorist and critic whose 1894 novel *The Autobiography of a Boy* satirized Wilde and Douglas; Alice Meynell (1847–1922), poet and essayist, once complimented by Wilde (see *CL* 392) for her "graceful and clever pen."

have written. I waited for a letter. I felt sure that at last you would see that, if old affection, much-protested love, the thousand acts of ill-requited kindness I had showered on you, the thousand unpaid debts of gratitude you owed me—that if all these were nothing to you, mere duty itself, most barren of all bonds between man and man, should have made you write. You cannot say that you seriously thought I was obliged to receive none but business communications from members of my family. You knew perfectly well that every twelve weeks Robbie was writing to me a little budget[242] of literary news. Nothing can be more charming than his letters, in their wit, their clever concentrated criticism, their light touch: they are real letters: they are like a person talking to one: they have the quality of a French *causerie intime:*[243] and in his delicate modes of deference to me, appealing at one time to my judgment, at another to my sense of humour, at another to my instinct for beauty or to my culture, and reminding me in a hundred subtle ways that once I was to many an arbiter of style in Art, the supreme arbiter to some,[244] he shows how he has the tact of love as well as the tact of literature. His letters have been the little messengers between me and that beautiful unreal world of Art where once I was King, and would have remained King, indeed, had I not let myself be lured into the imperfect world of coarse uncompleted passions, of appetite without distinction, desire without limit[245] and formless greed. Yet, when all is said, surely you might have been able to understand, or conceive, at any rate, in your own mind, that, even on the ordinary grounds of mere psychological curiosity, it would have been more interesting to me to hear from *you* than to learn that Alfred Austin was trying to bring out a volume of poems, or that Street was writing dramatic criticisms for the *Daily Chronicle,* or that by one who cannot speak a panegyric without stammering Mrs. Meynell had been pronounced to be the new Sibyl of Style.[246]

Ah! had *you* been in prison—I will not say through any fault of mine, for that would be a thought too terrible for me to bear—but through fault of your own, error of your own, faith in some unworthy friend, slip in sensual mire, trust misapplied, or love ill-bestowed, or none, or all of

247. "house of bondage" and "despised of men" are phrases with biblical associations, as Ian Small observes (De Profundis; "Epistola: In Carcere et Vinculis," ed. Small, 241). In Deutronomy and Exodus, Egypt is frequently represented as a "house of bondage" to the enslaved children of Israel. In Isaiah 53:3, the Lord's servant is "despised and rejected of men; a man of sorrows, and acquainted with grief."

248. "of the joy" added to the manuscript as an afterthought.

249. "though seen through prison-bars and in a shape of shame" added to the manuscript as an afterthought.

250. "Preach the word; be instant in season, out of season; reprove, rebuke, exhort with all long suffering and doctrine" (Timothy 4:2).

251. Prison regulations dictated that Wilde could receive just one letter every quarter. Wilde is not known to have been given any unread letters on the day of his release. But his warder Thomas Martin testified years later that Governor Nelson circumvented prison regulations by personally receiving letters intended for Wilde but addressed to himself: "these [Nelson] would deliver personally and wait in the cell until they were read, then bring the letters away with him, but sometimes forgetting the envelope" (quoted in Hyde, Oscar Wilde: The Aftermath, 211).

252. It is unlikely that Wilde was thinking of Douglas when he incorporated this aphorism into chapter 15 of the twenty-chapter 1891 version of The Picture of Dorian Gray, where it is spoken by Lord Henry Wotton. Richard Ellmann, Wilde's preeminent biographer, says that Wilde first met Douglas only days before, in late June 1891 (Oscar Wilde, 324). Even if one accepts Wilde's suggestion that he first met Douglas some months before this date (see p. 56, n.6 above), by Wilde's own admission he had only met Douglas four times before May 1892, when he began to know Douglas more intimately.

253. Smash or crush.

these—do you think that I would have allowed you to eat your heart away in darkness and solitude without trying in some way, however slight, to help you to bear the bitter burden of your disgrace? Do you think that I would not have let you know that if you suffered, I was suffering too: that if you wept, there were tears in my eyes also: and that if you lay in the house of bondage and were despised of men,[247] I out of my very griefs had built a house in which to dwell until your coming, a treasury in which all that men had denied to you would be laid up for your healing, one hundredfold in increase? If bitter necessity, or prudence, to *me* more bitter still, had prevented my being near you, and robbed me of the joy[248] of your presence, though seen through prison-bars and in a shape of shame,[249] I would have written to you in season and out of season[250] in the hope that some mere phrase, some single word, some broken echo even of Love might reach you. If you had refused to receive my letters, I would have written none the less, so that you should have known that at any rate there were always letters waiting for you. Many have done so to me. Every three months people write to me, or propose to write to me. Their letters and communications are kept. They will be handed to me when I go out of prison.[251] I know that they are there. I know the names of the people who have written them. I know that they are full of sympathy, and affection, and kindness. That is sufficient for me. I need to know no more. Your silence has been horrible. Nor has it been a silence of weeks and months merely, but of years; of years even as they have to count them who, like yourself, live swiftly in happiness, and can hardly catch the gilt feet of the days as they dance by, and are out of breath in the chase after pleasure. It is a silence without excuse; a silence without palliation. I knew you had feet of clay. Who knew it better? When I wrote, among my aphorisms, that it was simply the feet of clay that made the gold of the image precious,[252] it was of you I was thinking. But it is no gold image with clay feet that you have made of yourself. Out of the very dust of the common highway that the hooves of horned things pash[253] into mire you have moulded your perfect semblance for me to look at, so that, whatever my secret desire might have been, it would be impossible

254. Shakespeare's Hamlet famously debates "Whether 'tis nobler in the mind to suffer / The slings and arrows of outrageous fortune / Or to take arms against a sea of troubles / And by opposing end them" (*Hamlet*, act 3, scene 1, ll. 56–59).

255. See too Wilde's comment later in *De Profundis*: "The poor thieves and outcasts who are imprisoned here with me are in many respects more fortunate than I am" (p. 179 below).

256. "under conditions of unspeakable humiliation" added to the manuscript as an afterthought. Wilde "found himself the object [of scrutiny] at the hands of [a] large number of well-dressed loafers and sightseers who occupied the back of the court," reported *Reynolds's Newspaper* of Wilde's second bankruptcy hearing (issue 2362, 17 November 1895). For Wilde's own description of his humiliating transfer from Wandsworth to Reading prison, see p. 235 below.

257. The threat was part of a battle over Wilde's life interest in his wife's marriage settlement, which was listed as an asset at his bankruptcy and thus scheduled to be sold at auction by the receiver to help pay Wilde's creditors. Constance wanted to buy Wilde's life interest for the benefit of her children in the event of her premature death, but Wilde's representatives, More Adey and Robert Ross, were determined to bid against her in an effort to secure it for Wilde himself. In mid-December 1896, Constance's lawyers wrote telling Wilde that unless Adey and Ross withdrew their competing bid, Constance would withdraw her previous offer to settle money on Wilde. It is only fair to recall that "Constance believed that Oscar would not emerge from jail penniless," her solicitors having been mistakenly informed that "two or three thousand pounds had been raised by Wilde's friends for his use" (Ashley H. Robins, *Oscar Wilde: The Great Drama of His Life* [Brighton, UK: Sussex Academic, 2011], 85).It also needs to be emphasized that Constance was acting in her children's best interests, since she believed, with good reason, that Wilde was profligate with money and could not be trusted to provide for the children in the event of her death.

258. On 1 March 1897 Wilde's parental rights were formally dissolved, on the grounds of his unfitness under the Guardianship of Children Act (1886), as the result of an action brought by his wife. See also Robins, *Oscar Wilde: The Great Drama of His Life*, 93; Hyde, *The Trials of Oscar Wilde*, 98.

for me now to have for you any feeling other than that of contempt and scorn, for myself any feeling other than that of contempt and scorn either. And setting aside all other reasons, your indifference, your worldly wisdom, your callousness, your prudence, whatever you may choose to call it, has been made doubly bitter to me by the peculiar circumstances that either accompanied or followed my fall.

Other miserable men, when they are thrown into prison, if they are robbed of the beauty of the world, are at least safe, in some measure, from the world's most deadly slings, most awful arrows.[254] They can hide in the darkness of their cells, and of their very disgrace make a mode of sanctuary.[255] The world, having had its will, goes its way, and they are left to suffer undisturbed. With me it has been different. Sorrow after sorrow has come beating at the prison doors in search of me. They have opened the gates wide and let them in. Hardly, if at all, have my friends been suffered to see me. But my enemies have had full access to me always. Twice in my public appearances at the Bankruptcy Court, twice again in my public transferences from one prison to another, have I been shown under conditions of unspeakable humiliation to the gaze and mockery of men.[256] The messenger of Death has brought me his tidings and gone his way, and in entire solitude, and isolated from all that could give me comfort, or suggest relief, I have had to bear the intolerable burden of misery and remorse that the memory of my mother placed upon me, and places on me still. Hardly has that wound been dulled, not healed, by time when violent and bitter and harsh letters come to me from my wife through her solicitor. I am, at once, taunted and threatened with poverty.[257] That I can bear. I can school myself to worse than that. But my two children are taken from me by legal procedure.[258] That is and always will remain to me a source of infinite distress, of infinite pain, of grief without end or limit. That the law should decide, and take upon itself to decide, that I am one unfit to be with my own children is something quite horrible to me. The disgrace of prison is as nothing compared to it. I envy the other men who tread the yard along with me. I am sure that their children wait for them, look for their corning, will be sweet to them. The poor are wiser,

259. Peter Stoneley writes that Wilde stood out among the Reading Prison population by virtue of his class and educational background: he was "very probably the only upper middle-class, university-educated person in the prison. He seems very unlikely to have had any fellow inmates who might have been described as middle-class" (" 'Looking at the Others': Oscar Wilde and the Reading Gaol Archive," *Journal of Victorian Culture* 19 [2014]: 474).

260. An allusion to the ghost of Hamlet's father, who appears dressed in armor at night, and of whom Hamlet asks:

> ... What may this mean
> That thou, dead corpse, again in complete steel,
> Revisits thus the glimpses of the moon,
> Making night hideous[?]

(*Hamlet*, act 1, scene 4, ll. 51–54.)

261. "us and help us, might bring balm to the bruised heart, and peace to the soul in pain" substituted in the manuscript for "our broken heart."

262. This sentence added to the manuscript as an afterthought.

263. "I know that you did not mean to do so" added to the manuscript as an afterthought.

264. Wilde is quoting himself from the two occasions on which he had used this phrase previously in the manuscript. See pp. 113 and 119 above.

265. When Wilde instructed Robert Ross to make copies of selected extracts from *De Profundis*, to be disseminated among readers "interested to know something of what is happening to my soul" (*CL* 782; see also "A Note on The Texts," p. 35 above), he insisted that Ross should begin here and should include everything up to "Between Art and myself there is none" on p. 233 below, "welded together with anything else ... good and nice in intention." Ross used Wilde's specifications as the rough basis for his 1905 edition.

266. "Break up your fallow ground, and sow not among thorns" (Jeremiah 4:3). As the critic Richard Hughes Gibson writes, in this

more charitable, more kind, more sensitive than we are. In their eyes prison is a tragedy in a man's life, a misfortune, a casualty, something that calls for sympathy in others. They speak of one who is in prison as of one who is "in trouble" simply. It is the phrase they always use, and the expression has the perfect wisdom of Love in it. With people of our rank it is different.[259] With us prison makes a man a pariah. I, and such as I am, have hardly any right to air and sun. Our presence taints the pleasures of others. We are unwelcome when we reappear. To revisit the glimpses of the moon is not for us.[260] Our very children are taken away. Those lovely links with humanity are broken. We are doomed to be solitary while our sons still live. We are denied the one thing that might heal us and help us, might bring balm to the bruised heart, and peace to the soul in pain.[261]

And to all this has been added the hard, small fact that by your actions and by your silence, by what you have done and by what you have left undone, you have made every day of my long imprisonment still more difficult for me to live through. The very bread and water of prison fare you have by your conduct changed. You have rendered the one bitter and the other brackish to me. The sorrow you should have shared you have doubled, the pain you should have sought to lighten you have quickened to anguish.[262] I have no doubt that you did not mean to do so. I know that you did not mean to do so.[263] It was simply that "one really fatal defect of your character, your entire lack of imagination."[264]

And the end of it all is that I have got to forgive you.[265] I must do so. I don't write this letter to put bitterness into your heart but to pluck it out of mine. For my own sake I must forgive you. One cannot always keep an adder in one's breast to feed on one, nor rise up every night to sow thorns in the garden of one's soul.[266] It will not be difficult at all for me to do so, if you help me a little. Whatever you did to me in old days I always readily forgave. It did you no good then. Only one whose life is without stain of any kind can forgive sins. But now when I sit in humiliation and disgrace it is different. My forgiveness should mean a great deal to you now. Some day you will realise it. Whether you do so early or late,

paragraph "Wilde has taken the received religious language of forgiveness and set it in a new virtue system, in effect given it a new grammar.... This bitterness is killing *me*, he says, and so I must forgive you for my own sake" (*Forgiveness in Victorian Literature* [London: Bloomsbury, 2015], 147–50).

267. "I am trying to do so, though you may not think it at the present moment" altered from "I am doing so at the present moment."

268. "without pity" added to the manuscript as an afterthought.

269. "I treated Art as the supreme reality, and life as a mere mode of fiction" added to the manuscript as an afterthought.

soon or not at all, my way is clear before me. I cannot allow you to go through life bearing in your heart the burden of having ruined a man like me. The thought might make you callously indifferent, or morbidly sad. I must take the burden from you and put it on my own shoulders. I must say to myself that neither you nor your father, multiplied a thousand times over, could possibly have ruined a man like me: that I ruined myself: and that nobody, great or small, can be ruined except by his own hand. I am quite ready to do so. I am trying to do so, though you may not think it at the present moment.[267] If I have brought this pitiless indictment against you, think what an indictment I bring without pity[268] against myself. Terrible as what you did to me was, what I did to myself was far more terrible still. I was a man who stood in symbolic relations to the art and culture of my age. I had realised this for myself at the very dawn of my manhood, and had forced my age to realise it afterwards. Few men hold such a position in their own lifetime and have it so acknowledged. It is usually discerned, if discerned at all, by the historian, or the critic, long after both the man and his age have passed away. With me it was different. I felt it myself, and made others feel it. Byron was a symbolic figure, but his relations were to the passion of his age and its weariness of passion. Mine were to something more noble, more permanent, of more vital issue, of larger scope. The Gods had given me almost everything. I had genius, a distinguished name, high social position, brilliancy, intellectual daring: I made art a philosophy, and philosophy an art: I altered the minds of men and the colours of things: there was nothing I said or did that did not make people wonder: I took the drama, the most objective form known to art, and made it as personal a mode of expression as the lyric or the sonnet, at the same time that I widened its range and enriched its characterisation: drama, novel, poem in rhyme, poem in prose, subtle or fantastic dialogue, whatever I touched I made beautiful in a new mode of beauty: to truth itself I gave what is false no less than what is true as its rightful province, and showed that the false and the true are merely forms of intellectual existence. I treated Art as the supreme reality, and life as a mere mode of fiction:[269] I awoke the imagination of my century so that it

270. "A lounger or ... idle 'man about town'" (OED).

271. "I amused myself with being a *flâneur,* a dandy, a man of fashion" added to the manuscript as an afterthought.

272. This oft-quoted sentence was added to the manuscript as an afterthought.

273. "It matters not how strait the gate, / How charged with punishments the scroll. / I am the master of my fate: / I am the captain of my soul" (W. E. Henley, "Invictus" [1875], repr. without the original title in his *Poems* [London: David Nutt, 1898], 119).

274. "anguish that wept aloud" added to the manuscript as an afterthought.

275. Wordsworth, "The Borderers," although Wordsworth gives "shares" for Wilde's "has." From December 1896 onward, Wilde possessed a one-volume edition of Wordsworth's *Complete Works* in his cell.

276. "The kingdom of heaven is like unto treasure hid in a field; the which when a man hath found, he hideth, and for joy thereof goeth" (Matthew 13:44).

created myth and legend around me: I summed up all systems in a phrase, and all existence in an epigram. Along with these things, I had things that were different. I let myself be lured into long spells of senseless and sensual ease. I amused myself with being a *flâneur*,[270] a dandy, a man of fashion.[271] I surrounded myself with the smaller natures and the meaner minds. I became the spendthrift of my own genius, and to waste an eternal youth gave me a curious joy.[272] Tired of being on the heights I deliberately went to the depths in the search for new sensations. What the paradox was to me in the sphere of thought, perversity became to me in the sphere of passion. Desire, at the end, was a malady, or a madness, or both. I grew careless of the lives of others. I took pleasure where it pleased me and passed on. I forgot that every little action of the common day makes or unmakes character, and that therefore what one has done in the secret chamber one has some day to cry aloud on the housetop. I ceased to be Lord over myself. I was no longer the Captain of my Soul,[273] and did not know it. I allowed you to dominate me, and your father to frighten me. I ended in horrible disgrace. There is only one thing for me now, absolute Humility: just as there is only one thing for you, absolute Humility also. You had better come down into the dust and learn it beside me. I have lain in prison for nearly two years. Out of my nature has come wild despair; an abandonment to grief that was piteous even to look at: terrible and impotent rage: bitterness and scorn: anguish that wept aloud:[274] misery that could find no voice: sorrow that was dumb. I have passed through every possible mood of suffering. Better than Wordsworth himself I know what Wordsworth meant when he said:

> Suffering is permanent, obscure, and dark
> And has the nature of Infinity.[275]

But while there were times when I rejoiced in the idea that my sufferings were to be endless, I could not bear them to be without meaning. Now I find hidden away in my nature something that tells me that nothing in the whole world is meaningless, and suffering least of all. That something hidden away in my nature, like a treasure in a field,[276] is Humility.

277. The capitalized Italian words for "new life," the title of Dante's great work of literary self-creation—at once a love poem (or series of poems) and the announcement of his arrival as a writer in the wake of the death of his beloved Beatrice.

278. In the late nineteenth century, an adherent of "the social theory which advocates the free and independent action of the individual, as opposed to communistic methods of organization and state interference" (OED). See "The Soul of Man" for Wilde's paradoxical effort to reconcile social theories of individualism and socialism.

279. But see the passage beginning nine sentences below, where Wilde says, "I know that to ask for alms on the highway is not to be my lot" and "I believe I am to have enough to live on for about eighteen months at any rate."

280. "A subsidiary structure or annexe attached to a wall of a main building, such as a shelter, a porch, a shed, an outhouse, etc." (OED).

281. Wilde is quoting from his own *A Woman of No Importance*, in which the penitent sexual renegade Mrs. Arbuthnot declares, "For me the world is shrivelled to a palm's breadth, and where I walk there are thorns" (*A Woman of No Importance*, ed. Small, act 4. p. 108). The phrase derives originally from Proverbs 22:5: "thorns and snares are in the way of the crooked."

282. This sentence was substituted in the manuscript for "Of course I know that things will not be so with me."

It is the last thing left in me, and the best: the ultimate discovery at which I have arrived: the starting-point for a fresh development. It has come to me right out of myself, so I know that it has come at the proper time. It could not have come before, nor later. Had anyone told me of it, I would have rejected it. Had it been brought to me, I would have refused it. As I found it, I want to keep it. I must do so. It is the one thing that has in it the elements of life, of a new life, a *Vita Nuova*[277] for me. Of all things it is the strangest. One cannot give it away, and another may not give it to one. One cannot acquire it, except by surrendering everything that one has. It is only when one has lost all things, that one knows that one possesses it.

Now that I realise that it is in me, I see quite clearly what I have got to do, what, in fact, I must do. And when I use such a phrase as that, I need not tell you that I am not alluding to any external sanction or command. I admit none. I am far more of an individualist[278] than I ever was. Nothing seems to me of the smallest value except what one gets out of oneself. My nature is seeking a fresh mode of self-realisation. That is all I am concerned with. And the first thing that I have got to do is to free myself from any possible bitterness of feeling against you. I am completely penniless, and absolutely homeless.[279] Yet there are worse things in the world than that. I am quite candid when I tell you that rather than go out from this prison with bitterness in my heart against you or against the world I would gladly and readily beg my bread from door to door. If I got nothing at the house of the rich, I would get something at the house of the poor. Those who have much are often greedy. Those who have little always share. I would not a bit mind sleeping in the cool grass in summer, and when winter came on sheltering myself by the warm close-thatched rick, or under the penthouse[280] of a great barn, provided I had love in my heart. The external things of life seem to me now of no importance at all. You can see to what intensity of individualism I have arrived, or am arriving rather, for the journey is long, and 'where I walk there are thorns.'[281] Of course I know that to ask for alms on the highway is not to be my lot, and that if ever I lie in the cool grass at night-time it will be to write sonnets to the Moon.[282] When I go out of prison, Robbie will

283. Wilde was greeted at the gate of Pentonville Prison on 19 May 1897 by More Adey and the Reverend Stewart Headlam. The former had taken care of Wilde's financial affairs during his imprisonment, while the latter had stood bail for him two years previously. Later that day, Adey accompanied Wilde on the overnight ferry to Dieppe, on the Normandy coast, where the next morning they were greeted by their friends Robert Ross and Reginald Turner, who had reserved and prepared rooms for Wilde at the Hôtel Sandwich. Wilde was never to return to Britain again. Ross and Turner were also present at Wilde's death in November 1900. See also the lines with which Wilde originally intended dedicating *The Ballad of Reading Gaol* to Ross, p. 318, n.1 below.

284. Although Wilde's writings contain trenchant criticisms of wealth, materialism, and class-based privilege, he had always romanticized poverty: the hero of "The Happy Prince" deliberately strips himself of all wealthy trappings in order to become "little better than a beggar." Similarly Baron Hausberg, one of the wealthiest men in Europe, commissions a portrait of himself dressed in disguise as a beggar, in "The Model Millionaire," with a coarse brown tattered cloak flung over his shoulder, holding out his hand for alms. As the portrait painter Alan Trevor remarks, "what you call rags I call romance. What seems poverty to you is picturesqueness to me."

285. "had I to accept . . . and scorn" added to the manuscript as an afterthought.

286. "When you really want it you will find it waiting for you" added to the manuscript as an afterthought.

287. "Neither Religion, Morality, nor Reason can help me at all" added to the manuscript as an afterthought.

288. An individual opposed to the obligatoriness of the moral law (OED).

289. Wilde's remark echoes that of the man called to judgment in his prose poem "The House of Judgment," who tells God that he cannot be sent to hell "because in Hell have I always lived."

290. The 1905 edition gives "Faithless," not "Fatherless," and this reading persists in some modern editions. However the manuscript clearly reads "Fatherless."

be waiting for me on the other side of the big iron-studded gate, and he is the symbol not merely of his own affection, but of the affection of many others besides.[283] I believe I am to have enough to live on for about eighteen months at any rate, so that, if I may not write beautiful books, I may at least read beautiful books, and what joy can be greater? After that, I hope to be able to recreate my creative faculty. But were things different: had I not a friend left in the world: were there not a single house open to me even in pity: had I to accept the wallet and ragged cloak of sheer penury:[284] still as long as I remained free from all resentment, hardness, and scorn,[285] I would be able to face life with much more calm and confidence than I would were my body in purple and fine linen, and the soul within it sick with hate. And I shall really have no difficulty in forgiving you. But to make it a pleasure for me you must feel that you want it. When you really want it you will find it waiting for you.[286] I need not say that my task does not end there. It would be comparatively easy if it did. There is much more before me. I have hills far steeper to climb, valleys much darker to pass through. And I have to get it all out of myself. Neither Religion, Morality, nor Reason can help me at all.[287]

Morality does not help me. I am a born antinomian.[288] I am one of those who are made for exceptions, not for laws. But while I see that there is nothing wrong in what one does, I see that there is something wrong in what one becomes. It is well to have learned that. Religion does not help me. The faith that others give to what is unseen, I give to what one can touch, and look at. My Gods dwell in temples made with hands, and within the circle of actual experience is my creed made perfect and complete: too complete it may be, for like many or all of those who have placed their Heaven in this earth, I have found in it not merely the beauty of Heaven but the horror of Hell also.[289] When I think about Religion at all, I feel as if I would like to found an order for those who cannot believe: the Confraternity of the Fatherless[290] one might call it, where on an altar, on which no taper burned, a priest, in whose heart peace had no dwelling, might celebrate with unblessed bread and a chalice empty

291. The unconsecrated accoutrements to Wilde's "Confraternity of the Fatherless" recall Wilde's neo-pagan assault on Christian mysticism in his prose poems, especially "The Master," in which a young contemporary of Christ laments that he too has performed miracles "and yet they have not crucified me."

292. "agnosticism" substituted in the manuscript for "scepticism." As Ian Small observes (*De Profundis*; "*Epistola: In Carcere et Vinculis*," ed. Small, 245), "agnosticism," meaning skepticism "with regard to the existence of anything beyond and behind material phenomena" (OED), was a term of comparatively recent invention. Its first use dates from 1870.

293. The last clause of this sentence, "and praise God daily for having hidden Himself from man," was added to the manuscript as an afterthought, while "sown" and "reap" were substituted for "had" and "have" respectively.

294. "Only that is spiritual which makes its own form" added to the manuscript as an afterthought.

of wine.[291] Everything to be true must become a religion. And agnosticism[292] should have its ritual no less than faith. It has sown its martyrs, it should reap its saints, and praise God daily for having hidden Himself from man.[293] But whether it be faith or agnosticism, it must be nothing external to me. Its symbols must be of my own creating. Only that is spiritual which makes its own form.[294] If I may not find its secret within myself, I shall never find it. If I have not got it already, it will never come to me. Reason does not help me. It tells me that the laws under which I am convicted are wrong and unjust laws, and the system under which I have suffered a wrong and unjust system. But, somehow, I have got to make both of these things just and right to me. And exactly as in Art one is only concerned with what a particular thing is at a particular moment to oneself, so it is also in the ethical evolution of one's character. I have got to make everything that has happened to me good for me. The plank-bed, the loathsome food, the hard ropes shredded into oakum till one's finger-tips grow dull with pain, the menial offices with which each day begins and finishes, the harsh orders that routine seems to necessitate, the dreadful dress that makes sorrow grotesque to look at, the silence, the solitude, the shame—each and all of these things I have to transform into a spiritual experience. There is not a single degradation of the body which I must not try and make into a spiritualising of the soul. I want to get to the point when I shall be able to say, quite simply and without affectation, that the two great turning points of my life were when my father sent me to Oxford, and when society sent me to prison. I will not say that it is the best thing that could have happened to me, for that phrase would savour of too great bitterness towards myself. I would sooner say, or hear it said of me, that I was so typical a child of my age that in my perversity, and for that perversity's sake, I turned the good things of my life to evil, and the evil things of my life to good. What is said, however, by myself or by others matters little. The important thing, the thing that lies before me, the thing that I have to do, or be for the brief remainder of my days one maimed, marred, and incomplete, is to absorb into my nature all that has been done to me, to make it part of me, to accept it without

295. "the rain falling...making it silver" added to the manuscript as an afterthought.

296. "Experience [is] of no ethical value. It [is] merely the name we [give] to our mistakes," reflects Lord Henry Wotton cynically in *The Picture of Dorian Gray*: yet Wotton's protégé, Dorian Gray, embraces a "new Hedonism" whose aim "was to be experience itself, and not the fruits of experience, sweet or bitter as they might be" (*The Picture of Dorian Gray*, ed. Frankel, 129, 192). The idea derives directly from Wilde's university tutor and friend Walter Pater, who had written in *The Renaissance*, "Not the fruit of experience, but experience itself, is the end.... The theory or idea or system which requires of us the sacrifice of any part of this experience...has no real claim upon us" (Pater, *The Renaissance*, ed. Hill, 188–89). As other verbal echoes of Pater later in this paragraph suggest, Wilde was still under the sway of Pater's aestheticism.

complaint, fear, or reluctance. The supreme vice is shallowness. Whatever is realised is right.

When first I was put into prison some people advised me to try and
forget who I was. It was ruinous advice. It is only by realising what I am
that I have found comfort of any kind. Now I am advised by others to try
on my release to forget that I have ever been in a prison at all. I know
that would be equally fatal. It would mean that I would be always haunted
by an intolerable sense of disgrace, and that those things that are meant
as much for me as for anyone else—the beauty of the sun and the moon,
the pageant of the seasons, the music of daybreak and the silence of great
nights, the rain falling through the leaves, or the dew creeping over the
grass and making it silver,[295] would all be tainted for me, and lose their
healing power and their power of communicating joy. To reject one's own
experiences is to arrest one's own development.[296] To deny one's own
experiences is to put a lie into the lips of one's own life. It is no less than a
denial of the Soul. For just as the body absorbs things of all kinds, things
common and unclean no less than those that the priest or a vision has
cleansed, and converts them into swiftness or strength, into the play of
beautiful muscles and the moulding of fair flesh, into the curves and colours of the hair, the lips, the eye: so the Soul, in its turn, has its nutritive
functions also, and can transform into noble moods of thought, and
passions of high import, what in itself is base, cruel, and degrading: nay
more, may find in these its most august modes of assertion, and can
often reveal itself most perfectly through what was intended to desecrate
or destroy. The fact of my having been the common prisoner of a common
gaol I must frankly accept, and, curious as it may seem to you, one of the
things I shall have to teach myself is not to be ashamed of it. I must accept it as a punishment, and if one is ashamed of having been punished,
one might just as well never have been punished at all. Of course there
are many things of which I was convicted that I had not done, but then
there are many things of which I was convicted that I had done, and a
still greater number of things in my life for which I was never indicted at
all. And as for what I have said in this letter, that the gods are strange,

297. But see Wilde's later acknowledgment of—and contempt for—"the Prisoners' Aid Society and other modern movements of the kind" (p. 225 below). Recidivism and the future of the discharged prisoner were hotly debated in the period leading up to the reforms of the 1898 Prisons Act, although "Discharged Prisoners' Aid Societies" had existed in many localities since the 1870s. "Some do admirable work, but it is impossible to form a definite opinion upon either the extent or the permanent effect of the aid given," commented the Gladstone Committee in its review of the prison system in 1895: "No doubt many prisoners are rescued by them, and much philanthropic effort is devoted to their welfare.... [But] it is most desirable that fuller scope should be given to their able efforts and philanthropic enterprise, and that other societies should be encouraged to work in the same spirit" (*Report from the Departmental Committee on Prisons*, 1895, p. 14).

298. "a creditor whose debt they cannot pay, or one" substituted for "those," and "an irreparable, an irredeemable" substituted for "a terrible" in the manuscript.

299. "The poor thieves and outcasts" substituted for "those" in the manuscript. Peter Stoneley writes that the vast majority of Wilde's fellow-prisoners at Reading "were working-class and a significant proportion of them were destitute, or close to destitute. Aside from those who were beggars, many of them had been tempted to steal very small items, such as rabbits, shirts on a line, nuts from a tree, pipes and tobacco, and so on. Even where the charge was not vagrancy, [some prisoners had committed] crimes that seem to relate to homelessness, such as 'lodging in an outhouse' in winter. Others—the repeat offenders—seem to have committed a series of more or less token crimes which gave them access to a prison regime which, however restrictive and unpleasant, provided them with shelter other than the hated workhouse, with regular meals, some rudimentary healthcare, some educational opportunity, and even a measure of community and fellow feeling" ("'Looking at the Others,'" 466–67).

300. A slight misquotation from *A Woman of No Importance*, Act IV. See p. 170, n.281 above.

301. "My words... were graven with an iron pen and lead in the rock for ever" (Job 19:23–24).

and punish us for what is good and humane in us as much as for what is evil and perverse, I must accept the fact that one is punished for the good as well as for the evil that one does. I have no doubt that it is quite right one should be. It helps one, or should help one, to realise both, and not to be too conceited about either. And if I then am not ashamed of my punishment, as I hope not to be, I shall be able to think, and walk, and live with freedom. Many men on their release carry their prison along with them into the air, hide it as a secret disgrace in their hearts, and at length like poor poisoned things creep into some hole and die. It is wretched that they should have to do so, and it is wrong, terribly wrong, of Society that it should force them to do so. Society takes upon itself the right to inflict appalling punishments on the individual, but it also has the supreme vice of shallowness, and fails to realise what it has done. When the man's punishment is over, it leaves him to himself: that is to say it abandons him at the very moment when its highest duty towards him begins.[297] It is really ashamed of its own actions, and shuns those whom it has punished, as people shun a creditor whose debt they cannot pay, or one on whom they have inflicted an irreparable, an irredeemable wrong.[298] I claim on my side that if I realise what I have suffered, Society should realise what it has inflicted on me: and there should be no bitterness or hate on either side.

Of course I know that from one point of view things will be made more difficult for me than for others; must indeed, by the very nature of the case, be made so. The poor thieves and outcasts[299] who are imprisoned here with me are in many respects more fortunate than I am. The little way in grey city or green field that saw their sin is small: to find those who know nothing of what they have done they need go no further than a bird might fly between the twilight before dawn and dawn itself: but for me "the world is shrivelled to a handsbreadth,"[300] and everywhere I turn my name is written on the rocks in lead.[301] For I have come, not from obscurity into the momentary notoriety of crime, but from a sort of eternity of fame to a sort of eternity of infamy, and sometimes seem to myself to have shown, if indeed it required showing, that between the famous and the infamous there is but one step, if so much as one. Still, in the

302. "Life" substituted for "Society" in the manuscript.

303. "Nor am I making any demands on Life. In all that I have said" added to the manuscript as an afterthought.

304. "It was always springtime once in my heart" added to the manuscript as an afterthought.

305. "strange" substituted for "great" in the manuscript.

306. In *The Renaissance*, as Ian Small observes, Walter Pater refers twice in close succession to "the judgment of Dante on those who willfully lived in sadness."

307. "Sad once we were / In the sweet air made gladsome by the sun" (Dante, *Inferno*, trans. Cary, 7:121–22). Wilde possessed Dante's *Divine Comedy* in both Italian and English editions in his prison cell.

308. Sloth, or apathy, one of the seven deadly sins.

very fact that people will recognise me wherever I go, and know all about my life, as far as its follies go, I can discern something good for me. It will force on me the necessity of again asserting myself as an artist, and as soon as I possibly can. If I can produce even one more beautiful work of art I shall be able to rob malice of its venom, and cowardice of its sneer, and to pluck out the tongue of scorn by the roots. And if life be, as it surely is, a problem to me, I am no less a problem to Life.[302] People must adopt some attitude towards me, and so pass judgment both on themselves and me. I need not say I am not talking of particular individuals. The only people I would care to be with now are artists and people who have suffered: those who know what Beauty is, and those who know what Sorrow is: nobody else interests me. Nor am I making any demands on Life. In all that I have said[303] I am simply concerned with my own mental attitude towards life as a whole: and I feel that not to be ashamed of having been punished is one of the first points I must attain to, for the sake of my own perfection, and because I am so imperfect.

Then I must learn how to be happy. Once I knew it, or thought I knew it, by instinct. It was always springtime once in my heart.[304] My temperament was akin to joy. I filled my life to the very brim with pleasure, as one might fill a cup to the very brim with wine. Now I am approaching life from a completely new standpoint, and even to conceive happiness is often extremely difficult for me. I remember during my first term at Oxford reading in Pater's *Renaissance*—that book which has had such a strange[305] influence over my life—how Dante places low in the Inferno those who wilfully live in sadness,[306] and going to the College Library and turning to the passage in the *Divine Comedy* where beneath the dreary marsh lie those who were "sullen in the sweet air," saying for ever through their sighs,

> Tristi fummo
> nell' aer dolce che dal sol s'allegra.[307]

I knew the Church condemned *accidia*,[308] but the whole idea seemed to me quite fantastic, just the sort of sin, I fancied, a priest who knew nothing

309. Dante, *Purgatorio*, 23: 81.

310. "to maim them with an alien sorrow: to mar them with my own pain" added as an afterthought, and "secret" substituted for "mystery" in the manuscript.

311. Probably 27 February 1897, when Ross visited Wilde at Reading accompanied by More Adey.

about real life would invent. Nor could I understand how Dante, who says that "sorrow remarries us to God,"[309] could have been so harsh to those who were enamoured of melancholy, if any such there really were. I had no idea that someday this would become to me one of the greatest temptations of my life. While I was in Wandsworth Prison I longed to die. It was my one desire. When after two months in the Infirmary I was transferred here, and found myself growing gradually better in physical health, I was filled with rage. I determined to commit suicide on the very day on which I left prison. After a time that evil mood passed away, and I made up my mind to live, but to wear gloom as a King wears purple: never to smile again: to turn whatever house I entered into a house of mourning: to make my friends walk slowly in sadness with me: to teach them that melancholy is the true secret of life: to maim them with an alien sorrow: to mar them with my own pain.[310] Now I feel quite differently. I see it would be both ungrateful and unkind of me to pull so long a face that when my friends came to see me they would have to make their faces still longer in order to show their sympathy, or, if I desired to entertain them, to invite them to sit down silently to bitter herbs and funeral baked meats. I must learn how to be cheerful and happy. The last two occasions on which I was allowed to see my friends here I tried to be as cheerful as possible, and to show my cheerfulness in order to make them some slight return for their trouble in coming all the way from town to visit me. It is only a slight return, I know, but it is the one, I feel certain, that pleases them most. I saw Robbie for an hour on Saturday week,[311] and I tried to give the fullest possible expression to the delight I really felt at our meeting. And that, in the views and ideas I am here shaping for myself, I am quite right is shown to me by the fact that now for the first time since my imprisonment I have a real desire to live. There is before me so much to do that I would regard it as a terrible tragedy if I died before I was allowed to complete at any rate a little of it. I see new developments in Art and Life, each one of which is a fresh mode of perfection. I long to live so that I can explore what is no less than a new world to me. Do you want to know what this new world is?

312. "They had no place in my philosophy" added to the manuscript as an afterthought. In fact, sorrow and suffering *had* found a place in Wilde's philosophy before his imprisonment: the title character in Wilde's story "The Happy Prince," a statue, remarks, "When I was alive and had a human heart...I did not know what tears were, for I lived in the Palace of Sans-Souci, where sorrow is not allowed to enter.... Round the garden ran a very lofty wall, but I never cared to ask what lay beyond it, everything about me was so beautiful. My courtiers called me the Happy Prince, and happy indeed I was, if pleasure be happiness. So I lived, and so I died. And now that I am dead...I can see all the ugliness and all the misery of my city, and though my heart is made of lead yet I cannot choose but weep" (Wilde, *Complete Shorter Fiction*, ed. Isobel Murray [Oxford: Oxford University Press, 1980], 97).

313. A slight misquotation from Johann Wolfgang von Goethe, *Wilhelm Meister's Apprenticeship: A Novel*, trans. Thomas Carlyle, 3 vols. (Edinburgh, 1824), 1:214. While nothing is known of the book which Carlyle gave to Lady Wilde, Carlyle's published translation has "darksome" for "midnight," "watching" for "waiting," "he knows ye not" for "he knows you not," and "gloomy Powers" for "Heavenly Powers."

314. Louise of Mecklenburg-Strelitz, Queen consort of Prussia from 1797 until her death in 1810 at the age of thirty-four. Following Prussia's defeat by Napoleon's forces at Jena in 1806, the pregnant Louise attempted personally to convince Napoleon to treat Prussia with leniency. Her unsuccessful intercession was all the more humiliating because Napoleon had previously slandered Louise by publicly suggesting that she had been unfaithful to her husband, King Friedrich Wilhelm III. From 1806 to 1809, Louise and Friedrich Wilhelm were effectively exiled—first in Königsberg, then briefly in St. Petersburg—as a result of Napoleon's occupation of Berlin.

315. The "troubles" of Lady Wilde's later life were the infidelities of her philandering husband, Sir William Wilde; the loss of her libel case in 1864 against Mary Travers, a young patient of her husband's, whose claim that Sir William had seduced her while under sedation—angrily denied by Lady Wilde—was upheld in court; the death of her only daughter (and Wilde's sister) Isola in 1867; and the poverty in which Sir William left her on his death in 1876, when his estate was found to be largely worthless.

I think you can guess what it is. It is the world in which I have been living.

Sorrow, then, and all that it teaches one, is my new world. I used to live entirely for pleasure. I shunned sorrow and suffering of every kind. I hated both. I resolved to ignore them as far as possible, to treat them, that is to say, as modes of imperfection. They were not part of my scheme of life. They had no place in my philosophy.[312] My mother, who knew life as a whole, used often to quote to me Goethe's lines—written by Carlyle in a book he had given her years ago—and translated, I fancy, by him also:

> Who never ate his bread in sorrow,
>   Who never spent the midnight hours
> Weeping and waiting for the morrow,
>   He knows you not, ye Heavenly Powers.[313]

They were the lines that noble Queen of Prussia, whom Napoleon treated with such coarse brutality, used to quote in her humiliation and exile:[314] they were lines my mother often quoted in the troubles of her later life:[315] I absolutely declined to accept or admit the enormous truth hidden in them. I could not understand it. I remember quite well how I used to tell her that I did not want to eat my bread in sorrow, or to pass any night weeping and watching for a more bitter dawn. I had no idea that it was one of the special things that the Fates had in store for me; that for a whole year of my life, indeed, I was to do little else. But so has my portion been meted out to me; and during the last few months I have, after terrible struggles and difficulties, been able to comprehend some of the lessons hidden in the heart of pain. Clergymen, and people who use phrases without wisdom, sometimes talk of suffering as a mystery. It is really a revelation. One discerns things that one never discerned before. One approaches the whole of history from a different standpoint. What one had felt dimly through instinct, about Art, is intellectually and emotionally realised with perfect clearness of vision and absolute intensity of apprehension. I now see that Sorrow, being the supreme emotion of which

316. "being the supreme emotion of which man is capable, is at once the type and test of all great Art" substituted in the manuscript for "is the supreme [illegible word] emotion."

man is capable, is at once the type and test of all great Art.[316] What the artist is always looking for is that mode of existence in which soul and body are one and indivisible: in which the outward is expressive of the inward: in which Form reveals. Of such modes of existence there are not a few: youth and the arts preoccupied with youth may serve as a model for us at one moment: at another, we may like to think that, in its subtlety and sensitiveness of impression, its suggestion of a spirit dwelling in external things and making its raiment of earth and air, of mist and city alike, and in the morbid sympathy of its moods, and tones and colours, modern landscape art is realising for us pictorially what was realised in such plastic perfection by the Greeks. Music, in which all subject is absorbed in expression and cannot be separated from it, is a complex example, and a flower or a child a simple example of what I mean: but Sorrow is the ultimate type both in life and Art. Behind Joy and Laughter there may be a temperament, coarse, hard and callous. But behind Sorrow there is always Sorrow. Pain, unlike Pleasure, wears no mask. Truth in Art is not any correspondence between the essential idea and the accidental existence; it is not the resemblance of shape to shadow, or of the form mirrored in the crystal to the form itself: it is no Echo coming from a hollow hill, any more than it is the well of silver water in the valley that shows the Moon to the Moon and Narcissus to Narcissus. Truth in Art is the unity of a thing with itself: the outward rendered expressive of the inward: the soul made incarnate: the body instinct with spirit. For this reason there is no truth comparable to Sorrow. There are times when Sorrow seems to me to be the only truth. Other things may be illusions of the eye or the appetite, made to blind the one and cloy the other, but out of Sorrow have the worlds been built, and at the birth of a child or a star there is pain. More than this, there is about Sorrow an intense, an extraordinary reality. I have said of myself that I was one who stood in symbolic relations to the art and culture of my age. There is not a single wretched man in this wretched place along with me who does not stand in symbolic relations to the very secret of life. For the secret of life is suffering. It is what is hidden behind everything. When we begin to

317. A slight misquotation from Algernon Swinburne, "Before Parting." Swinburne has "live on honeycomb," not "feed on honeycomb."

318. Wilde is describing his friend Adela Schuster, a wealthy spinster, whose sympathy and kindness had been expressed in her gift to Wilde of £1,000 for his personal use while he was out on bail awaiting his second criminal trial in May 1895. She maintained a close personal interest in Wilde during his imprisonment, corresponding frequently with More Adey, and around the time he began *De Profundis* Wilde was "greatly touched . . . that she should keep a gracious memory of me, and have trust or hope for me in the future" (*CL* 666). After finishing *De Profundis*, Wilde identified Schuster as one of two "sweet women" (the other was his friend Frankie Forbes-Robertson) to whom he wanted copied extracts from the manuscript of *De Profundis* sent, since she "will be interested to know something of what is happening to my soul" (*CL* 782).

319. "one for whom Beauty and Sorrow walk hand in hand and have the same message" added to the manuscript as an afterthought.

320. Wilde had considered the contradiction between pleasure and sorrow in his prose poem "The Artist," published nearly a year before his conviction. The poem's protagonist has fashioned and placed a bronze icon of *The Sorrow That Endureth for Ever* on the tomb of his dead lover. But creativity comes from the vanquishing of sorrow, which is less permanent than it seems at first: desiring to create a new icon, and finding no other bronze in the world except that from which he made *The Sorrow That Endureth for Ever*, the artist places the first icon in a furnace, melts it down, and creates instead an icon of *The Pleasure That Abideth for a Moment*.

321. A phrase loosely derived from Psalms (e.g., Psalm 46:3: "There is a river, the streams whereof shall make glad the city of God"), and from Revelations, where the twelve gates of the New Jerusalem "were twelve pearls, with each gate made of a single pearl (Revelations 21:21). Wilde's direct source might have been St. Augustine's *De civitate dei* ("Concerning the City of God"), which he had been sent at Pentonville (see p. 45, n.7 above), although from December 1896 onward he also possessed a Greek Testament in his Reading Prison cell.

live, what is sweet is so sweet to us, and what is bitter so bitter, that we inevitably direct all our desires towards pleasure, and seek not merely for "a month or twain to feed on honeycomb,"[317] but for all our years to taste no other food, ignorant the while that we may be really starving the soul.

I remember talking once on this subject to one of the most beautiful personalities I have ever known: a woman, whose sympathy and noble kindness to me both before and since the tragedy of my imprisonment have been beyond power of description:[318] one who has really assisted me, though she does not know it, to bear the burden of my troubles more than anyone else in the whole world has: and all through the mere fact of her existence: through her being what she is, partly an ideal and partly an influence, a suggestion of what one might become, as well as a real help towards becoming it, a soul that renders the common air sweet, and makes what is spiritual seem as simple and natural as sunlight or the sea, one for whom Beauty and Sorrow walk hand in hand and have the same message.[319] On the occasion of which I am thinking I recall distinctly how I said to her that there was enough suffering in one narrow London lane to show that God did not love man, and that wherever there was any sorrow, though but that of a child in some little garden weeping over a fault that it had or had not committed, the whole face of creation was completely marred. I was entirely wrong. She told me so, but I could not believe her. I was not in the sphere in which such belief was to be attained to. Now it seems to me that Love of some kind is the only possible explanation of the extraordinary amount of suffering that there is in the world. I cannot conceive any other explanation. I am convinced that there is no other, and that if the worlds have indeed, as I have said, been built out of Sorrow, it has been by the hands of Love, because in no other way could the Soul of man for whom the worlds are made reach the full stature of its perfection. Pleasure for the beautiful body, but Pain for the beautiful Soul.[320]

When I say that I am convinced of these things I speak with too much pride. Far off, like a perfect pearl, one can see the city of God.[321] It is so

322. A very slight misquotation from Wordsworth's "The Excursion," which has "heights which," not "heights that." The previous few sentences dimly echo Wordsworth's "Ode: Intimations of Immortality from Recollections of Early Childhood": "the growing boy ... beholds the light and whence it flows, / He sees it in his joy; / ... At length the man perceives it die away / And fade into the common light of day". From December 1896 onward, Wilde possessed a one-volume edition of Wordsworth in his cell.

323. "When the unclean spirit is gone out of a man, he walketh through dry places, seeking rest; and finding none, he saith, I will return unto my house whence I came out. And when he cometh, he findeth it swept and garnished" (Luke 11:24–25).

324. A reference to Acts 3:1–10, which describes how the Apostles Peter and Paul healed a lame man who had asked for alms "at the gate of the temple which is called Beautiful." According to the first-century historian Josephus, this gate, which separated the inner court from the outer "Court of the Gentiles" on the east, was "beautiful" because it "greatly excelled those that were only covered over with silver and gold."

325. "I sink in deep mire, where there is no standing. . . . I am become a stranger unto my brethren, and an alien unto my mother's children. . . . I made sackcloth also my garment; and I became a proverb to them. O God, in the multitude of thy mercy ... deliver me out of the mire, and let me not sink" (Psalms 69:2–14).

326. The fate suffered by the false prophet Barjesus, to whom the prophet Saul (Paul) says, "Behold, the hand of the Lord is upon thee, and thou shalt be blind, not seeing the sun for a season," whereupon "immediately there fell on him a mist and a darkness; and he went about seeking some to lead him by the hand" (Acts 13:11).

327. See p. 170, n.277 above.

328. For Magdalen, see p. 74, n.58 above. In his early poem "Magdalen Walks," Wilde writes:

The birds are singing for joy of the Spring's glad birth,
Hopping from branch to branch on the rocking trees.

wonderful that it seems as if a child could reach it in a summer's day. And so a child could. But with me and such as I am it is different. One can realise a thing in a single moment, but one loses it in the long hours that follow with leaden feet. It is so difficult to keep "heights that the soul is competent to gain."[322] We think in Eternity, but we move slowly through Time: and how slowly time goes with us who lie in prison I need not speak again, nor of the weariness and despair that creep back into one's cell, and into the cell of one's heart, with such strange insistence that one has, as it were, to garnish and sweep one's house for their coming,[323] as for an unwelcome guest, or a bitter master, or a slave whose slave it is one's chance or choice to be. And, though at present you may find it a thing hard to believe, it is true none the less that for you, living in freedom and idleness and comfort, it is more easy to learn the lessons of Humility than it is for me, who begin the day by going down on my knees and washing the floor of my cell. For prison-life, with its endless privations and restrictions, makes one rebellious. The most terrible thing about it is not that it breaks one's heart—hearts are made to be broken[—]but that it turns one's heart to stone. One sometimes feels that it is only with a front of brass and a lip of scorn that one can get through the day at all. And he who is in a state of rebellion cannot receive grace, to use the phrase of which the Church is so fond;[—]so rightly fond I dare say,[—]for in life, as in Art, the mood of rebellion closes up the channels of the soul, and shuts out the airs of heaven. Yet I must learn these lessons here, if I am to learn them anywhere, and must be filled with joy if my feet are on the right road, and my face set towards the "gate which is called Beautiful,"[324] though I may fall many times in the mire,[325] and often in the mist go astray.[326]

This new life, as through my love of Dante I like sometimes to call it,[327] is, of course, no new life at all, but simply the continuance, by means of development, and evolution, of my former life. I remember when I was at Oxford saying to one of my friends—as we were strolling round Magdalen's narrow bird-haunted walks one morning in the June before I took my degree[328]—that I wanted to eat of the fruit of all the trees in the

And all the woods are alive with the murmur and sound of Spring,
  And the rosebud breaks into pink on the climbing briar,
  And the crocus-bed is a quivering moon of fire
Girdled round with the belt of an amethyst ring.

(*Poems and Poems in Prose*, ed. Fong and Beckson, 55.)

329. "And the Lord God commanded the man, saying, Of every tree of the garden thou mayest freely eat: But of the tree of the knowledge of good and evil, thou shalt not eat of it: for in the day that thou eatest thereof thou shalt surely die" (Genesis 2:16–17).

330. "And so, indeed, I went out, and so I lived" added to the manuscript as an afterthought.

Garrick Palmer, wood-engraved frontispiece for Oscar Wilde, *The Ballad of Reading Gaol* (Llandogo, Gwent: The Old Stile Press, 1994).

garden of the world,[329] and that I was going out into the world with that passion in my soul. And so, indeed, I went out, and so I lived.[330] My only mistake was that I confined myself so exclusively to the trees of what seemed to me the sun-gilt side of the garden, and shunned the other side for its shadow and its gloom. Failure, disgrace, poverty, sorrow, despair, suffering, tears even, the broken words that come from the lips of pain,

331. In the Old Testament, sackcloth and ashes were worn as signs of mourning, misery, and penitence.

332. "I will feed them with wormwood, and make them drink the water of gall" (Jeremiah 23:15).

333. Wilde likens himself to Cleopatra, who, according to the Roman historian Pliny, dissolved a massive pearl in a cup of wine, prior to drinking it, in order to impress her lover Mark Antony. This sentence and the next two, from "I threw the pearl" to "lived on honeycomb," were added to the manuscript as an afterthought.

334. "A puffed and reckless libertine, / ... the primrose path of dalliance treads / And recks not his own rede" (*Hamlet*, act 1, scene 3, ll. 48–50).

335. In the Bible, honeycomb epitomizes ecstatic, often deceptive, gratification—e.g., "The full soul loatheth an honeycomb; but to the hungry soul every bitter thing is sweet" (Proverbs 27:7).

336. In marked contrast to other parts of *De Profundis*, the folio sheet on which roughly the next three thousand words (up to "To him what is dumb is dead," on p. 209 below) are written is one of the most pristine and error-free in Wilde's entire manuscript. This folio, in which Wilde discusses the secret and nature of Christ, is clearly a fair copy, not an early draft, and Wilde revised and polished it carefully.

337. In Wilde's story "The Young King" (1888), the eponymous protagonist prepares for his coronation dressed as a simple shepherd, rather than in the finery of state. When the young king enters the cathedral, a bishop (betraying his Christian mission) enjoins him in the name of Christ to "put on the raiment that beseemeth a king" ("The Young King," in Wilde, *The Complete* Stories, ed. John Sloan [Oxford: Oxford University Press, 2010], 151). The young king reacts by angrily striding past the bishop, remarking incredulously, "Sayeth thou that in this house?" and then kneeling before an image of Christ and bowing his head in prayer (152).

338. Wilde has here *reversed* the narrative of his prose poem "The Artist," whose protagonist—in accord with Paterian notions about life's brevity and the importance of living for the moment—fashions an image of "*The Pleasure that abideth for a Moment*" out of the bronze he used previously

remorse that makes one walk in thorns, conscience that condemns, self-abasement that punishes, the misery that puts ashes on its head, the anguish that chooses sackcloth for its raiment[331] and into its own drink puts gall[332]—all these were things of which I was afraid. And as I had determined to know nothing of them, I was forced to taste each one of them in turn, to feed on them, to have for a season, indeed, no other food at all. I don't regret for a single moment having lived for pleasure. I did it to the full, as one should do everything that one does to the full. There was no pleasure I did not experience. I threw the pearl of my soul into a cup of wine.[333] I went down the primrose path[334] to the sound of flutes. I lived on honeycomb.[335] But to have continued the same life would have been wrong because it would have been limiting. I had to pass on. The other half of the garden had its secrets for me also.

Of course all this is foreshadowed and prefigured in my art.[336] Some of it is in "The Happy Prince," some of it in "The Young King," notably in the passage where the Bishop says to the kneeling boy, "Is not He who made misery wiser than thou art?"[337] a phrase which when I wrote it seemed to me little more than a phrase: a great deal of it is hidden away in the note of Doom that like a purple thread runs through the gold cloth of *Dorian Gray:* in "The Critic as Artist" it is set forth in many colours: in *The Soul of Man* it is written down simply and in letters too easy to read: it is one of the refrains whose recurring *motifs* make *Salomé* so like a piece of music and bind it together as a ballad: in the prose-poem of the man who from the bronze of the image of the "Pleasure that liveth for a Moment" has to make the image of the "Sorrow that abideth for Ever" it is incarnate.[338] It could not have been otherwise. At every single moment of one's life one is what one is going to be no less than what one has been. Art is a symbol, because man is a symbol.

It is, if I can fully attain to it, the ultimate realisation of the artistic life. For the artistic life is simple self-development.[339] Humility in the artist is his frank acceptance of all experiences, just as Love in the artist is simply that sense of Beauty that reveals to the world its body and its soul. In *Marius the Epicurean* Pater seeks to reconcile the artistic life with the to make the image of "*The Sorrow that endureth for Ever.*" See p. 188, n.320 above.

339. See too "The Soul of Man under Socialism" (1891), where Wilde argues that with the abolition of private property and authoritarian institutions "we shall have true, beautiful healthy Individualism" and that "Art is the most intense mode of Individualism that the world has known" (*Criticism: "Historical Criticism," "Intentions," "The Soul of Man,"* ed. Josephine Guy, vol. 4 of *The Complete Works of Oscar Wilde* [Oxford: Oxford University Press, 2007], 238, 248).

340. *Marius the Epicurean: His Sensations and Ideas* (1885), a philosophical novel in which Walter Pater strives to reconcile aesthetics with religion. As the critic Guy Willoughby observes, "According to Wilde, Pater failed to reconcile ... [a] life based on artistic principles 'with the life of religion' in its ethical sense, because his hero ... Marius's limited aesthetic sense is directed only at appearances" (*Art and Christhood: The Aesthetics of Oscar Wilde* [London: Associated University Presses, 1993], 106). In *The Picture of Dorian Gray*—and most especially in the "New Hedonism" driving the protagonist's behavior—Wilde had implicitly criticized the spirit of detachment espoused in Pater's novel.

341. Wilde is misquoting from Walter Pater's essay on Wordsworth in *Appreciations,* where Pater paraphrases Wordsworth's preface to *Lyrical Ballads* to argue not merely that Wordsworth's is an "art of impassioned contemplation," designed to "withdraw the thoughts for a little while from the mere machinery of life, to fix them, with appropriate emotions, on the spectacle of those great facts in man's existence which no machinery affects," but also that "to witness this spectacle with appropriate emotions is the aim of all culture" (Pater, *Appreciations* [1889; repr., Evanston, IL: Northwestern University Press, 1987], 62–63). Wilde possessed Wordsworth's and Pater's works in his prison cell.

342. "Thou and thy sons with thee shall minister before the tabernacle of witness. And they shall keep thy charge, ... only they shall not come nigh the vessels of the sanctuary ... that neither they, nor ye also, die" (Numbers 18:2).

343. In "The Soul of Man under Socialism," Wilde had written, "The message of Christ to man was simply 'Be thyself.' That is the secret of

life of religion in the deep, sweet and austere sense of the word.[340] But Marius is little more than a spectator: an ideal spectator indeed, and one to whom it is given "to contemplate the spectacle of life with appropriate emotions," which Wordsworth defines as the poet's true aim:[341] yet a spectator merely, and perhaps a little too much occupied with the comeliness of the vessels of the Sanctuary[342] to notice that it is the Sanctuary of Sorrow that he is gazing at. I see a far more intimate and immediate connection between the true life of Christ and the true life of the artist, and I take a keen pleasure in the reflection that long before Sorrow had made my days her own and bound me to her wheel I had written in *The Soul of Man* that he who would lead a Christ-like life must be entirely and absolutely himself,[343] and had taken as my types not merely the shepherd on the hillside and the prisoner in his cell but also the painter to whom the world is a pageant and the poet for whom the world is a song. I remember saying once to André Gide, as we sat together in some Paris café, that while Metaphysics had but little real interest for me, and Morality absolutely none, there was nothing that either Plato or Christ had said that could not be transferred immediately into the sphere of Art, and there find its complete fulfilment. It was a generalisation as profound as it was novel. Nor is it merely that we can discern in Christ that close union of personality with perfection which forms the real distinction between classical and romantic Art and makes Christ the true precursor of the romantic movement in life, but the very basis of his nature was the same as that of the nature of the artist, an intense and flame-like imagination. He realised in the entire sphere of human relations that imaginative sympathy which in the sphere of Art is the sole secret of creation. He understood the leprosy of the leper, the darkness of the blind, the fierce misery of those who live for pleasure, the strange poverty of the rich. You can see now—can you not?—that when you wrote to me in my trouble, "When you are not on your pedestal you are not interesting. The next time you are ill I will go away at once," you were as remote from the true temper of the artist as you were from what Matthew Arnold calls "the secret of Jesus."[344] Either would have taught you

Christ.... And so he who would lead a Christ-like life is he who is perfectly and absolutely himself. He may be a great poet, or a great man of science; or a young student at a University, or one who watches sheep upon a moor.... It does not matter what he is, as long as he realizes the perfection of the soul that is within him" (in *Criticism*, ed. Guy, 240, 243).

344. A reference either to Matthew Arnold's essay "A Comment on Christmas," in his *"St. Paul and Protestantism," with Other Essays* (1883; London: Smith Elder, 1892), in which Arnold speaks of "the method and secret and temper of Jesus" (166), or else to Arnold's *Literature and Dogma: An Essay towards a Better Apprehension of the Bible*, 4th ed. (London: Smith Elder, 1874), in which Arnold explains that righteousness consists in "the method, secret, and sweet reasonableness of Jesus" (267).

345. A misquotation of the epigraph to Ralph Waldo Emerson's essay "History," which Wilde possessed in his prison cell. The epigraph actually runs:

> I am owner of the sphere,
> Of the seven stars and the solar year,
> Of Caesar's hand, and Plato's brain,
> Of Lord Christ's heart, and Shakespeare's strain.

("History," in *Essays: First Series*, intro. J. Slater, text established by Alfred R. Ferguson and Jean Ferguson Carr, vol. 1 of *The Collected Works of Ralph Waldo Emerson* [Cambridge, MA: Harvard University Press, 1979], 1.)

346. One who believes "that God is immanent in or identical with the universe;... that God is everything and everything is God" (OED).

347. "Priest of the Sun" refers to Marcus Aurelius Antoninus, emperor of Rome (218–222 CE), who called himself Elagabalus, meaning "formed god" or "plastic god," and was a worshipper of the Syrian sun god Elagabal, for whom he erected a temple in Rome. He fascinated Wilde, who mentions him in *The Picture of Dorian Gray* and at one point contemplated writing his life. See CL 972–73.

348. "There met him out of the tombs a man with an unclean spirit, who had his dwelling among the tombs.... And he asked him, What is thy name? And he answered, saying, My name is Legion: for we are many" (Mark 5:2–9).

that whatever happens to another happens to oneself, and if you want an inscription to read at dawn and at night-time and for pleasure or for pain, write up on the wall of your house in letters for the sun to gild and the moon to silver "Whatever happens to another happens to oneself," and should anyone ask you what such an inscription can possibly mean you can answer that it means "Lord Christ's heart and Shakespeare's brain."[345]

Christ's place indeed is with the poets. His whole conception of Humanity sprang right out of the imagination and can only be realised by it. What God was to the Pantheist,[346] man was to him. He was the first to conceive the divided races as a unity. Before his time there had been gods and men. He alone saw that on the hills of life there were but God and Man, and, feeling through the mysticism of sympathy that in himself each had been made incarnate, he calls himself the Son of the One or the son of the other, according to his mood. More than anyone else in history he wakes in us that temper of wonder to which Romance always appeals. There is still something to me almost incredible in the idea of a young Galilean peasant imagining that he could bear on his own shoulders the burden of the entire world: all that had been already done and suffered, and all that was yet to be done and suffered: the sins of Nero, of Caesar Borgia, of Alexander VI, and of him who was Emperor of Rome and Priest of the Sun:[347] the sufferings of those whose name is Legion and whose dwelling is among the tombs,[348] oppressed nationalities, factory children, thieves, people in prison, outcasts, those who are dumb under oppression and whose silence is heard only of God: and not merely imagining this but actually achieving it, so that at the present moment all who come in contact with his personality, even though they may neither bow to his altar nor kneel before his priest, yet somehow find that the ugliness of their sins is taken away and the beauty of their sorrow revealed to them.

I have said of him that he ranks with the poets. That is true. Shelley and Sophocles are of his company. But his entire life also is the most wonderful of poems. For "pity and terror" there is nothing in the entire cycle

349. "It is the business of the tragic poet to give that pleasure which arises from pity and terror through imitation" (Aristotle, *Poetics*, trans. T. Twining [London: Printed by Luke Hansard and Sons, 1815], sec. 13, p. 83).

350. "Let gorgeous Tragedy / In sceptred pall come sweeping by, / Presenting Thebes, or Pelops' line, / Or the tale of Troy divine" (Milton, "Il Penseroso," ll. 97–100).

351. "The change from prosperity to adversity should not be represented as happening to a virtuous character" (Aristotle, *Poetics*, trans. Twining, sec. 11, p. 81).

of Greek Tragedy to touch it.[349] The absolute purity of the protagonist raises the entire scheme to a height of romantic art from which the sufferings of "Thebes and Pelops' line"[350] are by their very horror excluded, and shows how wrong Aristotle was when he said in his treatise on the Drama that it would be impossible to bear the spectacle of one blameless in pain.[351] Nor in Aeschylus or Dante, those stern masters of tenderness, in Shakespeare, the most purely human of all the great artists, in the whole of Celtic myth and legend where the loveliness of the world is shown through a mist of tears, and the life of a man is no more than the life of a flower, is there anything that for sheer simplicity of pathos wedded and made one with sublimity of tragic effect can be said to equal or approach even the last act of Christ's Passion. The little supper with his companions, one of whom had already sold him for a price: the anguish in the quiet moonlit olive-garden: the false friend coming close to him so as to betray him with a kiss: the friend who still believed in him and on whom as on a rock he had hoped to build a House of Refuge for Man denying him as the bird cried to the dawn: his own utter loneliness, his submission, his acceptance of everything: and along with it all such scenes as the high priest of Orthodoxy rending his raiment in wrath, and the Magistrate of Civil Justice calling for water in the vain hope of cleansing himself of that stain of innocent blood that makes him the scarlet figure of History: the coronation-ceremony of Sorrow, one of the most wonderful things in the whole of recorded time: the crucifixion of the Innocent One before the eyes of his mother and of the disciple whom he loved: the soldiers gambling and throwing dice for his clothes: the terrible death by which he gave the world its most eternal symbol, and his final burial in the tomb of the rich man, his body swathed in Egyptian linen with costly spices and perfumes as though he had been a King's son—when one contemplates all this from the point of view of Art alone one cannot but be grateful that the supreme office of the Church should be the playing of the tragedy without the shedding of blood, the mystical presentation by means of dialogue and costume and gesture even of the Passion of her Lord, and it is always a source of pleasure and awe to me

352. A literary work that depicts and exalts pastoral virtues and scenes, typically those pertaining to a simple shepherd's life. As Willoughby notes, Wilde here "calls into play the entire pastoral tradition in Greek poetry. . . . Wilde's image of Christ the pastoral singer whose life was his song . . . represents a powerful and suggestive . . . example of human artistry, becoming, indeed, an image of our creative ability to transcend experience" (*Art and Christhood*, 111–12).

353. Wilde is quoting from the following lines of Milton's *Comus*:

> How charming is divine Philosophy!
> Not harsh and crabbed, as dull fools suppose,
> But musical as is Apollo's lute,
> And a perpetual feast of nectared sweets,
> Where no crude surfeit reigns.

(Milton, *Comus*, ll. 482–86.)

354. Wilde possessed a copy of Renan's *Vie de Jésus* in the original French in his prison cell. Renan writes: "To have made himself beloved, 'to the degree that after his death they ceased not to love him,' was the great work of Jesus" (Ernest Renan, *The Life of Jesus* [translator unknown, London: Trübner, 1864], 302). Renan is quoting here from Josephus, *Antiquities of the Jews*, Book 18, 3:3. The term "fifth Gospel" is used by Renan himself to describe *The Life of Jesus* (Introduction, 31), but Wilde half-jokingly calls Renan's account "the Gospel according to St Thomas" because he detects in it skepticism and spiritual doubt. "St Thomas" is a reference to the Apostle Thomas, mythologized in the phrase "doubting Thomas," who refused to believe in the Resurrection of Christ without the confirmation supplied by direct personal experience.

to remember that the ultimate survival of the Greek Chorus, lost elsewhere to art, is to be found in the servitor answering the priest at Mass.

Yet the whole life of Christ—so entirely may Sorrow and Beauty be made one in their meaning and manifestation—is really an idyll,[352] though it ends with the veil of the temple being rent, and the darkness coming over the face of the earth, and the stone rolled to the door of the sepulchre. One always thinks of him as a young bridegroom with his companions, as indeed he somewhere describes himself, or as a shepherd straying through a valley with his sheep in search of green meadow or cool stream, or as a singer trying to build out of music the walls of the city of God, or as a lover for whose love the whole world was too small. His miracles seem to me as exquisite as the coming of Spring, and quite as natural. I see no difficulty at all in believing that such was the charm of his personality that his mere presence could bring peace to souls in anguish, and that those who touched his garments or his hands forgot their pain: or that as he passed by on the highway of life people who had seen nothing of life's mysteries saw them clearly, and others who had been deaf to every voice but that of Pleasure heard for the first time the voice of Love and found it as "musical as is Apollo's lute":[353] or that evil passions fled at his approach, and men whose dull unimaginative lives had been but a mode of death rose as it were from the grave when he called them: or that when he taught on the hillside the multitude forgot their hunger and thirst and the cares of this world, and that to his friends who listened to him as he sat at meat the coarse food seemed delicate, and the water had the taste of good wine, and the whole house became full of the odour and sweetness of nard. Renan in his *Vie de Jésus*—that gracious Fifth Gospel, the Gospel according to St Thomas one might call it—says somewhere that Christ's great achievement was that he made himself as much loved after his death as he had been during his lifetime.[354] And certainly, if his place is among the poets, he is the leader of all the lovers. He saw that love was that lost secret of the world for which the wise men had been looking, and that it was only through love that one could approach either the heart of the leper or the feet of God.

355. Another echo (of many) of "The Soul of Man under Socialism." See p. 196, nn.339, 343 above. As Willoughby observes, Wilde offers an "explanation of both Christ's motive and his achievement that ignores purely theological or moral assumptions. . . . Like his fellow secular Christologists Ernest Renan and Matthew Arnold, Wilde conceives of Jesus as a charismatic human being, whose original impact on the world has been imaginatively transformed by later generations. . . . Wilde advances beyond Arnold and Renan, however, in his claims for Christ's relation to art. . . . The artist's ability to transform disparate elements into a complex symmetry, his 'sense of beauty,' was in Christ an ability to comprehend the inherent oneness of humanity" (*Art and Christhood*, 105).

356. A phrase used throughout the New Testament—e.g., "Except a man be born again, he cannot see the kingdom of God" (John 3:3).

357. "In your patience possess ye your souls" (Luke 21:19).

358. Emerson, "Success" (repr. in *Society and Solitude*, vol. 7 of *Complete Works of Ralph Waldo Emerson* [1904; repr., New York: AMS, 1979], 292). From August 1896 onward, Wilde possessed a copy of Emerson's essays in his prison cell.

And, above all, Christ is the most supreme of Individualists.[355] Humility, like the artistic acceptance of all experiences, is merely a mode of manifestation. It is man's soul that Christ is always looking for. He calls it "God's Kingdom"—ἡ βασιλεία τοῦ Θεοῦ[356]—and finds it in every one. He compares it to little things, to a tiny seed, to a handful of leaven, to a pearl. That is because one only realises one's soul by getting rid of all alien passions, all acquired culture, and all external possessions be they good or evil. I bore up against everything with some stubbornness of will and much rebellion of nature till I had absolutely nothing left in the world but Cyril. I had lost my name, my position, my happiness, my freedom, my wealth. I was a prisoner and a pauper. But I had still one beautiful thing left, my own eldest son. Suddenly he was taken away from me by the law. It was a blow so appalling that I did not know what to do, so I flung myself on my knees, and bowed my head, and wept and said "The body of a child is as the body of the Lord: I am not worthy of either." That moment seemed to save me. I saw then that the only thing for me was to accept everything. Since then—curious as it will no doubt sound to you—I have been happier.

It was of course my soul in its ultimate essence that I had reached. In many ways I had been its enemy, but I found it waiting for me as a friend. When one comes in contact with the soul it makes one simple as a child, as Christ said one should be. It is tragic how few people ever "possess their souls"[357] before they die. "Nothing is more rare in any man." says Emerson, "than an act of his own."[358] It is quite true. Most people are other people. Their thoughts are someone else's opinions, their life a mimicry, their passions a quotation. Christ was not merely the supreme Individualist, but he was the first in History. People have tried to make him out an ordinary Philanthropist, like the dreadful philanthropists of the nineteenth century, or ranked him as an Altruist with the unscientific and sentimental. But he was really neither one nor the other. Pity he has, of course, for the poor, for those who are shut up in prisons, for the lowly, for the wretched, but he has far more pity for the rich, for the hard Hedonists, for those who waste their freedom in becoming slaves to

359. Matthew 5:44, Luke 6:27, and Luke 6:35.

360. Matthew 19:21, Luke 18:22, and Mark 10:21.

361. "How salt a savour / Hath the bread of others, and how hard the path / To climb and descend the stranger's stairs" (Dante, *Paradiso*, 17). In 1302, Dante was falsely accused of corruption and banished from Florence.

362. "O Lord, give me strength and courage to look upon my own flesh and heart without disgust." A very slight misquotation of Baudelaire, "Un Voyage à Cythère," in *Les Fleurs du Mal* (Wilde reverses "corps" and "coeur," while giving "O Seigneur" for Baudelaire's "Ah! Seigneur").

things, for those who wear soft raiment and live in Kings' houses. Riches and Pleasure seemed to him to be really greater tragedies than Poverty and Sorrow. And as for Altruism, who knew better than he that it is vocation not volition that determines us, and that one cannot gather grapes off thorns or figs from thistles? To live for others as a definite self-conscious aim was not his creed. It was not the basis of his creed. When he says "Forgive your enemies,"[359] it is not for the sake of the enemy but for one's own sake that he says so, and because Love is more beautiful than Hate. In his entreaty to the young man whom when he looked on he loved, "Sell all that thou hast and give it to the poor,"[360] it is not of the state of the poor that he is thinking but of the soul of the young man, the lovely soul that wealth was marring. In his view of life he is one with the artist who knows that by the inevitable law of self-perfection the poet must sing, and the sculptor think in bronze and the painter make the world a mirror for his moods, as surely and as certainly as the hawthorn must blossom in Spring, and the corn burn to gold at harvest-time, and the Moon in her ordered wanderings change from shield to sickle, and from sickle to shield.

But while Christ did not say to men, "Live for others," he pointed out that there was no difference at all between the lives of others and one's own life. By this means he gave to man an extended, a Titan personality. Since his coming the history of each separate individual is, or can be made, the history of the world. Of course Culture has intensified the personality of man. Art has made us myriad-minded. Those who have the artistic temperament go into exile with Dante and learn how salt is the bread of others and how steep their stairs:[361] they catch for a moment the serenity and calm of Goethe, and yet know but too well why Baudelaire cried to God:

> O Seigneur, donnez-moi la force et le courage
> De contempler mon corps et mon coeur sans dégoût.[362]

Out of Shakespeare's sonnets they draw, to their own hurt it may be, the secret of his love and make it their own: they look with new eyes on modern life because they have listened to one of Chopin's nocturnes, or

363. Wilde is quoting from earlier in *De Profundis:* see p. 199 above.

364. "Sun's disk crescent" substituted in the manuscript for "sun rising."

365. Wilde acknowledges that Apollo, the Greek god of music and poetry, was the ideal of masculine beauty and athleticism, but he also notes his heartless cruelty. According to Classical myth, Apollo flayed alive the faun Marsyas (often credited with inventing the flute) after vanquishing him in a contest of musicianship adjudicated by the Muses, who had stipulated that the contest's winner might do what he liked with the loser. Together with his sister Artemis, Apollo also killed the fourteen children of Niobe because the latter had boasted of her superiority to Leto, their own mother.

366. According to Greek legend, Pallas Athena, the goddess of wisdom, justice, and war, transformed Arachne into a spider upon vanquishing her following a weaving contest.

367. Peacocks—a symbol of her pride—were sacred to Hera, the Greek goddess of marriage and sister of Zeus.

368. Zeus, the father of gods and men, legendary for his promiscuity, fathered many mortal and semidivine offspring.

369. In ancient Greek religion and myth, Demeter presided over grains and the fertility of the earth. Often described as the goddess of the harvest, she also presided over the sanctity of marriage, sacred law, and the cycle of life and death. She was the mother of Persephone, known by the Romans as Proserpina.

370. According to Greek legend, Semele, the mortal mother of Dionysius, perished in a flash of lightning after asking Zeus to reveal himself in his full glory as a sign of his godhead. At the moment of her death, Zeus rescued the fetal Dionysius, sewed the infant into his thigh, and Dionysius emerged newly born a few months later.

handled Greek things, or read the story of the passion of some dead man for some dead woman whose hair was like threads of fine gold and whose mouth was as a pomegranate. But the sympathy of the artistic temperament is necessarily with what has found expression. In words or in colour, in music or in marble, behind the painted masks of an Aeschylean play or through some Sicilian shepherd's pierced and jointed reeds the man and his message must have been revealed. To the artist, expression is the only mode under which he can conceive life at all. To him what is dumb is dead. But to Christ it was not so. With a width and wonder of imagination, that fills one almost with awe, he took the entire world of the inarticulate, the voiceless world of pain, as his kingdom, and made of himself its eternal mouthpiece. Those of whom I have spoken, who are dumb under oppression and "whose silence is heard only of God,"[363] he chose as his brothers. He sought to become eyes to the blind, ears to the deaf, and a cry on the lips of those whose tongue had been tied. His desire was to be to the myriads who had found no utterance a very trumpet through which they might call to Heaven. And feeling, with the artistic nature of one to whom Sorrow and Suffering were modes through which he could realise his conception of the Beautiful, that an idea is of no value till it becomes incarnate and is made an image, he makes of himself the image of the Man of Sorrows, and as such has fascinated and dominated Art as no Greek God ever succeeded in doing. For the Greek Gods, in spite of the white and red of their fair fleet limbs, were not really what they appeared to be. The curved brow of Apollo was like the sun's disk crescent[364] over a hill at dawn, and his feet were as the wings of the morning, but he himself had been cruel to Marsyas and had made Niobe childless:[365] in the steel shields of the eyes of Pallas there had been no pity for Arachne:[366] the pomp and peacocks of Hera were all that was really noble about her:[367] and the Father of the Gods himself had been too fond of the daughters of men.[368] The two deep suggestive figures of Greek mythology were, for religion, Demeter, an earth-goddess, not one of the Olympians,[369] and, for art, Dionysus, the son of a mortal woman to whom the moment of his birth had proved the moment of her death also.[370]

371. Cithaeron, a mountain range in central Greece, was the scene of Bacchanalian orgies in honour of Dionysius, the god of the grape harvest, wine, and wine making; the fields or meadows of Enna, in central Sicily, were celebrated in Classical myth as the site where Persephone (Proserpina) was carried off to the underworld by Pluto.

372. Isaiah 53:3.

373. The so-called "Messianic" Fourth Eclogue of the Roman poet Virgil (70–19 BCE) was later widely understood as prophesying the birth of Christ.

374. Isaiah 52:14.

375. Wilde is quoting himself, from earlier in De Profundis. See p. 187 above. As Willoughby notes, Wilde's identification with Christ is premised on seeing him as "the great historical model and inspiration" for his own "reformulated aestheticism" (Art and Christhood, 103).

But Life itself from its lowliest and most humble sphere produced one far more marvellous than the mother of Proserpina or the son of Semele. Out of the carpenter's shop at Nazareth had come a personality infinitely greater than any made by myth or legend, and one, strangely enough, destined to reveal to the world the mystical meaning of wine and the real beauty of the lilies of the field as none, either on Cithaeron or at Enna,[371] had ever done it. The song of Isaiah, "He is despised and rejected of men, a man of sorrows and acquainted with grief: and we hid as it were our faces from him,"[372] had seemed to him to be a prefiguring of himself, and in him the prophecy was fulfilled. We must not be afraid of such a phrase. Every single work of art is the fulfilment of a prophecy. For every work of art is the conversion of an idea into an image. Every single human being should be the fulfilment of a prophecy. For every human being should be the realisation of some ideal, either in the mind of God or in the mind of man. Christ found the type, and fixed it, and the dream of a Virgilian poet,[373] either at Jerusalem or at Babylon, became in the long progress of the centuries incarnate in him for whom the world was waiting. *"His visage was marred more than any man's, and his form more than the sons of men"*[374] are among the signs noted by Isaiah as distinguishing the new ideal, and as soon as Art understood what was meant it opened like a flower at the presence of one in whom truth in Art was set forth as it had never been before. For is not truth in Art, as I have said, "that in which the outward is expressive of the inward; in which the soul is made flesh, and the body instinct with spirit: in which Form reveals?"[375]

To me one of the things in history the most to be regretted is that the Christ's own Renaissance which had produced the Cathedral of Chartres, the Arthurian cycle of legends, the life of St. Francis of Assisi, the art of Giotto, and Dante's *Divine Comedy,* was not allowed to develop on its own lines but was interrupted and spoiled by the dreary classical Renaissance that gave us Petrarch, and Raphael's frescoes, and Palladian architecture, and formal French tragedy, and St. Paul's Cathedral, and Pope's poetry, and everything that is made from without and by dead rules, and does not spring from within through some spirit informing it.

376. "The Rime of the Ancyent Marinere," by Samuel Taylor Coleridge, retitled (and substantially altered) as "The Rime of the Ancient Mariner" in 1817, nineteen years after its first publication; "La Belle Dame Sans Merci: A Ballad," by John Keats; "An Excelente Balad of Charitie," by Thomas Chatterton.

377. The campanile of the Cathedral of Sta. Maria del Fiore, in Florence, described by Wilde in his early poem "Ravenna" as rising like "a marble lily under sapphire skies."

378. "Tannhaüser" should be "Tannhäuser": Wilde has misplaced the umlaut. For the legend of Tannhäuser, see p. 356, n.69 below.

379. Gothic architecture.

380. "grown-up" and the final clause in this sentence, from "and the life" to "narcissus," added to the manuscript as an afterthought.

381. Francis Bacon, "Of Beauty" (1612), in *Bacon's Essays*, ed. F. G. Selby (London: Macmillan, 1889), 111.

382. John 3:8.

But wherever there is a romantic movement in Art, there somehow, and under some form, is Christ, or the soul of Christ. He is in *Romeo and Juliet,* in *The Winter's Tale,* in Provençal poetry, in "The Ancient Mariner," in "La Belle Dame sans Merci," and in Chatterton's "Ballad of Charity."[376] We owe to him the most diverse things and people. Hugo's *Les Misérables,* Baudelaire's *Fleurs du Mal,* the note of pity in Russian novels, the stained glass and tapestries and quattrocento work of Burne-Jones and Morris[.] Verlaine and Verlaine's poems belong to him no less than the Tower of Giotto,[377] Lancelot and Guinevere, Tannhäuser,[378] the troubled romantic marbles of Michael Angelo, pointed architecture,[379] and the love of children and flowers—for both of whom, indeed, in classical art there was but little place, hardly enough for them to grow or play in, but who from the twelfth century down to our own day have been continually making their appearance in art, under various modes and at various times, coming fitfully and wilfully as children and flowers are apt to do, Spring always seeming to one as if the flowers had been hiding, and only came out into the sun because they were afraid that grown-up people would grow tired of looking for them and give up the search, and the life of a child being no more than an April day on which there is both rain and sun for the narcissus.[380]

And it is the imaginative quality of Christ's own nature that makes him this palpitating centre of romance. The strange figures of poetic drama and ballad are made by the imagination of others, but out of his own imagination entirely did Jesus of Nazareth create himself. The cry of Isaiah had really no more to do with his coming than the song of the nightingale has to do with the rising of the moon—no more, though perhaps no less. He was the denial as well as the affirmation of prophecy. For every expectation that he fulfilled, there was another that he destroyed. In all beauty, says Bacon, there is "some strangeness of proportion,"[381] and of those who are born of the spirit, of those, that is to say, who like himself are dynamic forces, Christ says that they are like the wind that "bloweth where it listeth and no man can tell whence it cometh or whither it goeth?"[382] That is why he is so fascinating to artists. He has

383. "The lunatic, the lover, and the poet / Are of imagination all compact" (Shakespeare, *A Midsummer Night's Dream*, act 5, scene 1, ll. 7–8).

384. *The Picture of Dorian Gray*, ed. Frankel, 96. Wilde's remark is an adaptation of Walter Pater's notion that "the world is but a thought, or series of thoughts.... It exists, therefore, solely in the mind" (*Imaginary Portraits, with "The Child in the House" and Gaston de Latour*, intro. Bill Beckley [New York: Allworth, 1997], 76).

385. "studying the four prose-poems about Christ with some diligence" substituted in the manuscript for "reading a great deal about Christ." The four "prose-poems" are, of course, the Gospels, although it is significant that Wilde refers to them as artistic and literary texts, rather than as sacred books. Wilde requested a Greek Testament in July 1896, though he did not receive it till Christmas, he says in the next sentence, and the second half of *De Profundis*, with its frequent references and quotations from the four "prose-poems," bears out his claim that he studied them vigilantly.

386. Very words. As Willoughby observes, by insisting on the importance of reading the Gospels in Greek, Wilde, while "drawing on contemporary theories that Greek was the *lingua franca* of the entire ancient world," heals the "Hellenic-Hebraic divide" that had troubled the earlier Victorian cultural critics Arnold and Pater (*Art and Christhood*, 111–12).

387. "I am the good shepherd" (John 10:11 and 10:14).

all the colour-elements of life: mystery, strangeness, pathos, suggestion, ecstasy, love. He appeals to the temper of wonder, and creates that mood by which alone he can be understood. And it is to me a joy to remember that if he is "of imagination all compact,"[383] the world itself is of the same substance. I said in *Dorian Gray* that the great sins of the world take place in the brain,[384] but it is in the brain that everything takes place. We know now that we do not see with the eye or hear with the ear. They are merely channels for the transmission, adequate or inadequate, of sense-impressions. It is in the brain that the poppy is red, that the apple is odorous, that the skylark sings.

Of late I have been studying the four prose-poems about Christ with some diligence.[385] At Christmas I managed to get hold of a Greek Testament, and every morning, after I have cleaned my cell and polished my tins, I read a little of the Gospels, a dozen verses taken by chance anywhere. It is a delightful way of opening the day. To you, in your turbulent, ill-disciplined life, it would be a capital thing if you would do the same. It would do you no end of good, and the Greek is quite simple. Endless repetition, in and out of season, has spoiled for us the *naïveté*, the freshness, the simple romantic charm of the Gospels. We hear them read far too often, and far too badly, and all repetition is anti-spiritual. When one returns to the Greek it is like going into a garden of lilies out of some narrow and dark house. And to me the pleasure is doubled by the reflection that it is extremely probable that we have the actual terms, the *ipsissima verba*,[386] used by Christ. It was always supposed that Christ talked in Aramaic. Even Renan thought so. But now we know that the Galilean peasants, like the Irish peasants of our own day, were bilingual, and that Greek was the ordinary language of intercourse all over Palestine, as indeed all over the Eastern world. I never liked the idea that we only knew of Christ's own words through a translation of a translation. It is a delight to me to think that as far as his conversation was concerned, Charmides might have listened to him, and Socrates reasoned with him, and Plato understood him: that he really said ἐγώ εἰμι ὁ ποιμὴν ὁ καλός:[387] that when he thought of the lilies of the field and how they

388. Matthew 6:28,

389. "It is finished" (John 19:30).

390. The Greek woman.

391. Mark 7:26–30.

392. "We live by Admiration, Hope, and Love" (Wordsworth, *The Excursion*, 4:763).

neither toil nor spin,[388] his absolute expression was καταμάθετε τὰ κρίνα τοῦ ἀγροῦ, πῶς αὐξάνει: οὐ κοπιᾷ, οὐδὲ νήθει and that his last word when he cried out "My life has been completed, has reached its fulfilment, has been perfected" was exactly as St John tells us it was: τετέλεσται:[389] no more.

And while in reading the Gospels—particularly that of St John himself, or whatever early Gnostic took his name and mantle—I see this continual assertion of the imagination as the basis of all spiritual and material life, I see also that to Christ imagination was simply a form of Love, and that to him Love was Lord in the fullest meaning of the phrase. Some six weeks ago I was allowed by the Doctor to have white bread to eat instead of the coarse black or brown bread of ordinary prison fare. It is a great delicacy. To you it will sound strange that dry bread could possibly be a delicacy to anyone. I assure you that to me it is so much so that at the close of each meal I carefully eat whatever crumbs may be left on my tin plate, or have fallen on the rough towel that one uses as a cloth so as not to soil one's table: and do so not from hunger—I get now quite sufficient food—but simply in order that nothing should be wasted of what is given to me. So one should look on love. Christ, like all fascinating personalities, had the power not merely of saying beautiful things himself, but of making other people say beautiful things to him; and I love the story St Mark tells us about the Greek woman—the γυνὴ Ἑλληνίς[390]—who, when as a trial of her faith he said to her that he could not give her the bread of the children of Israel, answered him that the little dogs—κυνάρια, "little dogs" it should be rendered—who are under the table eat of the crumbs that the children let fall.[391] Most people live *for* love and admiration. But it is *by* love and admiration that we should live.[392] If any love is shown us we should recognise that we are quite unworthy of it. Nobody is worthy to be loved. The fact that God loves man shows that in the divine order of ideal things it is written that eternal love is to be given to what is eternally unworthy. Or if that phrase seems to you a bitter one to hear, let us say that everyone is worthy of love, except he who thinks that he is. Love is a sacrament that should be taken

393. "Lord, I am not worthy," originally spoken by a Roman centurion to Christ (Matthew 8:8), now recited by communicants at Holy Communion.

394. Wilde is probably thinking of Christ's injunction "why take ye thought for raiment? Consider the lilies of the field, how they grow; they toil not, neither do they spin" (Matthew 6:28; Luke 12:27). Cf. "He cometh forth like a flower, and is cut down" (Job 14:2) and also "As for man, his days are as grass: as a flower of the field, so he flourisheth" (Psalms 103:15).

395. "The rising generation of America . . . spare no pains at all to bring up their parents properly and to give them a suitable, if somewhat late, education. From its earliest years every American child spends most of its time in correcting the faults of its father and mother. . . . In America the young are always ready to give to those who are older than themselves the full benefits of their inexperience" (Wilde, "The American Invasion" [1887], in *The Artist as Critic*, ed. Ellmann, 56–57). See also Wilde's article "The Child Philosopher" (1887), in which he observes that "we may all learn wisdom from the lips of babes and sucklings" (*Journalism: Part One*, ed. John Stokes and Mark W. Turner, vol. 6 of *The Complete Works of Oscar Wilde* [Oxford: Oxford University Press, 2013], 151). Wilde's employment of the term "use" is ironic: he held a profound contempt for utilitarianism, as his comment "if what is perfect should have a use" perhaps implies.

396. "Like a young girl, weeping and laughing like a child" (Dante, *Purgatory*, 16:86–87).

397. "Behold the fowls of the air: for they sow not, neither do they reap, nor gather into barns; yet your heavenly Father feedeth them. Are ye not much better than they?" (Matthew 6:26).

398. "Take no thought for your life, what ye shall eat, or what ye shall drink; nor yet for your body, what ye shall put on. Is not the life more than meat, and the body than raiment? . . . Take therefore no thought for the morrow" (Matthew 6:25).

399. Luke 7:47.

400. Luke 16:20–22.

kneeling, and *Domine, non sum dignus*[393] should be on the lips and in the hearts of those who receive it. I wish you would sometimes think of that. You need it so much.

If I ever write again, in the sense of producing artistic work, there are just two subjects on which and through which I desire to express myself: one is "Christ, as the precursor of the Romantic movement in life": the other is "the Artistic life considered in its relation to Conduct." The first is, of course, intensely fascinating, for I see in Christ not merely the essentials of the supreme romantic type, but all the accidents, the wilfulnesses even, of the romantic temperament also. He was the first person who ever said to people that they should live "flower-like" lives.[394] He fixed the phrase. He took children as the type of what people should try to become. He held them up as examples to their elders, which I myself have always thought the chief use of children, if what is perfect should have a use.[395] Dante describes the soul of man as coming from the hand of God "weeping and laughing like a little child," and Christ also saw that the soul of each one should be "a guisa di fanciulla, che piangendoe ridendo pargoleggia."[396] He felt that life was changeful, fluid, active, and that to allow it to be stereotyped into any form was death. He said that people should not be too serious over material, common interests: that to be unpractical was a great thing: that one should not bother too much over affairs. "The birds didn't, why should man?"[397] He is charming when he says, "Take no thought for the morrow. Is not the *soul* more than meat? Is not the *body* more than raiment?"[398] A Greek might have said the latter phrase. It is full of Greek feeling. But only Christ could have said both, and so summed up life perfectly for us. His morality is all sympathy, just what morality should be. If the only thing that he had ever said had been "Her sins are forgiven her because she loved much,"[399] it would have been worth while dying to have said it. His justice is all poetical justice, exactly what justice should be. The beggar goes to heaven because he had been unhappy.[400] I can't conceive a better reason for his being sent there. The people who work for an hour in the vineyard in the cool of the evening receive just as much reward as those who had

401. Matthew 20:1–14.

402. "as if anybody . . . in the world" added to the manuscript as an afterthought.

403. "He that is without sin among you, let him first cast a stone at her" (John 8:7).

404. "Woe unto you, lawyers! for ye have taken away the key of knowledge: ye entered not in yourselves, and them that were entering in ye hindered" (Luke 11:52).

405. "Upon this rock I will build my church. . . . And I will give unto thee the keys of the kingdom of heaven" (Matthew 16:18–19).

406. Wilde refers loosely to the biblical Philistines (see p. 80, n.73 above) and by analogy to the unenlightened wealthy classes of England, of whom Matthew Arnold had written: "It may be thought that the characteristic which I have occasionally mentioned as proper to aristocracies—their natural inaccessibility, as children of the established fact, to ideas—points to our extending to this class the designation of *Philistines*; the Philistine being, as is well known, the enemy of the children of light or servant of the idea. Nevertheless . . . if we look into the thing closely, we shall find that the term *Philistine* gives the notion of something particularly stiff-necked and perverse in the resistance to light and its children; and therein it specially suits our middle-class" (Matthew Arnold, *Culture and Anarchy*, in *Culture and Anarchy and Other Writings*, ed. Stefan Collini [Cambridge: Cambridge University Press, 1993], 104).

407. "Woe unto you, scribes and Pharisees, hypocrites! for ye are like unto whited sepulchres, which indeed appear beautiful outward, but are within full of dead men's bones, and of all uncleanness" (Matthew 23:27).

toiled there all day long in the hot sun.[401] Why shouldn't they? Probably no one deserved anything. Or perhaps they were a different kind of people. Christ had no patience with the dull lifeless mechanical systems that treat people as if they were things, and so treat everybody alike: as if anybody, or anything for that matter, was like aught else in the world.[402] For him there were no laws: there were exceptions merely. That which is the very keynote of romantic art was to him the proper basis of actual life. He saw no other basis. And when they brought him one taken in the very act of sin and showed him her sentence written in the law and asked him what was to be done, he wrote with his finger on the ground as though he did not hear them, and finally, when they pressed him again and again, looked up and said "Let him of you who has never sinned be the first to throw the stone at her."[403] It was worth while living to have said that.

Like all poetical natures, he loved ignorant people. He knew that in the soul of one who is ignorant there is always room for a great idea. But he could not stand stupid people, especially those who are made stupid by education—people who are full of opinions not one of which they can understand, a peculiarly modern type, and one summed up by Christ when he describes it as the type of one who has the key of knowledge, can't use it himself, and won't allow other people to use it,[404] though it may be made to open the gate of God's Kingdom.[405] His chief war was against the Philistines. That is the war every child of light has to wage.[406] Philistinism was the note of the age and community in which he lived. In their heavy inaccessibility to ideas, their dull respectability, their tedious orthodoxy, their worship of vulgar success, their entire preoccupation with the gross materialistic side of life, and their ridiculous estimate of themselves and their importance, the Jew of Jerusalem in Christ's day was the exact counterpart of the British Philistine of our own. Christ mocked at the "whited sepulchres" of respectability,[407] and fixed that phrase for ever. He treated worldly success as a thing to be absolutely despised. He saw nothing in it at all. He looked on wealth as an encumbrance to a man. He would not hear of life being sacrificed to any system

408. A "Sabbatarian" is either "a Jewish observer of the Sabbath" or "a Christian who regards the Lord's Day as a Sabbath.... Also, and more commonly, one whose opinion and practice with regard to Sunday observance are unusually strict" (OED). Wilde refers here to Jesus's remark "The sabbath was made for man, and not man for the sabbath" (Mark 2:27), delivered in reply to Pharisees who had questioned the lawfulness of gathering corn on the Sabbath (Mark 2:23–24).

409. "middle-class mind" substituted in the manuscript for "righteous in their airs."

410. Wilde here once again echoes Pater, who had written in *The Renaissance* that "what we have to do is to be for ever testing new opinions and courting new impressions, never acquiescing in a facile orthodoxy" (Pater, *The Renaissance*, ed. Hill, 189).

411. "Woe unto you, Pharisees! for ye tithe mint and rue and all manner of herbs, and pass over judgment and the love of God" (Luke 11:42). Tithing is literally the granting, bestowal, or payment of "one tenth of (one's goods, earnings, etc.), esp. to the support of the church" (OED), although Wilde uses the word figuratively to mean "dividing" or "be[ing] conspicuously scrupulous in minutiæ" (OED).

412. Wilde confuses Mary Magdalen with the "Mary" who, according to John 12:3, anointed Christ's feet with nard taken from an alabaster box prior to his crucifixion. A similar incident is related in Luke 7:36–38, Matthew 26:6–13, and Mark 14:3–9, although here the woman remains unnamed and in two of the Gospels she anoints Christ's head, not his feet. Ruth is the heroine of the book of Ruth, the seventh book of the Old Testament, and Beatrice is Dante's inspiration and guide through Paradise in *The Divine Comedy*. In Cantos 31–32 of the *Paradiso*, Dante is given a vision of the holy host "in [the] form of a pure white rose" that includes Beatrice sitting alongside Mary Magdalen, Ruth, and other holy women of the Bible.

of thought or morals. He pointed out that forms and ceremonies were made for man, not man for forms and ceremonies. He took Sabbatarianism as a type of the things that should be set at nought.[408] The cold philanthropies, the ostentatious public charities, the tedious formalisms so dear to the middle-class mind,[409] he exposed with utter and relentless scorn. To us, what is termed Orthodoxy is merely a facile unintelligent acquiescence,[410] but to them, and in their hands, it was a terrible and paralysing tyranny. Christ swept it aside. He showed that the spirit alone was of value. He took a keen pleasure in pointing out to them that though they were always reading the Law and the Prophets they had not really the smallest idea of what either of them meant. In opposition to their tithing of each separate day into its fixed routine of prescribed duties, as they tithed mint and rue, he preached the enormous importance of living completely for the moment.[411] Those whom he saved from their sins are saved simply for beautiful moments in their lives. Mary Magdalen, when she sees Christ, breaks the rich vase of alabaster that one of her seven lovers had given her and spills the odorous spices over his tired dusty feet, and for that one moment's sake sits for ever with Ruth and Beatrice in the tresses of the snow-white Rose of Paradise.[412] All that Christ says to us by way of a little warning is that *every* moment should be beautiful, that the soul should *always* be ready for the coming of the Bridegroom, *always* waiting for the voice of the Lover. Philistinism being simply that side of man's nature that is not illumined by the imagination, he sees all the lovely influences of life as modes of Light: the imagination itself is the world-light, τὸ Φῶς τοῦ κοσμοῦ: the world is made by it, and yet the world cannot understand it: that is because the imagination is simply a manifestation of Love, and it is love, and the capacity for it, that distinguishes one human being from another. But it is when he deals with the Sinner that he is most romantic, in the sense of most real. The world had always loved the Saint as being the nearest possible approach to the perfection of God. Christ, through some divine instinct in him, seems to have always loved the sinner as being the nearest possible approach to the perfection of man. His primary desire was not

413. For Discharged Prisoners' Aid Societies, see p. 178, n.297 above.

414. For Christ's parable of the conversion of the publican, see Luke 18:9–14. A publican was "a person who farms the public taxes; a tax-gatherer, esp. any of those in Judaea and Galilee in the New Testament period, who were generally regarded as traitorous and impious on account of their service of Rome and their extortion" (OED). A Pharisee was "a member of a religious party within Judaism between the 2nd cent. B.C. and New Testament times, distinguished by its rigorous interpretation and observance of the written Mosaic law as well as the traditions of the elders" (OED).

415. Hart-Davis (*Letters of Oscar Wilde,* 752, n.2) suggests that Wilde, a brilliant Classicist in his youth, is thinking here of Aristotle's *Ethics* ("This only is denied even to God, the power to make what has been done undone," Aristotle, *Ethics,* 6:2, 6) and Pindar's *Olympian Odes* ("Once deeds are done . . . not even Time, the father of all, could undo their outcome," Pindar, *Olympian Odes,* 2:17). Ian Small (*De Profundis;* "Epistola: In Carcere et Vinculis," ed. Small, 271) suggests Aristotle's *Nicomachean Ethics* ("This only is denied even to God, the power to make what has been done undone") as a more likely reference.

416. For the parable of the prodigal son, who "wasted his substance with riotous living," "devoured [his father's] living with harlots," and then in hunger "would fain have filled his belly with the husks that the swine did eat," see Luke 15:11–32.

417. "If so, it may be worth while going to prison" added to the manuscript as an afterthought.

to reform people, any more than his primary desire was to relieve suffering. To turn an interesting thief into a tedious honest man was not his aim. He would have thought little of the Prisoners' Aid Society[413] and other modern movements of the kind. The conversion of a Publican into a Pharisee would not have seemed to him a great achievement by any means.[414] But in a manner not yet understood of the world he regarded sin and suffering as being in themselves beautiful, holy things, and modes of perfection. It *sounds* a very dangerous idea. It is so. All great ideas *are* dangerous. That it was Christ's creed admits of no doubt. That it is the true creed I don't doubt myself. Of course the sinner must repent. But why? Simply because otherwise he would be unable to realise what he had done. The moment of repentance is the moment of initiation. More than that. It is the means by which one alters one's past. The Greeks thought that impossible. They often say in their gnomic aphorisms "Even the Gods cannot alter the past."[415] Christ showed that the commonest sinner could do it. That it was the one thing he could do. Christ, had he been asked, would have said—I feel quite certain about it—that the moment the prodigal son fell on his knees and wept he really made his having wasted his substance with harlots, and then kept swine and hungered for the husks they ate,[416] beautiful and holy incidents in his life. It is difficult for most people to grasp the idea. I dare say one has to go to prison to understand it. If so, it may be worth while going to prison.[417] There is something so unique about Christ. Of course, just as there are false dawns before the dawn itself, and winter-days so full of sudden sunlight that they will cheat the wise crocus into squandering its gold before its time, and make some foolish bird call to its mate to build on barren boughs, so there were Christians before Christ. For that we should be grateful. The unfortunate thing is that there have been none since. I make one exception, St. Francis of Assisi. But then God had given him at his birth the soul of a poet, and he himself when quite young had in mystical marriage taken Poverty as his bride; and with the soul of a poet and the body of a beggar he found the way to perfection not difficult. He understood Christ, and so he became like him. We do not require the *Liber*

418. The *Liber Conformitatum* (1385–1389), by Bartholomew of Pisa (c. 1335–1401), draws elaborate parallels between Francis of Assisi and Christ; *De Imitatio Christi* [The Imitation of Christ] (c. 1418–1427), by Thomas à Kempis (c. 1380–1471), is perhaps the most widely read devotional work next to the Bible.

419. Village, sixty furlongs from Jerusalem, to which Peter and other disciples walked following Christ's crucifixion and burial, and where Christ appeared to them in resurrected form. See Luke 24. As Willoughby notes, the previous sentences enshrine Wilde's determination "to save the Nazarene for a secular world, and to recharge that world with the integrity of art" (*Art and Christhood*, 113).

420. Officer, bailiff, or minor functionary, appointed by the parish to deliver and enforce proclamations. In civic life, the position was made largely redundant by the growth and expansion of police forces in the nineteenth century.

421. See p. 56, n.11 above. Wilde had previously written in "The Soul of Man under Socialism" that "'Know thyself!' was written over the portal of the antique world" (in *Criticism*, ed. Guy, 240).

422. A phrase derived from Sonnet 31 of Sir Philip Sidney's *Astrophil and Stella* ("With how sad steps, O moon, though climb'st the skies"), although Wilde may have known it as well from Wordsworth's Sonnet 14, which opens by quoting Sidney's line verbatim.

423. Consecrating oil.

424. An allusion to Saul who, when sent seeking for the asses of his father, Kish, was anointed by the prophet Samuel, saying, "The Spirit of the Lord will come upon thee, and thou shalt prophesy...and shalt be turned into another man" (1 Samuel 10:6).

Conformitatum to teach us that the life of St. Francis was the true *Imitatio Christi:*[418] a poem compared to which the book that bears that name is merely prose. Indeed, that is the charm about Christ, when all is said. He is just like a work of art himself. He does not really teach one anything, but by being brought into his presence one becomes something. And everybody is predestined to his presence. Once at least in his life each man walks with Christ to Emmaus.[419]

As regards the other subject, the relation of the artistic life to conduct, it will no doubt seem strange to you that I should select it. People point to Reading Gaol, and say "There is where the artistic life leads a man." Well, it might lead one to worse places. The more mechanical people, to whom life is a shrewd speculation dependent on a careful calculation of ways and means, always know where they are going, and go there. They start with the desire of being the Parish Beadle,[420] and in whatever sphere they are placed, they succeed in being the Parish Beadle and no more. A man whose desire is to be something separate from himself, to be a Member of Parliament, or a successful grocer, or a prominent Solicitor, or a judge, or something equally tedious, invariably succeeds in being what he wants to be. That is his punishment. Those who want a mask have to wear it. But with the dynamic forces of life, and those in whom those dynamic forces become incarnate, it is different. People whose desire is solely for self-realisation never know where they are going. They can't know. In one sense of the word it is, of course, necessary, as the Greek oracle said, to know oneself.[421] That is the first achievement of knowledge. But to recognise that the soul of a man is unknowable is the ultimate achievement of Wisdom. The final mystery is oneself. When one has weighed the sun in a balance, and measured the steps of the moon,[422] and mapped out the seven heavens star by star, there still remains oneself. Who can calculate the orbit of his own soul? When the son of Kish went out to look for his father's asses, he did not know that a man of God was waiting for him with the very chrism[423] of coronation and that his own soul was already the Soul of a King.[424] I hope to live long enough, and to produce work of such a character, that I shall be able at the end of

425. Paul Verlaine (1844–1896), widely influential French Symbolist poet; and Prince Peter Kropotkin (1842–1921), exiled Russian nobleman, geographer, scientist, and one of the founding fathers of anarcho-communist thought. Wilde met Verlaine in 1883 and again in 1891. Since Wilde helped publicize a series of lectures by Kropotkin in 1889 (see CL 396), it seems highly likely that he met Kropotkin on this occasion and possibly on others too.

426. An allusion to Major James O. Nelson (1859–1914), who became governor of Reading Prison in July 1896 and immediately transformed the lives of the prisoners under his jurisdiction. Wilde called him "most sympathetic … and full of kindness" (CL 808) and "the most Christ-like man I have ever met." After his release into self-imposed exile, Wilde sent Nelson copies of his books, at one point signing a lengthy letter of gratitude to Nelson "your sincere and grateful friend, Oscar Wilde" (CL 863). For his public tribute to Nelson, see pp. 313–15 below.

427. Wilde's reflection on the healing potential of punishment is timely, since James Nelson's accession to the governorship of Reading Prison in July 1896 foreshadowed larger reforms that were about to take place in the British penal system. Nelson's predecessor as governor of Reading Prison, Lieutenant-Colonel Henry B. Isaacson, had unflinchingly carried out the regime of "hard labour, hard board, and hard fare" mandated in all British prisons by Major-General Sir Edmund Du Cane, the first chairman of the Prison Commission, upon his appointment in 1877. Reformation and / or rehabilitation had no place in this regime: for men like Isaacson and Du Cane, the prisoner's punishment was simply a warning to others, and it "painfully imprinted the results of crime on [the prisoner] himself" (Sean McConville, English Local Prisons 1860–1900 [London: Routledge, 1995], 181). Du Cane recognized that the harsh prison regime involved prisoners in considerable distress and pain, but his concern was only "whether the suffering was rationally conceived, officially sanctioned, at an appropriate stage of the sentence, and in accordance with the scientific regulations emanating from one of his committees" (McConville, English Local Prisons, 173). However, Du Cane was forced to resign in April 1895 after a series of newspaper exposés prompted a wide-ranging government inquiry, leading ultimately to the 1898 Prisons Act. While it was Wilde's misfortune to be imprisoned under the Du Cane regime, before the reforms contained in the 1898 Act took effect, the appointment of Nelson by Du Cane's

my days to say, "Yes: this is just where the artistic life leads a man." Two of the most perfect lives I have come across in my own experience are the lives of Verlaine and of Prince Kropotkin:[425] both of them men who passed years in prison: the first, the one Christian poet since Dante, the other a man with the soul of that beautiful white Christ that seems coming out of Russia. And for the last seven or eight months, in spite of a succession of great troubles reaching me from the outside world almost without intermission, I have been placed in direct contact with a new spirit working in this prison through men and things, that has helped me beyond any possibility of expression in words; so that while for the first year of my imprisonment I did nothing else, and can remember doing nothing else, but wring my hands in impotent despair, and say "What an ending! What an appalling ending!," now I try to say to myself, and sometimes when I am not torturing myself do really and sincerely say, "What a beginning! What a wonderful beginning!" It may really be so. It may become so. If it does, I shall owe much to this new personality that has altered every man's life in this place.[426]

Things in themselves are of little importance, have indeed—let us for once thank Metaphysics for something that she has taught us—no real existence. The spirit alone is of importance. Punishment may be inflicted in such a way that it will heal, not make a wound, just as alms may be given in such a manner that the bread changes to a stone in the hands of the giver.[427] What a change there is—not in the regulations, for they are fixed by iron rule, but in the spirit that uses them as its expression—you can realise when I tell you that had I been released last May, as I tried to be,[428] I would have left this place loathing it and every official in it with a bitterness of hatred that would have poisoned my life. I have had a year longer of imprisonment, but Humanity has been in the prison along with us all, and now when I go out I shall always remember great kindnesses that I have received here from almost everybody, and on the day of my release will give my thanks to many people and ask to be remembered by them in turn. The prison-system is absolutely and entirely wrong. I would give anything to be able to alter it when I go out. I intend to try.[429]

successor, Sir Evelyn Ruggles-Brise, was clearly a sign of things to come, and Nelson didn't hesitate to bend the existing regulations to ensure that Wilde was treated humanely and compassionately. *De Profundis* is itself a document attesting to the "healing" concept of punishment inculcated at Reading by Nelson.

428. Wilde petitioned the home secretary for early release in July 1896; see pp. 41–51 above.

429. "I intend to try" added to the manuscript as an afterthought.

430. "the Christ who is not in Churches" substituted in the manuscript for "Christ." See too Wilde's witty remark, "I cannot stand Christians because they are never Catholics, and I cannot stand Catholics because they are never Christians. Otherwise I am at one with the Indivisible Church" (*CL* 1191).

431. Wilde is quoting from St. Francis's "Canticle of Brother Sun," as follows:

> Praise be yours, my Lord, through Brothers Wind and Air,
> And fair and stormy, all the weather's moods,
> By which you cherish all that you have made.
> All praise be yours, my Lord, through Sister Water,
> So useful, lowly, precious and pure.

("The Canticle of Brother Sun" [begun 1225], trans. Benen Fahy O. F. M., in *St. Francis of Assisi: Writings and Early Biographies*, ed. Marion A. Habig [Chicago: Franciscan Herald Press, 1973], 130.)

But there is nothing in the world so wrong but that the spirit of Humanity, which is the spirit of Love, the spirit of the Christ who is not in Churches,[430] may make it, if not right, at least possible to be borne without too much bitterness of heart.

I know also that much is waiting for me outside that is very delightful, from what St. Francis of Assisi calls "my brother the wind" and "my sister the rain,"[431] lovely things both of them, down to the shopwindows and sunsets of great cities. If I made a list of all that still remains to me, I don't know where I should stop: for, indeed, God made the world just as much for me as for anyone else. Perhaps I may go out with something I had not got before. I need not tell you that to me Reformations in Morals are as meaningless and vulgar as Reformations in Theology. But while to propose to be a better man is a piece of unscientific cant, to have become a *deeper* man is the privilege of those who have suffered. And such I think I have become. You can judge for yourself. If after I go out a friend of mine gave a feast, and did not invite me to it, I shouldn't mind a bit. I can be perfectly happy by myself. With freedom, books, flowers, and the moon, who could not be happy? Besides, feasts are not for me any more. I have given too many to care about them. That side of life is over for me, very fortunately I dare say. But if, after I go out, a friend of mine had a sorrow, and refused to allow me to share it, I should feel it most bitterly. If he shut the doors of the house of mourning against me I would come back again and again and beg to be admitted, so that I might share in what I was entitled to share in. If he thought me unworthy, unfit to weep with him, I should feel it as the most poignant humiliation, as the most terrible mode in which disgrace could be inflicted on me. But that could not be. I have a right to share in Sorrow, and he who can look at the loveliness of the world, and share its sorrow, and realise something of the wonder of both, is in immediate contact with divine things, and has got as near to God's secret as anyone can get.

Perhaps there may come into my art also, no less than into my life, a still deeper note, one of greater unity of passion, and directness of impulse. Not width but intensity is the true aim of modern Art. We are no

432. Dante, *Paradiso*, 1, 20. For Apollo's victory over Marsyas, the flute player—referred to by Wilde a few sentences below as the "Phyrgian Faun," after the region of Phyrgia, in what is now southern Turkey—see p. 208, n.365 above. "Tacitean" means "resembling the style of the Roman historian Tacitus."

433. Matthew Arnold, "Empedocles on Etna," 3, 125–28.

434. "Thyrsis" and "The Scholar Gypsy" are the titles of poems by Arnold: Wilde possessed a one-volume edition of Arnold's poems in his cell.

435. Wilde's phrasing here echoes—and revises—his assertion earlier (p. 63 above) that Douglas stood "persistently between Art and myself."

longer in Art concerned with the type. It is with the exception we have to do. I cannot put my sufferings into any form they took, I need hardly say. Art only begins where Imitation ends. But something must come into my work, of fuller harmony of words perhaps, of richer cadences, of more curious colour-effects, of simpler architectural-order, of some aesthetic quality at any rate. When Marsyas was "torn from the scabbard of his limbs"—*della vagina delle membre sue,* to use one of Dante's most terrible, most Tacitean phrases—he had no more song, the Greeks said.[432] Apollo had been victor. The lyre had vanquished the reed. But perhaps the Greeks were mistaken. I hear in much modern Art the cry of Marsyas. It is bitter in Baudelaire, sweet and plaintive in Lamartine, mystic in Verlaine. It is in the deferred resolutions of Chopin's music. It is in the discontent that haunts the recurrent faces of Burne-Jones's women. Even Matthew Arnold, whose song of Callicles tells of "the triumph of the sweet per-suasive lyre," and the "famous final victory," in such a clear note of lyrical beauty[433]—even he, in the troubled undertone of doubt and distress that haunts his verse, has not a little of it. Neither Goethe nor Wordsworth could heal him, though he followed each in turn, and when he seeks to mourn for "Thyrsis" or to sing of "The Scholar Gipsy,"[434] it is the reed that he has to take for the rendering of his strain. But whether or not the Phrygian Faun was silent, I cannot be. Expression is as necessary to me as leaf and blossom are to the black branches of the trees that show them-selves above the prison wall and are so restless in the wind. Between my art and the world there is now a wide gulf, but between Art and myself there is none.[435]

I hope at least that there is none. To each of us different fates have been meted out. Freedom, pleasure, amusements, a life of ease have been your lot, and you are not worthy of it. My lot has been one of public in-famy, of long imprisonment, of misery, of ruin, of disgrace, and I am not worthy of it either—not yet, at any rate. I remember I used to say that I thought I could bear a real tragedy if it came to me with purple pall and a mask of noble sorrow, but that the dreadful thing about modernity was that it put Tragedy into the raiment of Comedy, so that the great realities

436. For Wilde's transfer to Reading Prison from London's Wandsworth Prison—on 20 November 1895, *not* 13 November, as Wilde states—see p. 144, n.216 above.

437. "save that of scorn" added to the manuscript as an afterthought.

seemed commonplace or grotesque or lacking in style. It is quite true about modernity. It has probably always been true about actual life. It is said that all martyrdoms seemed mean to the looker-on. The nineteenth century is no exception to the general rule. Everything about my tragedy has been hideous, mean, repellent, lacking in style. Our very dress makes us grotesques. We are the zanies of sorrow. We are clowns whose hearts are broken. We are specially designed to appeal to the sense of humour. On November 13th 1895 I was brought down here from London.[436] From two o'clock till half-past two on that day I had to stand on the centre platform of Clapham Junction in convict dress and handcuffed, for the world to look at. I had been taken out of the Hospital Ward without a moment's notice being given to me. Of all possible objects I was the most grotesque. When people saw me they laughed. Each train as it came up swelled the audience. Nothing could exceed their amusement. That was of course before they knew who I was. As soon as they had been informed, they laughed still more. For half an hour I stood there in the grey November rain surrounded by a jeering mob. For a year after that was done to me I wept every day at the same hour and for the same space of time. That is not such a tragic thing as possibly it sounds to you. To those who are in prison, tears are a part of every day's experience. A day in prison on which one does not weep is a day on which one's heart is hard, not a day on which one's heart is happy. Well, now I am really beginning to feel more regret for the people who laughed than for myself. Of course when they saw me I was not on my pedestal. I was in the pillory. But it is a very unimaginative nature that only cares for people on their pedestals. A pedestal may be a very unreal thing. A pillory is a terrific reality. They should have known also how to interpret sorrow better. I have said that behind Sorrow there is always Sorrow. It were still wiser to say that behind sorrow there is always a soul. And to mock at a soul in pain is a dreadful thing. Unbeautiful are their lives who do it. In the strangely simple economy of the world people only get what they give, and to those who have not enough imagination to penetrate the mere outward of things and feel pity, what pity can be given save that of scorn?[437]

Jean-Gabriel Daragnès, wood-engraved illustration for *Ballade de La Geôle de Reading, par C.3.3.*, trans. Henry-D. Davray (Paris: Léon Pichon, 1918).

I have told you this account of the mode of my being conveyed here simply that you should realise how hard it has been for me to get anything out of my punishment but bitterness and despair. I have however to do it, and now and then I have moments of submission and acceptance. All the spring may be hidden in a single bud, and the low ground-nest of the lark may hold the joy that is to herald the feet of many rose-red dawns, and so perhaps whatever beauty of life still remains to me is contained in some moment of surrender, abasement and humiliation. I can, at any rate, merely proceed on the lines of my own development, and by accepting all that has happened to me make myself worthy of it. People used to say of me that I was too individualistic. I must be far more of an individualist than I ever was. I must get far more out of myself than I ever got, and ask far less of the world than I ever asked. Indeed my ruin came, not from too great individualism of life, but from too little. The one disgraceful, unpardonable, and to all time contemptible action of my life was my allowing myself to be forced into appealing to Society for help and protection against your father. To have made such an appeal against

438. Bow Street Police Court, where Wilde was formally charged on 6 April 1895 with offenses under the 1885 Criminal Law Amendment Act, and where he appeared again on 11 and 19 April, prior to being committed for trial. Since these appearances did not constitute "trials" as such, by "three trials" Wilde means his failed libel action (conducted at the Old Bailey 3–5 April) against Queensberry and his two subsequent trials on the criminal charges on which he was eventually convicted.

439. *The Picture of Dorian Gray*, ed. Frankel, 80. The line is spoken by the urbane Lord Henry Wotton, who is often understood as Wilde's own fictional stand-in by virtue of his iconoclastic humor and witty speech mannerisms.

anyone would have been from the individualist point of view bad enough, but what excuse can there ever be put forward for having made it against one of such nature and aspect?

Of course once I had put into motion the forces of Society, Society turned on me and said, "Have you been living all this time in defiance of my laws, and do you now appeal to those laws for protection? You shall have those laws exercised to the full. You shall abide by what you have appealed to." The result is I am in gaol. And I used to feel bitterly the irony and ignominy of my position when in the course of my three trials, beginning at the Police Court,[438] I used to see your father bustling in and out in the hopes of attracting public attention, as if anyone could fail to note or remember the stableman's gait and dress, the bowed legs, the twitching hands, the hanging lower lip, the bestial and half-witted grin. Even when he was not there, or was out of sight, I used to feel conscious of his presence, and the blank dreary walls of the great Court-room, the very air itself, seemed to me at times to be hung with multitudinous masks of that apelike face. Certainly no man ever fell so ignobly, and by such ignoble instruments, as I did. I say, in *Dorian Gray* somewhere, that "a man cannot be too careful in the choice of his enemies."[439] I little thought that it was by a pariah that I was to be made a pariah myself.

This urging me, forcing me to appeal to Society for help, is one of the things that make me despise you so much, that make me despise myself so much for having yielded to you. Your not appreciating me as an artist was quite excusable. It was temperamental. You couldn't help it. But you might have appreciated me as an Individualist. For that no culture was required. But you didn't, and so you brought the element of Philistinism into a life that had been a complete protest against it, and from some points of view a complete annihilation of it. The Philistine element in life is not the failure to understand Art. Charming people such as fishermen, shepherds, ploughboys, peasants and the like know nothing about Art, and are the very salt of the earth. He is the Philistine who upholds and aids the heavy, cumbrous, blind mechanical forces of Society, and who does not recognise the dynamic force when he meets it either

440. This sentence added to the manuscript as an afterthought.

441. Respectively, the benign airy spirit and the half-human savage who feature in Shakespeare's *The Tempest*.

442. Robert Henry Cliburn and William Allen were notorious felons who blackmailed Wilde over an incriminating letter to Douglas that came into their possession, although they did not testify against Wilde. For Atkins, see p. 126, n.174 above. Atkins is probably a slip for Allen.

443. Boredom.

444. "This is where the paths of evil lead," an allusion to the title of Part 3 of Honoré de Balzac's novel *Splendeurs et misères des courtisanes* (1839–1847), translated into English variously as *The Splendors and Miseries of Courtesans*, *The Harlot's Progress*, and *A Harlot High and Low*.

in a man or a movement. People thought it dreadful of me to have entertained at dinner the evil things of life, and to have found pleasure in their company. But they, from the point of view through which I, as an artist in life, approached them, were delightfully suggestive and stimulating. It was like feasting with panthers. The danger was half the excitement. I used to feel as the snake-charmer must feel when he lures the cobra to stir from the painted cloth or reed-basket that holds it, and makes it spread its hood at his bidding, and sway to and fro in the air as a plant sways restfully in a stream. They were to me the brightest of gilded snakes. Their poison was part of their perfection.[440] I did not know that when they were to strike at me it was to be at your piping and for your father's pay. I don't feel at all ashamed of having known them. They were intensely interesting. What I do feel ashamed of is the horrible Philistine atmosphere into which you brought me. My business as an artist was with Ariel. You set me to wrestle with Caliban.[441] Instead of making beautiful coloured, musical things such as *Salomé,* and the *Florentine Tragedy,* and *La Sainte Courtisane,* I found myself forced to send long lawyer's letters to your father and constrained to appeal to the very things against which I had always protested. Clibborn and Atkins were wonderful in their infamous war against life.[442] To entertain them was an astounding adventure. Dumas *père,* Cellini, Goya, Edgar Allan Poe, or Baudelaire, would have done just the same. What is loathsome to me is the memory of interminable visits paid by me to the solicitor Humphreys in your company, when in the ghastly glare of a bleak room you and I would sit with serious faces telling serious lies to a bald man, till I really groaned and yawned with *ennui.*[443] *There* is where I found myself after two years' friendship with you, right in the centre of Philistia, away from everything that was beautiful, or brilliant, or wonderful, or daring. At the end I had to come forward, on your behalf, as the champion of Respectability in conduct, of Puritanism in life, and of Morality in Art. *Voilà où mènent les mauvais chemins!*[444]

And the curious thing to me is that you should have tried to imitate your father in his chief characteristics. I cannot understand why he was to you an exemplar, where he should have been a warning, except that

whenever there is hatred between two people there is bond or brother-
hood of some kind. I suppose that, by some strange law of the antipathy
of similars, you loathed each other, not because in so many points you
were so different, but because in some you were so like. In June 1893 when
you left Oxford, without a degree and with debts, petty in themselves,
but considerable to a man of your father's income, your father wrote you
a very vulgar, violent and abusive letter. The letter you sent him in reply
was in every way worse, and of course far less excusable, and consequently you were extremely proud of it. I remember quite well your
saying to me with your most conceited air that you could beat your father
"at his own trade." Quite true. But what a trade! What a competition! You
used to laugh and sneer at your father for retiring from your cousin's
house where he was living in order to write filthy letters to him from a
neighbouring hotel. You used to do just the same to me. You constantly
lunched with me at some public restaurant, sulked or made a scene during
luncheon, and then retired to White's Club and wrote me a letter of the
very foulest character. The only difference between you and your father
was that after you had dispatched your letter to me by special messenger,
you would arrive yourself at my rooms some hours later, not to apologise, but to know if I had ordered dinner at the Savoy, and if not, why
not. Sometimes you would actually arrive before the offensive letter had
been read. I remember on one occasion you had asked me to invite to
luncheon at the Café Royal two of your friends, one of whom I had never
seen in my life. I did so, and at your special request ordered beforehand
a specially luxurious luncheon to be prepared. The *chef,* I remember, was
sent for, and particular instructions given about the wines. Instead of
coming to luncheon you sent me at the Café an abusive letter, timed so
as to reach me after we had been waiting half an hour for you. I read the
first line, and saw what it was, and putting the letter in my pocket, explained to your friends that you were suddenly taken ill, and that the rest
of the letter referred to your symptoms. In point of fact I did not read
the letter till I was dressing for dinner at Tite Street that evening. As I
was in the middle of its mire, wondering with infinite sadness how you

445. The *Royal Blue Book* for 1897 lists several solicitors named Lumley connected to the firm of *Lumley and Lumley* at 37 Conduit Street.

446. 18 Cadogan Place, the London home of Douglas's mother.

447. For Wood, see p. 100, n.114 above. For Douglas's realization of "the immense opportunities afforded by the open postcard," see p. 116, n.149 above.

could write letters that were really like the froth and foam on the lips of an epileptic, my servant came in to tell me that you were in the hall and were very anxious to see me for five minutes. I at once sent down and asked you to come up. You arrived, looking I admit very frightened and pale, to beg my advice and assistance, as you had been told that a man from Lumley the Solicitor[445] had been enquiring for you at Cadogan Place,[446] and you were afraid that your Oxford trouble or some new danger was threatening you. I consoled you, told you, what proved to be the case, that it was merely a tradesman's bill probably, and let you stay to dinner, and pass your evening with me. You never mentioned a single word about your hideous letter, nor did I. I treated it as simply an unhappy symptom of an unhappy temperament. The subject was never alluded to. To write to me a loathsome letter at 2.30, and fly to me for help and sympathy at 7.15 the same afternoon, was a perfectly ordinary occurrence in your life. You went quite beyond your father in such habits, as you did in others. When his revolting letters to you were read in open Court he naturally felt ashamed and pretended to weep. Had your letters to him been read by his own Counsel still more horror and repugnance would have been felt by everyone. Nor was it merely in style that you "beat him at his own trade," but in mode of attack you distanced him completely. You availed yourself of the public telegram, and the open postcard. I think you might have left such modes of annoyance to people like Alfred Wood whose sole source of income it is.[447] Don't you? What was a profession to him and his class was a pleasure to you, and a very evil one. Nor have you given up your horrible habit of writing offensive letters, after all that has happened to me through them and for them. You still regard it as one of your accomplishments, and you exercise it on my friends, on those who have been kind to me in prison like Robert Sherard and others. That is disgraceful of you. When Robert Sherard heard from me that I did not wish you to publish any article on me in the *Mercure de France,* with or without letters, you should have been grateful to him for having ascertained my wishes on the point, and for having saved you from, without intending it, inflicting more pain on me than you had

448. Wilde refers chiefly to Robert Ross and More Adey, who had gone to great lengths—and were to go to still greater lengths—to put Wilde's life and reputation back on a secure footing. But shortly after completing *De Profundis*, Wilde wrote vituperatively to and about these friends too, chiefly in connection with their misguided efforts to secure Wilde's life-interest in his wife's marriage settlement from the bankruptcy receiver on Wilde's behalf, against his wife's wishes (see p. 162, n.257 above). For example, on 13 May 1897, Wilde wrote to Ross: "You and my other friends have so little imagination, so little sympathy, so little power of appreciating what was beautiful, noble, lovely, and of good report.... You pose as the generous friends.... Now that I reflect on your conduct and More Adey's to me in this matter I feel I have been unjust to [Alfred Douglas]" (*CL* 818, 823). All such declarations of animosity need to be understood as reflections of Wilde's misery in prison, as well as his sadness at the dissolution of his marriage, and they should not be taken at face value.

449. William More Adey (1858–1942), art connoisseur and partner of Robert Ross, with whom he jointly ran the Carfax Gallery; James Thomas (Frank) Harris (1856–1931), editor of the *Fortnightly Review* (in which he published "Pen, Pencil and Poison," "The Soul of Man under Socialism," and other pieces by Wilde) and also of *Saturday Review* (in which he published Wilde's "A Few Maxims"); Arthur Bellamy Clifton (1862–1932), solicitor and art dealer. For Ross and Sherard, see p. 68, n.39, and p. 130, n.183 above. Harris was instrumental in bringing about a radical improvement in Wilde's treatment in prison, and he was also to offer Wilde many kindnesses in the last three years of his life (see Frankel, *Oscar Wilde: The Unrepentant Years*, pp. 238–46). But Wilde fell out more than once with Harris too; and on 12 May 1897, within six weeks of finishing *De Profundis*, Wilde was to class Frank Harris unfairly among "the ostentatious, the false who ask one to a rich banquet and then when one is hungry and in want shut the door of house and heart," adding, "I have nothing but contempt for them. The Frank Harrises of life are a dreadful type" (*CL* 813–14).

done already. You must remember that a patronising and Philistine letter about "fair play" for a "man who is down" is all right for an English newspaper. It carries on the old traditions of English journalism in regard to their attitude towards artists. But in France such a tone would have exposed me to ridicule and you to contempt. I could not have allowed any article till I had known its aim, temper, mode of approach and the like. In art, good intentions are not of the smallest value. All bad art is the result of good intentions.

Nor is Robert Sherard the only one of my friends to whom you have addressed acrimonious and bitter letters because they sought that my wishes and my feelings should he consulted in matters concerning myself, the publication of articles on me, the dedication of your verses, the surrender of my letters and presents, and such like. You have annoyed or sought to annoy others also.

Does it ever occur to you what an awful position I would have been in if for the last two years, during my appalling sentence, I had been dependent on you as a friend? Do you ever think of that? Do you ever feel any gratitude to those who by kindness without stint, devotion without limit, cheerfulness and joy in giving, have lightened my black burden for me, have visited me again and again, have written to me beautiful and sympathetic letters, have managed my affairs for me, have arranged my future life for me, have stood by me in the teeth of obloquy, taunt, open sneer or insult even?[448] I thank God every day that he gave me friends other than you. I owe everything to them. The very books in my cell are paid for by Robbie out of his pocket-money. From the same source are to come clothes for me, when I am released. I am not ashamed of taking a thing that is given by love and affection. I am proud of it. But do you ever think of what my friends such as More Adey, Robbie, Robert Sherard, Frank Harris, and Arthur Clifton,[449] have been to me in giving me comfort, help, affection, sympathy and the like? I suppose that has never dawned on you. And yet—if you had any imagination in you—you would know that there is not a single person who has been kind to me in my prison-life, down to the warder who may give me a good-morning or a

450. Lord Percy Douglas (1868–1920), of whom Wilde later wrote, "When Percy is asked to fulfill his promise, he gets out of it like Frank Harris does.... People like that give me a sense of nausea" (CL 813). Percy Douglas had contributed to Wilde's bail in 1895.

451. Marie-Jeanne Phlippon Roland (1754–1793), influential member of the Girondist faction during the French Revolution.

good-night that is not one of his prescribed duties—down to the common policemen who in their homely rough way strove to comfort me on my journeys to and fro from the Bankruptcy Court under conditions of terrible mental distress—down to the poor thief who, recognising me as we tramped round the yard at Wandsworth whispered to me in the hoarse prison-voice men get from long and compulsory silence: "I am sorry for you: it is harder for the likes of you than it is for the likes of us"—not one of them all, I say, the very mire from whose shoes you should not be proud to be allowed to kneel down and clean.

Have you imagination enough to see what a fearful tragedy it was for me to have come across your family? What a tragedy it would have been for anyone at all, who had a great position, a great name, anything of importance to lose? There is hardly one of the elders of your family—with the exception of Percy,[450] who is really a good fellow—who did not in some way contribute to my ruin.

I have spoken of your mother to you with some bitterness, and I strongly advise you to let her see this letter, for your own sake chiefly. If it is painful to her to read such an indictment against one of her sons, let her remember that *my* mother, who intellectually ranks with Elizabeth Barrett Browning, and historically with Madame Roland,[451] died brokenhearted because the son of whose genius and art she had been so proud, and whom she had regarded always as a worthy continuer of a distinguished name, had been condemned to the treadmill for two years. You will ask me in what way your mother contributed to my destruction. I will tell you. Just as you strove to shift on to me all your immoral responsibilities, so your mother strove to shift on to me all her moral responsibilities with regard to you. Instead of speaking directly to you about your life, as a mother should, she always wrote privately to me with earnest, frightened entreaties not to let you know that she was writing to me. You see the position in which I was placed between you and your mother. It was one as false, as absurd, and as tragic as the one in which I was placed between you and your father. In August 1892, and on the 8th of November in the same year, I had two long interviews with your

452. Wilde may have erred in the dating and number of these interviews. Ellmann states that Lady Queensberry "decided to invite the Wildes to her house at Bracknell and consult them about her son . . . in October 1892" (*Oscar Wilde,* 385) a date confirmed by Wilde himself earlier in *De Profundis.* 8 November was the date *in 1893* when Wilde wrote to Lady Queensberry pleading with her to "do something" lest Douglas "come to grief of some kind" (*CL* 575). Wilde will say later that he told her "a good deal about" Douglas in December 1893 (see p. 265 below).

453. The Rt. Hon. George Wyndham (1863–1913), well-connected Conservative M. P. and member of "The Souls," the elite social group of England's leading intellectuals and politicians, and a cousin of Alfred Douglas's.

mother about you.[452] On both occasions I asked her why she did not speak directly to you herself. On both occasions she gave the same answer: "I am afraid to: he gets so angry when he is spoken to." The first time, I knew you so slightly that I did not understand what she meant. The second time, I knew you so well that I understood perfectly. (During the interval you had had an attack of jaundice and been ordered by the doctor to go for a week to Bournemouth, and had induced me to accompany you as you hated being alone.) But the first duty of a mother is not to be afraid of speaking seriously to her son. Had your mother spoken seriously to you about the trouble she saw you were in in July 1892 and made you confide in her it would have been much better, and much happier ultimately for both of you. All the underhand and secret communications with me were wrong. What was the use of your mother sending me endless little notes, marked "Private" on the envelope, begging me not to ask you so often to dinner, and not to give you any money, each note ending with an earnest postscript "On no account let Alfred know that I have written to you?" What good could come of such a correspondence? Did you ever wait to be asked to dinner? Never. You took all your meals as a matter of course with me. If I remonstrated, you always had one observation: "If I don't dine with you, where am I to dine? You don't suppose that I am going to dine at home?" It was unanswerable. And if I absolutely refused to let you dine with me, you always threatened that you would do something foolish, and always did it. What possible result could there be from letters such as your mother used to send me, except that which did occur, a foolish and fatal shifting of the moral responsibility on to my shoulders? Of the various details in which your mother's weakness and lack of courage proved so ruinous to herself, to you, and to me, I don't want to speak any more, but surely, when she heard of your father coming down to my house to make a loathsome scene and create a public scandal, she might then have seen that a serious crisis was impending, and taken some serious steps to try and avoid it? But all she could think of doing was to send down plausible George Wyndham[453] with his pliant tongue to propose to me . . . what?

454. As Ian Small observes (*De Profundis*; "*Epistola: In Carcere et Vinculis*," ed. Small, 279), Wilde is recalling (and slightly misquoting) a speech he deleted from a draft of *A Woman of No Importance*, in which Lord Illingworth observes: "Every now and then this England of ours finds that one of its sores shows through its rags and shrieks for the nonconformists. Caliban for nine months of the year, it is Tartuffe for the other three" (*A Woman of No Importance*, ed. Ian Small, 2nd ed. [London: A. & C. Black, 1993], 119–20). Tartuffe is the hypocritical protagonist of Molière's 1664 play *Tartuffe, ou l'Imposteur* (Tartuffe, or the Imposter); his name is a byword for a hypocrite who feigns virtue—especially religious virtue—that he does not possess. For Caliban, see p. 240, n.441 above.

That I should "gradually drop you!" As if it had been possible for me to gradually drop you! I had tried to end our friendship in every possible way, going so far as actually to leave England and give a false address abroad in the hopes of breaking at one blow a bond that had become irksome, hateful, and ruinous to me. Do you think that I *could* have "gradually dropped" you? Do you think that would have satisfied your father? You know it would not. What your father wanted, indeed, was not the cessation of our friendship, but a public scandal. That is what he was striving for. His name had not been in the papers for years. He saw the opportunity of appearing before the British public in an entirely new character, that of the affectionate father. His sense of humour was roused. Had I severed my friendship with you it would have been a terrible disappointment to him, and the small notoriety of a second divorce suit, however revolting its details and origin, would have proved but little consolation to him. For what he was aiming at was popularity, and to pose as a champion of purity, as it is termed, is, in the present condition of the British public, the surest mode of becoming for the nonce a heroic figure. Of this public I have said in one of my plays that if it is Caliban for one half of the year, it is Tartuffe for the other,[454] and your father, in whom both characters may be said to have become incarnate, was in this way marked out as the proper representative of Puritanism in its aggressive and most characteristic form. No gradual dropping of you would have been of any avail, even had it been practicable. Don't you feel now that the only thing for your mother to have done was to have asked me to come to see her, and had you and your brother present, and said definitely that the friendship must absolutely cease? She would have found in me her warmest seconder, and with Drumlanrig and myself in the room she need not have been afraid of speaking to you. She did not do so. She was afraid of her responsibilities, and tried to shift them on to me. One letter she did certainly write to me. It was a brief one, to ask me not to send the lawyer[']s letter to your father warning him to desist. She was quite right. It was ridiculous my consulting lawyers and seeking their protection. But she nullified any effect her letter might have produced

455. In Victorian England, an area was a sunken court, shut off from the sidewalk by railings, and approached by a flight of steps, giving access to the basement of city houses. Wilde uses "*area*-gate" as a euphemism for "furtive" or "secretive."

456. See p. 72, n.52 above.

457. Interrupting the judge's summing-up on the final day of Wilde's second criminal trial, the foreman of the jury asked, "Was a warrant ever issued for the apprehension of Lord Alfred Douglas?" For this question and the judge's contemptuous dismissal of it, see Hyde, *The Trials of Oscar Wilde*, 264–66.

by her usual postscript: "On no account let Alfred know that I have written to you." You were entranced at the idea of my sending lawyers['] letters to your father, as well as yourself. It was your suggestion. I could not tell you that your mother was strongly against the idea, for she had bound me with the most solemn promises never to tell you about her letters to me, and I foolishly kept my promise to her. Don't you see that it was wrong of her not to speak directly to you? That all the backstairs-interviews with me, and the area-gate[455] correspondence were wrong? Nobody can shift their responsibilities on anyone else. They always return ultimately to the proper owner. Your one idea of life, your one philosophy, if you are to be credited with a philosophy, was that whatever you did was to be paid for by someone else: I don't mean merely in the financial sense—that was simply the practical application of your philosophy to everyday life—but in the broadest, fullest sense of transferred responsibility. You made that your creed. It was very successful as far as it went. You forced me into taking the action because you knew that your father would not attack your life or yourself in any way, and that I would defend both to the utmost, and take on my own shoulders whatever would be thrust on me. You were quite right. Your father and I, each from different motives of course, did exactly as you counted on our doing. But somehow, in spite of everything, you have not really escaped. The "Infant Samuel theory," as for brevity's sake one may term it,[456] is all very well as far as the general world goes. It may be a good deal scorned in London, and a little sneered at in Oxford, but that is merely because there are a few people who know you in each place, and because in each place you left traces of your passage. Outside of a small set in those two cities, the world looks on you as the good young man who was very nearly tempted into wrong-doing by the wicked and immoral artist, but was rescued just in time by his kind and loving father. It sounds all right. And yet, you know you have not escaped. I am not referring to a silly question asked by a silly juryman, which was of course treated with contempt by the Crown and by the Judge.[457] No one cared about that. I am referring perhaps principally to yourself. In your own eyes, and some day you

458. Constance visited Wilde in Reading Prison on 19 February 1896 to break personally the news of his mother's death.

459. Adrian Charles Francis Hope (1858–1904), secretary to the Great Ormond Street Hospital for Sick Children, president of the Hospital Officers' Association, and at one time private secretary to the governor of Ceylon. In the end, Wilde's confidence in Hope was ill-judged. After Constance died suddenly in April 1898, Hope "did not take [the] duties he had towards us very seriously," Vyvyan Holland, Wilde's youngest son, later wrote, and the children scarcely ever saw their legal guardian (Vyvyan Holland, *Son of Oscar Wilde* [1954; repr., New York: Oxford University Press, 1988], 134). Hope did not permit the children to attend either of their parents' funerals—indeed he did not even inform them of their father's death.

460. Vyvyan Holland, born Vyvyan Wilde (1886–1967), younger son of Oscar Wilde. Although christened "Vyvyan," his parents usually spelled his name Vivian, as here. For Cyril, see p. 130, n.181 above.

will have to think of your conduct, you are not, cannot be quite satisfied at the way in which things have turned out. Secretly you must think of yourself with a good deal of shame. A brazen face is a capital thing to show the world, but now and then when you are alone, and have no audience, you have, I suppose, to take the mask off for mere breathing purposes. Else, indeed, you would be stifled.

And in the same manner your mother must at times regret that she tried to shift her grave responsibilities on someone else, who already had enough of a burden to carry. She occupied the position of both parents to you. Did she really fulfil the duties of either? If I bore with your bad temper and your rudeness and your scenes, she might have borne with them too. When last I saw my wife—fourteen months ago now[458]—I told her that she would have to be to Cyril a father as well as a mother. I told her everything about your mother[']s mode of dealing with you in every detail as I have set it down in this letter, only of course far more fully. I told her the reason of the endless notes with "Private" on the envelope that used to come to Tite Street from your mother, so constantly that my wife used to laugh and say that we must be collaborating in a society novel or something of that kind. I implored her not to be to Cyril what your mother was to you. I told her that she should bring him up so that if he shed innocent blood he would come and tell her, that she might cleanse his hands for him first, and then teach him how by penance or expiation to cleanse his soul afterwards. I told her that if she was frightened of facing the responsibility of the life of another, though her own child, she should get a guardian to help her. That she has, I am glad to say, done. She has chosen Adrian Hope[,] a man of high birth and culture and fine character,[459] her own cousin, whom you met once at Tite Street, and with him Cyril and Vivian[460] have a good chance of a beautiful future. Your mother, if she was afraid of talking seriously to you, should have chosen someone amongst her own relatives to whom you might have listened. But she should not have been afraid. She should have had it out with you and faced it. At any rate, look at the result. Is she satisfied and pleased?

461. Popular Victorian drink, comprised of *hock* (white Rhine wine, from the German *Hochheimer Wein*) and seltzer water, a naturally carbonated mineral water originally from the Prussian spa of Selters. "I always take hock-and-seltzer," proclaims the eponymous protagonist of Wilde's only novel (*The Picture of Dorian Gray*, ed. Frankel, 114). According to Frank Harris, Wilde, in the hours before his arrest, "sat as if glued to his chair, and drank hock and seltzer steadily in almost unbroken silence" (Harris, *Oscar Wilde*, 141).

I know she puts the blame on me. I hear of it, not from people who know you, but from people who do not know you, and do not desire to know you. I hear of it often. She talks of the influence of an elder over a younger man, for instance. It is one of her favourite attitudes towards the question, and it is always a successful appeal to popular prejudice and ignorance. I need not ask you what influence I had over you. You know I had none. It was one of your frequent boasts that I had none, and the only one indeed that was well-founded. What was there, as a mere matter of fact, in you that I could influence? Your brain? It was undeveloped. Your imagination? It was dead. Your heart? It was not yet born. Of all the people who have ever crossed my life you were the one, and the only one, I was unable in any way to influence in any direction. When I lay ill and helpless in a fever caught from tending on you, I had not sufficient influence over you to induce you to get me even a cup of milk to drink, or to see that I had the ordinary necessaries of a sickroom, or to take the trouble to drive a couple of hundred yards to a bookseller's to get me a book at my own expense. When I was actually engaged in writing, and penning comedies that were to beat Congreve for brilliancy, and Dumas *fils* for philosophy, and I suppose everybody else for every other quality, I had not sufficient influence with you to get you to leave me undisturbed as an artist should be left. Wherever my writing room was, it was to you an ordinary lounge, a place to smoke and drink hock-and-seltzer[461] in, and chatter about absurdities. The "influence of an elder over a younger man" is an excellent theory till it comes to my ears. Then it becomes grotesque. When it comes to your ears, I suppose you smile—to yourself. You are certainly entitled to do so.

I hear also much of what she says about money. She states, and with perfect justice, that she was ceaseless in her entreaties to me not to supply you with money. I admit it. Her letters were endless, and the postscript *"Pray do not let Alfred know that I have written to you"* appears in them all. But it was no pleasure to me to have to pay every single thing for you from your morning-shave to your midnight hansom. It was a horrible bore. I used to complain to you again and again about it. I used to tell

462. "The only excuse for making a useless thing is that one admires it intensely. All art is quite useless" ("Appendix B: The 1891 Preface to *The Picture of Dorian Gray*," in *The Picture of Dorian Gray*, ed. Frankel, 237).

463. The equivalent of roughly £140,000 or US$180,000 in 2018.

464. Spirit of the age.

465. Public holiday.

you—you remember, don't you?—how I loathed your regarding me as a "useful" person, how no artist wishes to be so regarded or so treated; artists, like art itself, being of their very essence quite useless.[462] You used to get very angry when I said it to you. The truth always made you angry. Truth, indeed, is a thing that is most painful to listen to and most painful to utter. But it did not make you alter your views or your mode of life. Every day I had to pay for every single thing you did all day long. Only a person of absurd good nature or of indescribable folly would have done so. I unfortunately was a complete combination of both. When I used to suggest that your mother should supply you with the money you wanted, you always had a very pretty and graceful answer. You said that the income allowed her by your father—some £1500 a year I believe[463]—was quite inadequate to the wants of a lady of her position, and that you could not go to her for more money than you were getting already. You were quite right about her income being one absolutely unsuitable to a lady of her position and tastes, but you should not have made that an excuse for living in luxury on me: it should on the contrary have been a suggestion to you for economy in your own life. The fact is that you were, and are I suppose still, a typical sentimentalist. For a sentimentalist is simply one who desires to have the luxury of an emotion without paying for it. To propose to spare your mother's pocket was beautiful. To do so at my expense was ugly. You think that one can have one's emotions for nothing. One cannot. Even the finest and the most self-sacrificing emotions have to be paid for. Strangely enough, that is what makes them fine. The intellectual and emotional life of ordinary people is a very contemptible affair. Just as they borrow their ideas from a sort of circulating library of thought—the *Zeitgeist*[464] of an age that has no soul—and send them back soiled at the end of each week, so they always try to get their emotions on credit, and refuse to pay the bill when it comes in. You should pass out of that conception of life. As soon as you have to pay for an emotion you will know its quality, and be the better for such knowledge. And remember that the sentimentalist is always a cynic at heart. Indeed sentimentality is merely the bank-holiday[465] of cynicism. And delightful as

466. The Cynic philosopher Diogenes (c. 412–323 BCE) is purported to have lived in a large jar or tub. Wilde means that cynicism has extended far beyond original narrow limits to reach London Clubland.

467. By his own account, the friend was Frank Harris. See Harris, *Oscar Wilde*, 167.

cynicism is from its intellectual side, now that it has left the Tub for the Club,[466] it never can be more than the perfect philosophy for a man who has no soul. It has its social value, and to an artist all modes of expression are interesting, but in itself it is a poor affair, for to the true cynic nothing is ever revealed. I think that if you look back now to your attitude towards your mother's income, and your attitude towards my income, you will not feel proud of yourself, and perhaps you may someday, if you don't show your mother this letter, explain to her that your living on me was a matter in which my wishes were not consulted for a moment. It was simply a peculiar, and to me personally most distressing form that your devotion to me took. To make yourself dependent on me for the smallest as well as the largest sums lent you in your own eyes all the charm of childhood, and in the insisting on my paying for every one of your pleasures you thought that you had found the secret of eternal youth. I confess that it pains me when I hear of your mother's remarks about me, and I am sure that on reflection you will agree with me that if she has no word of regret or sorrow for the ruin your race has brought on mine it would be better if she remained silent. Of course there is no reason she should see any portion of this letter that refers to any mental development I have been going through, or to any point of departure I hope to attain to. It would not be interesting to her. But the parts concerned purely with your life I should show her if I were you.

If I were you, in fact, I would not care about being loved on false pretences. There is no reason why a man should show his life to the world. The world does not understand things. But with people whose affection one desires to have it is different. A great friend of mine—a friend of ten years standing—came to see me some time ago and told me that he did not believe a single word of what was said against me, and wished me to know that he considered me quite innocent,[467] and the victim of a hideous plot concocted by your father. I burst into tears at what he said, and told him that while there was much amongst your father's definite charges that was quite untrue and transferred to me by revolting malice, still that my life had been full of perverse pleasures and strange passions, and that

468.   In "The Decay of Lying," Wilde had celebrated "the true liar, with his frank, fearless statements, his superb responsibility," and proclaimed that "lying, the telling of beautiful untrue things, is the proper aim of Art" (*Criticism*, ed. Guy, 74, 103).

469.   Sir Frank Lockwood (1847–1897), the solicitor-general, who led the prosecution at Wilde's final trial.

470.   Tacitus (c. 56–113 CE), Roman historian and senator (for Dante's "most Tacitean phrases," see p. 233 above); Girolamo Savonarola (1452–1498), Italian Dominican friar who denounced clerical corruption, despotic rule, and the exploitation of the poor. A defiant opponent of Pope Alexander VI, he was excommunicated then hanged and burned in the Piazza della Signoria in Florence.

471.   Many pages of the holograph manuscript of *De Profundis* are indeed full of corrections, errata, and "signs of passion or pain." See *De Profundis: A Facsimile*, intro. Merlin Holland (London: British Library, 2000). But other pages are written neatly, with no discernible blots, errors, or revisions. The former are clearly early drafts, while the latter constitute "fair copies" of earlier, less legible drafts and revisions. As Wilde suggests, his processes of revision and self-correction are self-evident from the manuscript, and they bear out the concern he expresses here that his words should be an absolute expression of his thoughts, as well as his contention that "language requires to be tuned, like a violin." But Wilde's pristine fair copies also suggest his concern with the literary end-product—with the letter's future readership and audience. They imply that Wilde took pleasure in the performance of his "finely-tuned instrument," even if he knew in his heart that *De Profundis* would never be widely appreciated in his own lifetime.

unless he accepted that fact as a fact about me and realised it to the full, I could not possibly be friends with him any more, or ever be in his company. It was a terrible shock to him, but we are friends, and I have not got his friendship on false pretences. I have said to you that to speak the truth is a painful thing. To be forced to tell lies is much worse.[468] I remember as I was sitting in the dock on the occasion of my last trial listening to Lockwood's[469] appalling denunciation of me—like a thing out of Tacitus, like a passage in Dante, like one of Savonarola's indictments of the Popes at Rome[470]—and being sickened with horror at what I heard. Suddenly it occurred to me, "How splendid it would be, if I was saying all this about myself!" I saw then at once that what is said of a man is nothing. The point is, who says it. A man's very highest moment is, I have no doubt at all, when he kneels in the dust, and beats his breast, and tells all the sins of his life. So with you. You would be much happier if you let your mother know a little at any rate of your life from yourself. I told her a good deal about it in December 1893, but of course I was forced into reticences and generalities. It did not seem to give her any more courage in her relations with you. On the contrary. She avoided looking at the truth more persistently than ever. If you told her yourself it would be different. My words may perhaps be often too bitter to you. But the facts you cannot deny. Things were as I have said they were, and if you have read this letter as carefully as you should have done you have met yourself face to face.

I have now written, and at great length, to you in order that you should realise what you were to me before my imprisonment, during those three years' fatal friendship: what you have been to me during my imprisonment, already within two moons of its completion almost: and what I hope to be to myself and to others when my imprisonment is over. I cannot reconstruct my letter, or rewrite it. You must take it as it stands, blotted in many places with tears, in some with the signs of passion or pain, and make it out as best you can, blots, corrections and all. As for the corrections and *errata*,[471] I have made them in order that my words should be an absolute expression of my thoughts, and err neither through surplusage nor through being inadequate. Language requires to be tuned,

472. Is greatly outweighed.

473. Winner in intercollegiate boat races.

like a violin: and just as too many or too few vibrations in the voice of the singer or the trembling of the string will make the note false, so too much or too little in words will spoil the message. As it stands, at any rate, my letter has its definite meaning behind every phrase. There is in it nothing of rhetoric. Wherever there is erasion or substitution, however slight, however elaborate, it is because I am seeking to render my real impression, to find for my mood its exact equivalent. Whatever is first in feeling comes always last in form.

I will admit that it is a severe letter. I have not spared you. Indeed you may say that, after admitting that to weigh you against the smallest of my sorrows, the meanest of my losses, would be really unfair to you, I have actually done so, and made scruple by scruple the most careful assay of your nature. That is true. But you must remember that you put yourself into the scales.

You must remember that, if when matched with one mere moment of my imprisonment the balance in which you lie kicks the beam,[472] Vanity made you choose the balance, and Vanity made you cling to it. *There* was the one great psychological error of our friendship, its entire want of proportion. You forced your way into a life too large for you, one whose orbit transcended your power of vision no less than your power of cyclic motion, one whose thoughts, passions and actions were of intense import, of wide interest, and fraught, too heavily indeed, with wonderful or awful consequence. Your little life of little whims and moods was admirable in its own little sphere. It was admirable at Oxford, where the worst that could happen to you was a reprimand from the Dean or a lecture from the President, and where the highest excitement was Magdalen becoming head of the river,[473] and the lighting of a bonfire in the quad as a celebration of the august event. It should have continued in its own sphere after you left Oxford. In yourself, you were all right. You were a very complete specimen of a very modern type. It was simply in reference to me that you were wrong. Your reckless extravagance was not a crime. Youth is always extravagant. It was your forcing me to pay for your extravagances that was disgraceful. Your desire to have a friend with

474. Tasty snack.

475. For White's, see p. 60, n.18 above.

476. "The Critic as Artist," in *Criticism,* ed. Guy, 173.

whom you could pass your time from morning to night was charming. It was almost idyllic. But the friend you fastened on should not have been a man of letters, an artist, one to whom your continual presence was as utterly destructive of all beautiful work as it was actually paralysing to the creative faculty. There was no harm in your seriously considering that the most perfect way of passing an evening was to have a champagne dinner at the Savoy, a box at a Music-Hall to follow, and a champagne supper at Willis's as a *bonne-bouche*[474] for the end. Heaps of delightful young men in London are of the same opinion. It is not even an eccentricity. It is the qualification for becoming a member of White's.[475] But you had no right to require of me that I should become the purveyor of such pleasures for you. It showed your lack of any real appreciation of my genius. Your quarrel with your father, again, whatever one may think about its character, should obviously have remained a question entirely between the two of you. It should have been carried on in a backyard. Such quarrels, I believe, usually are. Your mistake was in insisting on its being played as a tragi-comedy on a high stage in History, with the whole world as the audience, and myself as the prize for the victor in the contemptible contest. The fact that your father loathed you, and that you loathed your father, was not a matter of any interest to the English public. Such feelings are very common in English domestic life, and should be confined to the place they characterise: the home. Away from the home-circle they are quite out of place. To translate them is an offence. Family-life is not to be treated as a red flag to be flaunted in the streets, or a horn to be blown hoarsely on the housetops. You took Domesticity out of its proper sphere, just as you took yourself out of your proper sphere.

And those who quit their proper sphere change their surroundings merely, not their natures. They do not acquire the thoughts or passions appropriate to the sphere they enter. It is not in their power to do so. Emotional forces, as I say somewhere in *Intentions,* are as limited in extent and duration as the forces of physical energy.[476] The little cup that is made to hold so much can hold so much and no more, though all the purple vats of Burgundy be filled with wine to the brim, and the treaders

477. "Like a pale martyr in his shirt of fire" (Alexander Smith, "A Life-Drama," in his *Poems* [Boston: Ticknor, Reed, and Fields, 1853], 20). See too the "sheet of flame" in which the corpse of the executed felon lies wrapped in *The Ballad of Reading Gaol* (see p. 355 below).

478. See *Hamlet*, act 2, scene 2.

479. When still a child, Lucius Junius Brutus, founder of the Roman Republic and traditionally one of Rome's first consuls, saw his father and brothers cruelly executed by the tyrant Tarquinius Superbus, and escaped only by feigning mental instability. Later, when his kinswoman Lucretia committed suicide by stabbing herself after being raped by Tarquinius's son, Brutus supposedly grabbed the dagger from Lucretia's breast and shouted for the overthrow of the Tarquins.

480. Pranks.

481. *Hamlet*, act 2, scene 2, ll. 194–95.

stand knee-deep in the gathered grapes of the stony vineyards of Spain. There is no error more common than that of thinking that those who are the causes or occasions of great tragedies share in the feelings suitable to the tragic mood: no error more fatal than expecting it of them. The martyr in his "shirt of flame"[477] may be looking on the face of God, but to him who is piling the faggots or loosening the logs for the blast the whole scene is no more than the slaying of an ox is to the butcher, or the felling of a tree to the charcoal-burner in the forest, or the fall of a flower to one who is mowing down the grass with a scythe. Great passions are for the great of soul, and great events can be seen only by those who are on a level with them. I know of nothing in all Drama more incomparable from the point of view of Art, or more suggestive in its subtlety of observation, than Shakespeare's drawing of Rosencrantz and Guildenstern.[478] They are Hamlet's college friends. They have been his companions. They bring with them memories of pleasant days together. At the moment when they come across him in the play he is staggering under the weight of a burden intolerable to one of his temperament. The dead have come armed out of the grave to impose on him a mission at once too great and too mean for him. He is a dreamer, and he is called upon to act. He has the nature of the poet and he is asked to grapple with the common complexities of cause and effect, with life in its practical realisation, of which he knows nothing, not with life in its ideal essence, of which he knows much. He has no conception of what to do, and his folly is to feign folly. Brutus used madness as a cloak to conceal the sword of his purpose, the dagger of his will,[479] but to Hamlet madness is a mere mask for the hiding of weakness. In the making of mows[480] and jests he sees a chance of delay. He keeps playing with action, as an artist plays with a theory. He makes himself the spy of his proper actions, and listening to his own words knows them to be but "words, words, words."[481] Instead of trying to be the hero of his own history, he seeks to be the spectator of his own tragedy. He disbelieves in everything, including himself, and yet his doubt helps him not, as it comes not from scepticism but from a divided will. Of all this, Guildenstern and

482. *Hamlet*, act 2, scene 2, l. 540.

483. Wilde is quoting himself (and misquoting Pater); see p. 197 above.

484. Trap.

485. A slight adaptation of *Hamlet*, act 5, verse 2, ll. 349–51 and 357–60.

486. Angelo is the mendacious and despotic deputy to the Duke of Venice, in Shakespeare's *Measure for Measure*. For Tartuffe, see p. 252, n.454 above.

487. *De Amicitia* is a treatise on friendship by the Roman statesman and author Marcus Tullius Cicero, written in 44 BCE. Cicero lived near Rome in the town of Tusculum, which lent its name to his *Tusculanae Disputationes* (Tuscular Disputations), a series of books written around 45 BCE attempting to popularize Stoic philosophy.

488. *Hamlet*, act 2, scene 2, ll. 33–34.

Rosencrantz realise nothing. They bow and smirk and smile, and what the one says the other echoes with sicklier iteration. When at last by means of the play within the play and the puppets in their dalliance, Hamlet "catches the conscience" of the King,[482] and drives the wretched man in terror from his throne, Guildenstern and Rosencrantz see no more in his conduct than a rather painful breach of court-etiquette. That is as far as they can attain to in "the contemplation of the spectacle of life with appropriate emotions."[483] They are close to his very secret and know nothing of it. Nor would there be any use in telling them. They are the little cups that can hold so much and no more. Towards the close it is suggested that caught in a cunning springe[484] set for another, they have met, or may meet with a violent and sudden death. But a tragic ending of this kind, though touched by Hamlet's humour with something of the surprise and justice of comedy, is really not for such as they. They never die. Horatio who, in order to "report Hamlet and his cause aright to the unsatisfied,"

> Absents him from felicity a while
> And in the harsh world draws his breath in pain,[485]

dies, though not before an audience, and leaves no brother. But Guildenstern and Rosencrantz are as immortal as Angelo and Tartuffe,[486] and should rank with them. They are what modern life has contributed to the antique ideal of friendship. He who writes a new *De Amicitia* must find a niche for them and praise them in Tusculan prose.[487] They are types fixed for all time. To censure them would show a lack of appreciation. They are merely out of their sphere: that is all. In sublimity of soul there is no contagion. High thoughts and high emotions are by their very existence isolated. What Ophelia herself could not understand was not to be realised by "Guildenstern and gentle Rosencrantz," by "Rosencrantz and gentle Guildenstern."[488] Of course I do not propose to compare you. There is a wide difference between you. What with them was chance, with you was choice. Deliberately and by me uninvited you thrust yourself into my sphere, usurped there a place for which you had neither

489. More Adey had written to Wilde in early March 1897 about these and other distressing consequences of Wilde's bankruptcy. See Wilde's detailed reply to Adey of 8 March 1897 (*CL* 679–92).

right nor qualifications, and having by curious persistence, and by the rendering of your very presence a part of each separate day, succeeded in absorbing my entire life, could do no better with that life than break it in pieces. Strange as it may sound to you, it was but natural that you should do so. If one gives to a child a toy too wonderful for its little mind, or too beautiful for its but half-awakened eyes, it breaks the toy, if it is wilful; if it is listless it lets it fall and goes its way to its own companions. So it was with you. Having got hold of my life, you did not know what to do with it. You couldn't have known. It was too wonderful a thing to be in your grasp. You should have let it slip from your hands and gone back to your own companions at their play. But unfortunately you were wilful, and so you broke it. That, when everything is said, is perhaps the ultimate secret of all that has happened. For secrets are always smaller than their manifestations. By the displacement of an atom a world may be shaken. And that I may not spare myself any more than you I will add this: that dangerous to me as my meeting with you was, it was rendered fatal to me by the particular moment in which we met. For you were at that time of life when all that one does is no more than the sowing of the seed, and I was at that time of life when all that one does is no less than the reaping of the harvest.

There are some few things more about which I must write to you. The first is about my Bankruptcy. I heard some days ago, with great disappointment I admit, that it is too late now for your family to pay your father off, that it would be illegal, and that I must remain in my present painful position for some considerable time to come.[489] It is bitter to me because I am assured on legal authority that I cannot even publish a book without the permission of the Receiver to whom all the accounts must be submitted. I cannot enter into a contract with the manager of a theatre, or produce a play without the receipts passing to your father and my few other creditors. I think that even you will admit now that the scheme of "scoring off" your father by allowing him to make me a bankrupt has not really been the brilliant all round success you imagined it was going to turn out. It has not been so to me at any rate, and my feelings of pain and humiliation at my pauperism should have been consulted rather than

Jean-Gabriel Daragnès, wood-engraved illustration for *Ballade de La Geôle de Reading, par C.3.3.*, trans. Henry-D. Davray (Paris: Léon Pichon, 1918).

your own sense of humour, however caustic or unexpected. In point of actual fact in permitting my Bankruptcy, as in urging me on to the original trial, you really were playing right into your father's hands, and doing just what he wanted. Alone, and unassisted, he would from the very outset have been powerless. In you—though you did not mean to hold such a horrible office—he has always found his chief ally.

I am told by More Adey in his letter that last summer you really did express on more than one occasion your desire to repay me "a little of what I spent" on you. As I said to him in my answer, unfortunately I spent on you my art, my life, my name, my place in history, and if your family had all the marvellous things in the world at their command, or what the world holds as marvellous, genius, beauty, wealth, high position and the like, and laid them all at my feet, it would not repay me for one tithe of the smallest things that have been taken from me, or one tear of the least tears that I have shed. However, of course everything one does has to be paid for. Even to the Bankrupt it is so. You seem to be under the impression that Bankruptcy is a convenient means by which a man can avoid paying his debts, a "score off his creditors" in fact. It is quite the other way. It is the method by which a man's creditors "score off" him, if we are to continue your favourite phrase, and by which the Law by the confiscation of all his property forces him to pay every one of his debts, and if he fails to do so leaves him as penniless as the commonest mendicant who stands in an archway, or creeps down a road, holding out his hand for the alms for which, in England at any rate, he is afraid to ask. The Law has taken from me not merely all that I have, my books, furniture, pictures, my copyright in my published works, my copyright in my plays, everything in fact from *The Happy Prince* and *Lady Windermere's Fan* down to the stair-carpets and door-scraper of my house, but also all that I am ever going to have. My interest in my marriage-settlement, for instance, was sold. Fortunately I was able to buy it in through my friends. Otherwise, in case my wife died, my two children during my lifetime would be as penniless as myself. My interest in our Irish estate, entailed on me by my own father, will I suppose have to go next. I feel very bitterly

490. Jeweler and goldsmith, located at 172 New Bond Street, one of two jewelers to whom Wilde owed over £43 at the time of his bankruptcy (*The Real Trial of Oscar Wilde*, 321 n.206).

about its being sold, but I must submit. Your father's seven hundred pence—or pounds is it?—stand in the way, and must be refunded. Even when I am stripped of all I have, and am ever to have, and am granted a discharge as a hopeless Insolvent, I have still got to pay my debts. The Savoy dinners—the clear turtle-soup, the luscious ortolans wrapped in their crinkled Sicilian vineleaves, the heavy amber-coloured, indeed almost amber-scented champagne—Dagonet 1880, I think, was your favourite wine?—all have still to be paid for. The suppers at Willis's, the special *cuvée* of Perrier-Jouet reserved always for us, the wonderful *pâtés* procured directly from Strasburg, the marvellous *fin[e] champagne* served always at the bottom of great bell-shaped glasses that its bouquet might be the better savoured by the true epicures of what was really exquisite in life—these cannot be left unpaid, as bad debts of a dishonest *client.* Even the dainty sleeve-links—four heart-shaped moonstones of silver mist, girdled by alternate ruby and diamond for their setting—that I designed, and had made at Henry Lewis's[490] as a special little present to you, to celebrate the success of my second comedy—these even—though I believe you sold them for a song a few months afterwards—have to be paid for. I cannot leave the jeweller out of pocket for the presents I gave you, no matter what you did with them. So, even if I get my discharge, you see I have still my debts to pay. And what is true of a bankrupt is true of every one else in life. For every single thing that is done someone has to pay. Even you yourself—with all your desire for absolute freedom from all duties, your insistence on having everything supplied to you by others, your attempts to reject any claim on your affection, or regard, or gratitude—even you will have someday to reflect seriously on what you have done, and try, however unavailingly, to make some attempt at atonement. The fact that you will not be able really to do so will be part of your punishment. You can't wash your hands of all responsibility, and propose with a shrug or a smile to pass on to a new friend and a freshly spread feast. You can't treat all that you have brought upon me as a sentimental reminiscence to be served up occasionally with the cigarettes and *liqueurs,* a picturesque background to a modern life of pleasure like an old tapestry

491. See p. 64, n.31 above.

hung in a common inn. It may for the moment have the charm of a new sauce or a fresh vintage, but the scraps of a banquet grow stale, and the dregs of a bottle are bitter. Either today, or tomorrow, or someday you have got to realise it. Otherwise you may die without having done so, and then what a mean, starved, unimaginative life you would have had. In my letter to More I have suggested one point of view from which you had better approach the subject as soon as possible. He will tell you what it is. To understand it you will have to cultivate your imagination. Remember that imagination is the quality that enables one to see things and people in their real as in their ideal relations. If you cannot realise it by yourself, talk to others on the subject. I have had to look at my past face to face. Look at your past face to face. Sit down quietly and consider it. The supreme vice is shallowness. Whatever is realised is right. Talk to your brother about it. Indeed the proper person to talk to *is* Percy. Let him read this letter, and know all the circumstances of our friendship. When things are clearly put before him, no judgment is better. Had we told him the truth, what a lot would have been saved to me of suffering and disgrace! You remember I proposed to do so, the night you arrived in London from Algiers.[491] You absolutely refused. So when he came in after dinner we had to play the comedy of your father being an insane man subject to absurd and unaccountable delusions. It was a capital comedy while it lasted, none the less so because Percy took it all quite seriously. Unfortunately it ended in a very revolting manner. The subject on which I write now is one of its results, and if it be a trouble to you, pray do not forget that it is the deepest of my humiliations, and one I must go through. I have no option. You have none either.

The second thing about which I have to speak to you is with regard to the conditions, circumstances, and place of our meeting when my term of imprisonment is over. From extracts from your letter to Robbie written in the early summer of last year I understand that you have sealed up in two packages my letters and my presents to you—such at least as remain of either—and are anxious to hand them personally to me. It is, of course, necessary that they should be given up. You did not understand why

492. See p. 172, n.283 above. Within days of arriving in Dieppe, on the morning after his release, Wilde had moved with Robert Ross to a "little seaside village," Berneval sur Mer, five miles further up the coast. Wilde remained in Berneval, where he was visited by a number of old friends, for the next three months. Ross returned to England shortly after Wilde's arrival, although he would return for a second lengthy visit in August 1897.

493. "In one of his plays about Iphigenia" and the phrase in Greek, meaning "the sea doth wash away all the ills of the world," added to the manuscript as an afterthought. The phrase comes from Euripedes's play *Iphigenia in Tauris*, not his later *Iphigenia at Aulis*.

494. "one so modern as I am, 'enfant de mon siècle' [child of my century]" was added to the manuscript as an afterthought.

I wrote beautiful letters to you, any more than you understood why I gave you beautiful presents. You failed to see that the former were not meant to be published, any more than the latter were meant to be pawned. Besides, they belong to a side of life that is long over, to a friendship that somehow you were unable to appreciate at its proper value. You must look back with wonder now to the days when you had my entire life in your hands. I too look back to them with wonder, and with other, with far different, emotions.

I am to be released, if all goes well with me, towards the end of May, and hope to go at once to some little seaside village abroad with Robbie and More Adey.[492] The sea, as Euripides says in one of his plays about Iphigenia, washes away the stains and wounds of the world. θάλασσα κλύζει πάντα τ'ἀνθρώπων κακά.[493] I hope to be at least a month with my friends, and to gain, in their healthful and affectionate company, peace, and balance, and a less troubled heart, and a sweeter mood. I have a strange longing for the great simple primeval things, such as the Sea, to me no less of a mother than the Earth. It seems to me that we all look at Nature too much, and live with her too little. I discern great sanity in the Greek attitude. They never chattered about sunsets, or discussed whether the shadows on the grass were really mauve or not. But they saw that the sea was for the swimmer, and the sand for the feet of the runner. They loved the trees for the shadow that they cast, and the forest for its silence at noon. The vineyard-dresser wreathed his hair with ivy that he might keep off the rays of the sun as he stooped over the young shoots, and for the artist and the athlete, the two types that Greece gave us, they plaited into garlands the leaves of the bitter laurel and of the wild parsley which else had been of no service to man. We call ourselves a utilitarian age, and we do not know the uses of any single thing. We have forgotten that Water can cleanse, and Fire purify, and that the Earth is mother to us all. As a consequence our Art is of the Moon and plays with shadows, while Greek art is of the Sun and deals directly with things. I feel sure that in elemental forces there is purification, and I want to go back to them and live in their presence. Of course, to one so modern as I am, "enfant de mon siècle,"[494]

495. Carl Linnaeus (1707–1778), Swedish botanist and zoologist, the father of modern taxonomy, who laid the foundations for the modern scheme of binomial nomenclature and visited England in 1736. According to Florence Caddy, "the first time Linnaeus crossed Putney Heath the sight of the gorse blossom in its blaze of May made him fall on his knees in rapture" (*Through the Fields with Linnaeus* [Boston: Little Brown, 1887], 1:329).

496. The French poet and man of letters Théophile Gautier (1811–1872) is widely credited with having popularized the slogan "art for art's sake" (*l'art pour l'art*), a rallying cry for the artists and writers associated with the aesthetic movement. He was a formative influence on Wilde. Gautier's 1857 comment "Je suis un homme pour qui le monde visible existe [I am a man for whom the visible world exists]" is quoted in *Selections from Edmond and Jules de Goncourt*, ed. Arnold G. Cameron (New York: American Book, 1898), 147.

497. "weep undisturbed" substituted in the manuscript for "forget." Wilde's self-description here and in the next sentence is replete with Biblical echoes, especially of Psalm 51 ("Cleanse me with hyssop, and I will be clean; wash me, and I will be whiter than snow") and the Song of Solomon, 2:14: "My dove in the clefts of the rock, in the hiding places on the mountainside, show me your face, let me hear your voice; for your voice is sweet, and your face is lovely."

merely to look at the world will be always lovely. I tremble with pleasure when I think that on the very day of my leaving prison both the laburnum and the lilac will be blooming in the gardens, and that I shall see the wind stir into restless beauty the swaying gold of the one, and make the other toss the pale purple of its plumes so that all the air shall be Arabia for me. Linnaeus fell on his knees and wept for joy when he saw for the first time the long heath of some English upland made yellow with the tawny aromatic blossoms of the common furze,[495] and I know that for me, to whom flowers are part of desire, there are tears waiting in the petals of some rose. It has always been so with me from my boyhood. There is not a single colour hidden away in the chalice of a flower, or the curve of a shell, to which, by some subtle sympathy with the very soul of things, my nature does not answer. Like Gautier I have always been one of those "pour qui le monde visible existe."[496] Still, I am conscious now that behind all this Beauty, satisfying though it be, there is Some Spirit hidden of which the painted forms and shapes are but modes of manifestation, and it is with this Spirit that I desire to become in harmony. I have grown tired of the articulate utterances of men and things. The Mystical in Art, the Mystical in Life, the Mystical in Nature—this is what I am looking for, and in the great symphonies of Music, in the initiation of Sorrow, in the depths of the Sea I may find it. It is absolutely necessary for me to find it somewhere. All trials are trials for one's life, just as all sentences are sentences of death, and three times have I been tried. The first time I left the box to be arrested, the second time to be led back to the House of Detention, the third time to pass into a prison for two years. Society, as we have constituted it, will have no place for me, has none to offer; but Nature, whose sweet rains fall on unjust and just alike, will have clefts in the rocks where I may hide, and secret valleys in whose silence I may weep undisturbed.[497] She will hang the night with stars so that I may walk abroad in the darkness without stumbling, and send the wind over my footprints so that none may track me to my hurt: she will cleanse me in great waters, and with bitter herbs make me whole.

498. Wilde did indeed meet Douglas in some quiet foreign town—but in Rouen, in Normandy, not Bruges, in Belgium, and not till three months after Wilde's release. During this meeting, they resolved to live together in Naples, in southern Italy, for which they departed some days later. See Frankel, *Oscar Wilde: The Unrepentant Years*, 123–27.

499. "so musical in the mouth of Fame" substituted in the manuscript for "so wonderful to the world and to myself." Wilde's name was a compression of Oscar Fingal O'Flahertie Wills Wilde, and for some time in his youth he was known by friends as "Wills Wilde." Some of his earliest publications were signed "Oscar F. O'F. Wills Wilde." But shortly after arriving on English shores in 1874, he dropped the Irish and Celtic elements and became famous simply as "Oscar Wilde." Although Wilde means "musical in the mouth of fame" metaphorically (he is speaking of journalists' and gossip columnists' obsession with him in the 1880s and early 1890s), his name had been "musical" in a more literal sense when, during his American lecture tour of 1882, he found himself the subject of widely selling parlor songs and dances such as F. H. Snow's *The Oscar Wilde Galop*. His lecture tour was conceived, moreover, to support an American touring production of Gilbert and Sullivan's comic opera *Patience*, in which Wilde was affectionately mocked in song as a "greenery-yallery, Grosvenor Gallery, foot-in-the-grave young man" (*The Complete Annotated Gilbert and Sullivan*, intro. and ed. Ian Bradley [Oxford: Oxford University Press, 2001], 347).

500. Knowing that his real name was publicly unmentionable, Wilde took the pseudonym Sebastian Melmoth upon release. There was symbolism in the assumed name: St. Sebastian, who has been called the patron saint of homosexuals, was an early Christian martyr, persecuted and savagely killed at the hands of the Romans. Even before Wilde's adoption of his name, St. Sebastian had become a "coded means of articulating same-sex desire" (Richard A. Kaye, "'Determined Raptures': St. Sebastian and the Victorian Discourse of Decadence," *Victorian Literature and Culture* 27 [1999]: 271), at least among writers with homosexual and Catholic allegiances. In his youth Wilde had fallen in love with a painted depiction of the martyred saint, by Guido Reni, on first seeing the painting in Genoa in 1877. "Melmoth" alludes to the Gothic novel *Melmoth the Wanderer* by Wilde's Irish great-uncle Charles Maturin, whose Faust-like protagonist, half hero and half villain, having sold his soul to the devil in exchange for an extended life, wanders

At the end of a month, when the June roses are in all their wanton opulence, I will, if I feel able, arrange through Robbie to meet you in some quiet foreign town like Bruges, whose grey houses and green canals and cool still ways had a charm for me, years ago.[498] For the moment you will have to change your name. The little title of which you were so vain—and indeed it made your name sound like the name of a flower—you will have to surrender, if you wish to see *me;* just as *my* name, once so musical in the mouth of Fame,[499] will have to be abandoned by me, in turn.[500] How narrow, and mean, and inadequate to its burdens is this century of ours! It can give to Success its palace of porphyry, but for Sorrow and Shame it does not keep even a wattled house in which they may dwell: all it can do for *me* is to bid me alter my name into some other name, where even mediaevalism would have given me the cowl of the monk or the face-cloth of the leper behind which I might be at peace.

I hope that our meeting will be what a meeting between you and me should be, after every thing that has occurred. In old days there was always a wide chasm between us, the chasm of achieved Art and acquired culture: there is a still wider chasm between us now, the chasm of Sorrow: but to Humility there is nothing that is impossible, and to Love all things are easy.

As regards your letter to me in answer to this, it may be as long or as short as you choose. Address the envelope to "The Governor, HM Prison, Reading."[501] Inside, in another, and an open envelope, place your own letter to me: if your paper is very thin do not write on both sides, as it makes it hard for others to read. I have written to you with perfect freedom. You can write to me with the same. What I must know from you is why you have never made any attempt to write to me, since the August of the year before last, more especially after, in the May of last year, eleven months ago now, you knew, and admitted to others that you knew, how you had made me suffer, and how I realised it. I waited month after month to hear from you. Even if I had not been waiting but had shut the doors against you, you should have remembered that no one can possibly shut the doors against Love for ever. The unjust judge in the

the earth as the appointed day of his death draws near, haunting the dreams of men while hoping that one of them will absolve him of his pact.

For the names with which Wilde signed *De Profundis* and *The Ballad of Reading Gaol*, see p. 290, n.506, and p. 370, n.87 below. For those with which he signed his letters to the *Daily Chronicle*, see pp. 315 and 383 below.

501. Having his correspondents address their letters to Governor Nelson rather than to himself was, for Wilde, a way of circumventing the prison regulation mandating that prisoners receive only one letter per quarter. The compassionate Governor Nelson, who clearly felt that Wilde's rehabilitation was contingent on maintaining old friendships, was complicit in this arrangement. See p. 160, n.251 above.

502. For the parable of the unjust judge, who delivers just vengeance despite his disregard of God and man, see Luke 18:1–6.

503. "Which of you shall have a friend, and shall go unto him at midnight, and say unto him, Friend, lend me three loaves?... I say unto you, though he will not rise and give him, because he is his friend, yet because of his importunity he will rise and give him as many as he needeth" (Luke 11:5–8).

504. John Keats, "Sonnet ['If by dull rhymes our English must be chained']" (1819), in *Complete Poems and Selected Letters of John Keats*, intro. E. Hirsch (New York: Modern Library, 2001). Wilde possessed a copy of Keats's poems in his cell. Midas was the legendary and miserly king of Phyrgia, who fell victim to his own wish (granted by Bacchus) that everything he touched might be turned into gold. Wilde is here enjoining Douglas to "see what may be gained / By ear industrious, and attention meet," as Keats puts it.

505. Wilde appears to be conflating William Blake's caption ("When all the morning Stars sang together & all the sons of God shouted together") to one of his engraved *Illustrations to the Book of Job* (1826) with Blake's "Vision of the Last Judgment" ("I assert for My self that I do not behold the Outward Creation & that to me it is hindrance & not Action.... What it will be Questiond When the Sun rises do you not see a round Disk of fire somewhat like a Guinea O no no I see an Innumerable company of the Heavenly host crying Holy Holy Holy is the Lord God Almighty" [*Complete Poetry & Prose of William Blake*, ed. Erdman, 565–66]).

Gospels rises up at length to give a just decision because Justice comes knocking daily at his door;[502] and at night-time the friend, in whose heart there is no real friendship, yields at length to his friend "because of his importunity."[503] There is no prison in any world into which Love cannot force an entrance. If you did not understand that, you did not understand anything about Love at all. Then, let me know all about your article on me for the *Mercure de France.* I know something of it. You had better quote from it. It is set up in type. Also, let me know the exact terms of your Dedication of your poems. If it is in prose, quote the prose; if in verse, quote the verse. I have no doubt that there will be beauty in it. Write to me with full frankness about yourself: about your life: your friends: your occupations: your books. Tell me about your volume and its reception. Whatever you have to say for yourself, say it without fear. Don't write what you don't mean: that is all. If anything in your letter is false or counterfeit I shall detect it by the ring at once. It is not for nothing, or to no purpose, that in my lifelong cult of literature I have made myself

> Miser of sound and syllable, no less
> Than Midas of his coinage.[504]

Remember also that I have yet to know you. Perhaps we have yet to know each other.

For yourself, I have but this last thing to say. Do not be afraid of the past. If people tell you that it is irrevocable, do not believe them. The past, the present and the future are but one moment in the sight of God, in whose sight we should try to live. Time and space, succession and extension, are merely accidental conditions of Thought. The Imagination can transcend them, and move in a free sphere of ideal existences. Things, also, are in their essence what we choose to make them. A thing *is,* according to the mode in which one looks at it. "Where others," says Blake, "see but the Dawn coming over the hill, I see the sons of God shouting for joy."[505] What seemed to the world and to myself my future I lost irretrievably when I let myself be taunted into taking the action against your father: had, I dare say, lost it really long before that. What

506. It is striking that Wilde ends *De Profundis* by signing his own name given that earlier he said that it will "have to be abandoned" henceforth (p. 287 above) and that in prison he had become "merely the figure and letter of a little cell in a long gallery, one of a thousand lifeless numbers, as of a thousand lifeless lives" (p. 135 above). The composition of *De Profundis*, one might infer, had allowed him to rediscover and reaffirm his own identity. By contrast, Wilde insisted some months later that *The Ballad of Reading Gaol* should conclude with his prison cell number, telling his publisher that the cell number was "the actual name for eighteen months of the man who wrote the poem."

lies before me is my past. I have got to make myself look on that with different eyes, to make the world look on it with different eyes, to make God look on it with different eyes. This I cannot do by ignoring it, or slighting it, or praising it, or denying it. It is only to be done by fully accepting it as an inevitable part of the evolution of my life and character: by bowing my head to everything that I have suffered. How far I am away from the true temper of soul, this letter in its changing, uncertain moods, its scorn and bitterness, its aspirations and its failure to realise those aspirations, shows you quite clearly. But do not forget in what a terrible school I am sitting at my task. And incomplete, imperfect, as I am, yet from me you may have still much to gain. You came to me to learn the Pleasure of Life and the Pleasure of Art. Perhaps I am chosen to teach you something much more wonderful, the meaning of Sorrow, and its beauty. Your affectionate friend

Oscar Wilde[506]

* Wilde's letter appeared under the headline "The Case of Warder Martin" in the *Daily Chronicle* on 28 May 1897, nine days after Wilde's release and four days after the paper published a letter from Thomas Martin, a warder, recounting details of his dismissal from Reading Prison. Wilde's letter was subsequently published as a penny pamphlet titled *Children in Prison and Other Cruelties of Prison Life* (London: Murdoch and Co., n.d.). Martin, a native of Belfast, became a warder at Reading roughly seven weeks before Wilde's release, and he quickly befriended his fellow Irishman. Not a lot is known about him, but while Wilde was under his jurisdiction, the two men surreptitiously exchanged friendly notes, written on stray scraps of paper, and Martin broke prison rules and ran great risks so that Wilde and his fellow prisoners might be provided with a modicum of comfort. Martin supplied Wilde with contraband copies of the *Daily Chronicle* and the weekly reviews, for instance, as well as ginger biscuits. Anthony Stokes, who was himself for many years a warder at Reading Prison, surmises (albeit on thin evidence) that Martin was a "plant," placed in the prison by the Prison Commission to steer Wilde through his final weeks and then "cynically disposed of" after Wilde's release because he had served his purpose (*Pit of Shame: The Real Ballad of Reading Gaol* [Winchester: Waterside Press, 2007], 93). Nine months after being dismissed from Reading, Martin was still unemployed and hard up, but Christopher Millard tells us that he was later employed as a porter at Fulham Workhouse (Stuart Mason [Christopher Millard], *Bibliography of Oscar Wilde* [London: T. Werner Laurie, 1914], 52). Martin is purported to have contributed the chapter "The Poet in Prison" to Robert H. Sherard's *The Life of Oscar Wilde* (London: T. Werner Laurie, 1906), although the chapter—whose author Sherard identifies only as "one of the warders in Reading Gaol"—bears clear traces of Sherard's own hand.

The *Daily Chronicle*, closely affiliated with the Liberal Party, was England's leading progressive newspaper and "a vehicle for every group of thinkers and artists which was struggling to escape from the prison house of Victorian conventions" (H. N. Brailsford, quoted in Alfred F. Havighurst, *Radical Journalist: H. W. Massingham, 1860–1924* [London: Cambridge University Press, 1974], 60). For several years the paper had championed the cause of penal reform. From 1895 to 1899 its editor was Henry W. Massingham, to whom Wilde later sent a copy of the first edition of *The Ballad of Reading Gaol*.

Letter to the *Daily Chronicle**

27 May 1897

Sir,—I learn with great regret, through the columns of your paper, that the warder Martin, of Reading Prison, has been dismissed by the Prison Commissioners[1] for having given some sweet biscuits to a little hungry child. I saw the three children myself on the Monday preceding my release. They had just been convicted, and were standing in a row in the central hall in their prison dress, carrying their sheets under their arms previous to their being sent to the cells allotted to them. I happened to be passing along one of the galleries on my way to the reception room,[2] where I was to have an interview with a friend.[3] They were quite small children, the youngest—the one to whom the warder gave the biscuits—being a tiny little chap, for whom they had evidently been unable to find clothes small enough to fit. I had, of course, seen many children in prison during the two years during which I was myself confined. Wandsworth Prison especially contained always a large number of children.[4] But the little child I saw on the afternoon of Monday the 17th, at Reading, was tinier than any one of them. I need not say how utterly distressed I was to see these children at Reading, for I knew the treatment in store for them.[5] The cruelty that is practised by day and night on children in English prisons is incredible, except to those that have witnessed it and are aware of the brutality of the system.

People nowadays do not understand what cruelty is. They regard it as a sort of terrible mediæval passion, and connect it with the race of men like Eccelin da Romano,[6] and others, to whom the deliberate infliction

1. A statutory body set up by Parliament in 1877 to administer prisons in England and Wales, following their centralization and standardization in the 1877 Prison Act.

2. The room at Reading Prison set aside for prisoners to meet with their legal representatives. Prison regulations restricted visits by friends and family to just one per quarter, and these were expected to take place not in the reception room but in a room containing two crude hutch-like cages—one cage each for the prisoner and his / her visitor—separated by a space patrolled by a warder. However, in July 1896 Wilde successfully petitioned the home secretary to be allowed to discuss business matters with friends in the reception room, not the cage.

3. This visit was from Wilde's lawyer, Arthur D. Hansell, who had brought with him a copy of the separation agreement between Wilde and his wife, Constance, for the former to sign. One warder later stated that, unbeknownst to her husband, Constance was present and, through a peephole in the door, secretly witnessed her husband signing the document that effectively ended their marriage. There exists no independent evidence to corroborate the warder's account.

4. Wilde was imprisoned from 4 July to 20 November 1895 in London's Wandsworth Prison, which he later described as the worst of his five prisons (for a description of his time at Wandsworth, see Nicholas Frankel, *Oscar Wilde: The Unrepentant Years* [Cambridge, MA: Harvard University Press, 2017], 44–50). Until the creation of the Borstal system for young offenders in 1908, children and youths were imprisoned in adult jails. In all, 173 children under twelve years old were imprisoned in Britain from 1895 to 1897, the vast majority of them boys, along with another 4,981 children aged twelve to sixteen. Over the next decade these numbers declined steadily, to just four and 724 respectively in 1907. Records of the number of children admitted to Reading Prison during Wilde's time no longer survive, but according to Peter Stoneley, twenty-two children under the age of sixteen were admitted to Reading Prison in the roughly two-year period up till late 1894, including two under the age of twelve (" 'Looking at the Others': Oscar Wilde and the Reading Gaol Archive." *Journal of Victorian Culture* 19 [2014]: 470).

5. On seeing the three children, Wilde had written a contraband note to Martin asking, "Please find out for me ... the names of the children who are in for the rabbits, and the amount of the fine. Can I pay this, and get them out? If so I will get them out tomorrow. Please, dear friend, do this for me. I must get them out. Think what a thing for me it would be to be able to help the three little children. . . . If I can do this by paying the fine, tell the children that they are to be released tomorrow by a friend, and ask them to be happy, and not to tell anyone" (CL 831).

6. Ezzelino (or "Eccolino") da Romano (1192–1259) was a despot who ruled much of northern Italy in the mid-thirteenth century. His crimes were made legendary by poets after his death, and he lurks as a monstrous presence in the works of Byron and Dante. In *The Picture of Dorian Gray*, Wilde says that Ezzelino's "melancholy could be cured only by the spectacle of death" and that he "had a passion for red blood, as other men have for red wine" (*The Picture of Dorian Gray: An Annotated Uncensored Edition*, ed. Nicholas Frankel [Cambridge, MA: Harvard University Press, 2016], 208). See also p. 342, n.50 below.

7. That is, the prison commissioners.

8. Wilde had long protested the cruelty of well-intentioned officials. In "The Soul of Man under Socialism," he had written that "as one reads history … one is absolutely sickened, not by the crimes that the wicked have committed, but by the punishments that the good have inflicted; and a community is infinitely more brutalized by the habitual employment of punishment than it is by the occasional occurrence of crime" (*Criticism: "Historical Criticism," "Intentions," "The Soul of Man,"* ed. Josephine Guy, vol. 4 of *The Complete Works of Oscar Wilde* [Oxford: Oxford University Press, 2007], 244–45).

9. The so-called separate system, first introduced at Pentonville Prison in 1842 and extended to all English prisons in 1865, mandated that, regardless of age or sex, prisoners be housed each in a separate cell, where they must maintain absolute silence, forbidden to communicate with one another upon pain of further punishment. The system amounted to a sentence of solitary confinement for the full extent of the prisoner's jail term.

of pain gave a real madness of pleasure. But men of the stamp of Eccelin are merely abnormal types of perverted individualism. Ordinary cruelty is simply stupidity. It is the entire want of imagination. It is the result in our days of stereotyped systems, of hard-and-fast rules, and of stupidity. Wherever there is centralisation there is stupidity. What is inhuman in modern life is officialism. Authority is as destructive to those who exercise it as it is to those on whom it is exercised. It is the Prison Board,[7] and the system that it carries out, that is the primary source of the cruelty that is exercised on a child in prison. The people who uphold the system have excellent intentions.[8] Those who carry it out are humane in intention also. Responsibility is shifted on to the disciplinary regulations. It is supposed that because a thing is the rule it is right.

The present treatment of children is terrible, primarily from people not understanding the peculiar psychology of a child's nature. A child can understand a punishment inflicted by an individual, such as a parent or guardian, and bear it with a certain amount of acquiescence. What it cannot understand is a punishment inflicted by society. It cannot realise what society is. With grown people it is, of course, the reverse. Those of us who are either in prison or have been sent there, can understand, and do understand, what that collective force called society means, and whatever we may think of its methods or claims, we can force ourselves to accept it. Punishment inflicted on us by an individual, on the other hand, is a thing that no grown person endures, or is expected to endure.

The child consequently, being taken away from its parents by people whom it has never seen, and of whom it knows nothing, and finding itself in a lonely and unfamiliar cell,[9] waited on by strange faces, and ordered about and punished by the representatives of a system that it cannot understand, becomes an immediate prey to the first and most prominent emotion produced by modern prison life—the emotion of terror. The terror of a child in prison is quite limitless. I remember once in Reading, as I was going out to exercise, seeing in the dimly lit cell right opposite my own a small boy. Two warders—not unkindly men—were talking to him, with some sternness apparently, or perhaps giving him some useful

10. Awaiting his trial date.

11. With its provision of shelter and basic food, prison offered a last-ditch alternative to starvation for destitute and homeless prisoners. The "entirely ignorant" justices and magistrates may have been conscious of this fact when remanding destitute children in custody.

12. An important, if indirect, expression of the terror experienced by Wilde himself in the course of the first fourteen months of his prison sentence. As Jack London later wrote, "Oscar Wilde, God rest his soul, voices the cry of the prison child, which, in varying degree, is the cry of the prison man and woman" (*People of the Abyss* [London: Macmillan, 1903], 292).

13. Founded in 1884 as the London Society for the Prevention of Cruelty to Children, the National Society for the Prevention of Cruelty to Children (now known by its acronym NSPCC) was established in 1889 and received a Royal Charter in 1895.

advice about his conduct. One was in the cell with him, the other was standing outside. The child's face was like a white wedge of sheer terror. There was in his eyes the terror of a hunted animal. The next morning I heard him at breakfast-time crying, and calling to be let out. His cry was for his parents. From time to time I could hear the deep voice of the warder on duty telling him to keep quiet. Yet he was not even convicted of whatever little offence he had been charged with. He was simply on remand.[10] That I knew by his wearing his own clothes, which seemed neat enough. He was, however, wearing prison socks and shoes. This showed that he was a very poor boy, whose own shoes, if he had any, were in a bad state. Justices and magistrates, an entirely ignorant class as a rule, often remand children for a week, and then perhaps remit whatever sentence they are entitled to pass. They call this 'not sending a child to prison.' It is, of course, a stupid view on their part.[11] To a little child, whether he is in prison on remand or after conviction is not a subtlety of social position he can comprehend. To him the horrible thing is to be there at all. In the eyes of humanity it should be a horrible thing for him to be there at all.

This terror that seizes and dominates the child, as it seizes the grown man also,[12] is of course intensified beyond power of expression by the solitary cellular system of our prisons. Every child is confined to its cell for twenty-three hours out of the twenty-four. This is the appalling thing. To shut up a child in a dimly lit cell, for twenty-three hours out of the twenty-four, is an example of the cruelty of stupidity. If an individual, parent or guardian, did this to a child, he would be severely punished. The Society for the Prevention of Cruelty to Children would take the matter up at once.[13] There would be on all hands the utmost detestation of whomsoever had been guilty of such cruelty. A heavy sentence would, undoubtedly, follow conviction. But our own actual society does worse itself, and to the child to be so treated by a strange abstract force, of whose claims it has no cognisance, is much worse than it would be to receive the same treatment from its father or mother, or some one it knew. The inhuman treatment of a child is always inhuman, by whomsoever it is

14. A thin gruel consisting of coarse meal, suet, greasy cocoa, and water.

15. Reading Prison, constructed in 1844 and modeled closely on London's Pentonville Prison, contained multiple cell blocks, arranged in stories or "galleries," radiating from a central hallway. The prison architecture was designed to accommodate the separate system of solitary confinement in individual cells. The prison was decommissioned in 2013.

inflicted. But inhuman treatment by society is to the child the more terrible because there is no appeal. A parent or guardian can be moved, and let out a child from the dark lonely room in which it is confined. But a warder cannot. Most warders are very fond of children. But the system prohibits them from rendering the child any assistance. Should they do so, as Warder Martin did, they are dismissed.

The second thing from which a child suffers in prison is hunger. The food that is given to it consists of a piece of usually badly-baked prison bread and a tin of water for breakfast at half-past seven. At twelve o'clock it gets dinner, composed of a tin of coarse Indian meal stirabout,[14] and at half-past five it gets a piece of dry bread and a tin of water for its supper. This diet in the case of a strong grown man is always productive of illness of some kind, chiefly of course diarrhœa, with its attendant weakness. In fact in a big prison astringent medicines are served out regularly by the warders as a matter of course. In the case of a child, the child is, as a rule, incapable of eating the food at all. Anyone who knows anything about children knows how easily a child's digestion is upset by a fit of crying, or trouble and mental distress of any kind. A child who has been crying all day long, and perhaps half the night, in a lonely dimly-lit cell, and is preyed upon by terror, simply cannot eat food of this coarse, horrible kind. In the case of the little child to whom Warder Martin gave the biscuits, the child was crying with hunger on Tuesday morning, and utterly unable to eat the bread and water served to it for its breakfast. Martin went out after the breakfasts had been served, and bought the few sweet biscuits for the child rather than see it starving. It was a beautiful action on his part, and was so recognised by the child, who, utterly unconscious of the regulation of the Prison Board, told one of the senior warders how kind this junior warder had been to him. The result was, of course, a report and a dismissal.

I know Martin extremely well, and I was under his charge for the last seven weeks of my imprisonment. On his appointment at Reading he had charge of Gallery C,[15] in which I was confined, so I saw him constantly. I was struck by the singular kindness and humanity of the way in which

W. F. Poulton, lithograph of interior of Reading Prison (East Wing), 1846.

he spoke to me and to the other prisoners. Kind words are much in prison, and a pleasant "Good-morning" or "Good-evening" will make one as happy as one can be in a prison. He was always gentle and considerate. I happen to know another case in which he showed great kindness to one of the prisoners, and I have no hesitation in mentioning it. One of the most horrible things in prison is the badness of the sanitary arrangements. No prisoner is allowed under any circumstances to leave his cell after half-past five p.m. If, consequently, he is suffering from diarrhœa, he has to use his cell as a latrine, and pass the night in a most fetid and unwholesome atmosphere. Some days before my release Martin was going the rounds at half-past seven with one of the senior warders for the purpose of collecting the oakum and tools of the prisoners. A man just convicted, and suffering from violent diarrhœa in consequence of the food, as is always the case, asked the senior warder to allow him to empty the slops in his cell on account of the horrible odour of the cell and the possibility of illness again in the night. The senior warder refused absolutely; it was against the rules. The man had to pass the night in this dreadful condition. Martin, however, rather than see this wretched man in such a loathsome predicament, said he would empty the man's slops himself, and did so. A warder emptying a prisoner's slops is, of course, against the rules, but Martin did this act of kindness to the man out of the simple humanity of his nature, and the man was naturally most grateful.

As regards the children, a great deal has been talked and written lately about the contaminating influence of prison on young children. What is said is quite true. A child is utterly contaminated by prison life. But the contaminating influence is not that of the prisoners. It is that of the whole prison system—of the governor, the chaplain, the warders, the lonely cell, the isolation, the revolting food, the rules of the Prison Commissioners, the mode of discipline as it is termed, of the life. Every care is taken to isolate a child from the sight even of all prisoners over sixteen years of age. Children sit behind a curtain in chapel, and are sent to take exercise in small sunless yards—sometimes a stone-yard, sometimes a yard at the back of the mills—rather than that they should see the elder prisoners at

16. Thomas Carlyle, *Shooting Niagara: And After?* (London: Chapman and Hall, 1867), in which Carlyle writes of "the silent charm of rhythmic human companionship" (49).

exercise. But the only really humanising influence in prison is the influence of the prisoners. Their cheerfulness under terrible circumstances, their sympathy for each other, their humility, their gentleness, their pleasant smiles of greeting when they meet each other, their complete acquiescence in their punishments, are all quite wonderful, and I myself learned many sound lessons from them. I am not proposing that the children should not sit behind a curtain in chapel, or that they should take exercise in a corner of the common yard. I am merely pointing out that the bad influence on children is not, and could never be, that of the prisoners, but is, and will always remain, that of the prison system itself. There is not a single man in Reading Gaol that would not gladly have done the three children's punishment for them. When I saw them last it was on the Tuesday following their conviction. I was taking exercise at half-past eleven with about twelve other men, as the three children passed near us, in charge of a warder, from the damp, dreary stone-yard in which they had been at their exercise. I saw the greatest pity and sympathy in the eyes of my companions as they looked at them. Prisoners are, as a class, extremely kind and sympathetic to each other. Suffering and the community of suffering makes people kind, and day after day as I tramped the yard I used to feel with pleasure and comfort what Carlyle calls somewhere "the silent rhythmic charm of human companionship."[16] In this, as in all other things, philanthropists and people of that kind are astray. It is not the prisoners who need reformation. It is the prisons.

Of course no child under fourteen years of age should be sent to prison at all. It is an absurdity, and, like many absurdities, of absolutely tragic results. If, however, they are to be sent to prison, during the daytime they should be in a workshop or schoolroom with a warder. At night they should sleep in a dormitory, with a night-warder to look after them. They should be allowed exercise for at least three hours a day. The dark, badly ventilated, ill-smelling prison cells are dreadful for a child, dreadful indeed for any one. One is always breathing bad air in prison. The food given to children should consist of tea and bread-and-butter and soup. Prison soup is very good and wholesome. A resolution of the House of

17. By the mid-1800s, there were two distinct systems of imprisonment in operation in England. By "ordinary gaols," Wilde means the network of local prisons owned and administered by local and county magistrates, which housed prisoners sentenced to terms of up to two years, as distinct from nine large government-run prisons (called "convict prisons"), the foremost of which were London's Pentonville and Millbank Prisons. "Convict prisons" housed longer-term prisoners, who would in a previous era have been committed for transportation (banished to a penal settlement overseas). Although practical differences between the two systems blurred toward the end of the century, and Millbank was demolished in 1893, the distinction between "local" and "convict" prisons was formalized by the 1865 Prison Act and remained in place until 1948.

Commons could settle the treatment of children in half an hour. I hope you will use your influence to have this done. The way that children are treated at present is really an outrage on humanity and common sense. It comes from stupidity.

Let me draw attention now to another terrible thing that goes on in English prisons, indeed in prisons all over the world where the system of silence and cellular confinement is practised. I refer to the large number of men who become insane or weak-minded in prison. In convict prisons this is, of course, quite common; but in ordinary gaols also, such as that I was confined in, it is to be found.[17]

About three months ago I noticed amongst the prisoners who took exercise with me a young man who seemed to me to be silly or half-witted. Every prison, of course, has its half-witted clients, who return again and again, and may be said to live in the prison. But this young man struck me as being more than usually half-witted on account of his silly grin and idiotic laughter to himself, and the peculiar restlessness of his eternally twitching hands. He was noticed by all the other prisoners on account of the strangeness of his conduct. From time to time he did not appear at exercise, which showed me that he was being punished by confinement to his cell. Finally, I discovered that he was under observation, and being watched night and day by warders. When he did appear at exercise he always seemed hysterical, and used to walk round crying or laughing. At chapel he had to sit right under the observation of two warders, who carefully watched him all the time. Sometimes he would bury his head in his hands, an offence against the chapel regulations, and his head would be immediately struck up by a warder so that he should keep his eyes fixed permanently in the direction of the Communion-table. Sometimes he would cry—not making any disturbance—but with tears streaming down his face and an hysterical throbbing in the throat. Sometimes he would grin idiot-like to himself and make faces. He was on more than one occasion sent out of chapel to his cell, and of course he was continually punished. As the bench on which I used to sit in chapel was directly behind the bench at the end of which this unfortunate man

18. In the chapter of Sherard's *Life of Oscar Wilde* titled "The Poet in Prison" purportedly written by Martin, the latter states that Wilde kept his tins scrupulously clean "and in the mornings, after he had arranged them in their regulated order, he would step back, and view them with an air of child-like complacency" ([Thomas Martin], "The Poet in Prison" (1906), repr. in *Oscar Wilde: Interviews and Recollections*, ed. E. H. Mikhail [London: Macmillan, 1979], 2:332).

19. The minutes of the Reading Prison Visiting Committee confirm that on 15 May 1897 prisoner A 2. 11., named James Edward Prince, was "sentenced to 24 strokes of the birch rod over malingering" (quoted in Stoneley, "'Looking at the Others,'" 469). According to Anthony Stokes, the flogging would have taken place not in the basement but on the landing of cellblock B1, next to the dark cells, in the presence of the governor and the chief medical officer: "the prisoner was strapped to a wooden frame, his . . . hands were secured and with the prisoner facing the medical officer, the punishment would be carried out" (*Pit of Shame*, 49).

20. Prisoners exercised in the prison yard by walking in concentric rings, with the old and infirm in the center, supervised closely by the warders.

21. Reading Prison's A-yard, used principally for stone breaking and, in a previous era, for exercising imprisoned debtors.

was placed I had full opportunity of observing him. I also saw him, of course, at exercise continually, and I saw that he was becoming insane, and was being treated as if he was shamming.

On Saturday week last I was in my cell at about one o'clock occupied in cleaning and polishing the tins I had been using for dinner.[18] Suddenly I was startled by the prison silence being broken by the most horrible and revolting shrieks, or rather howls, for at first I thought some animal like a bull or a cow was being unskilfully slaughtered outside the prison walls. I soon realised, however, that the howls proceeded from the basement of the prison, and I knew that some wretched man was being flogged. I need not say how hideous and terrible it was for me, and I began to wonder who it was who was being punished in this revolting manner. Suddenly it dawned upon me that they might be flogging this unfortunate lunatic.[19] My feelings on the subject need not be chronicled; they have nothing to do with the question. The next day, Sunday 16th, I saw the poor fellow at exercise, his weak, ugly, wretched face bloated by tears and hysteria almost beyond recognition. He walked in the centre ring along with the old men, the beggars, and the lame people, so that I was able to observe him the whole time.[20] It was my last Sunday in prison, a perfectly lovely day, the finest day we had had the whole year, and there, in the beautiful sunlight, walked this poor creature—made once in the image of God—grinning like an ape, and making with his hands the most fantastic gestures, as though he was playing in the air on some invisible stringed instrument, or arranging and dealing counters in some curious game. All the while these hysterical tears, without which none of us ever saw him, were making soiled runnels on his white swollen face. The hideous and deliberate grace of his gestures made him like an antic. He was a living grotesque. The other prisoners all watched him, and not one of them smiled. Everybody knew what had happened to him, and that he was being driven insane—was insane already. After half an hour he was ordered in by the warder, and, I suppose, punished. At least he was not at exercise on Monday, though I think I caught sight of him at the corner of the stone-yard,[21] walking in charge of a warder.

22. A multi-tailed whip.

23. Wilde's informant was probably Martin. On Monday, 17 May 1897, the day before he left Reading Prison, Wilde asked Martin "Please find out for me the name of A. 2. 11" (*CL* 831).

On the Tuesday—my last day in prison—I saw him at exercise. He was worse than before, and again was sent in. Since then I know nothing of him, but I found out from one of the prisoners who walked with me at exercise that he had had twenty-four lashes in the cookhouse on Saturday afternoon, by order of the visiting justices on the report of the doctor. The howls that had horrified us all were his.

This man is undoubtedly becoming insane. Prison doctors have no knowledge of mental disease of any kind. They are as a class ignorant men. The pathology of the mind is unknown to them. When a man grows insane, they treat him as shamming. They have him punished again and again. Naturally the man becomes worse. When ordinary punishments are exhausted, the doctor reports the case to the justices. The result is flogging. Of course the flogging is not done with a cat-of-nine-tails.[22] It is what is called birching. The instrument is a rod; but the result on the wretched half-witted man may be imagined.

His number is, or was, A. 2. 11. I also managed to find out his name.[23] It is Prince. Something should be done at once for him. He is a soldier, and his sentence is one of court-martial. The term is six months. Three have yet to run.

May I ask you to use your influence to have this case examined into, and to see that the lunatic prisoner is properly treated?

No report by the Medical Commissioners is of any avail. It is not to be trusted. The medical inspectors do not seem to understand the difference between idiocy and lunacy—between the entire absence of a function or organ and the diseases of a function or organ. This man A. 2. 11. will, I have no doubt, be able to tell his name, the nature of his offence, the day of the month, the date of the beginning and expiration of his sentence, and answer any ordinary simple question; but that his mind is diseased admits of no doubt. At present it is a horrible duel between himself and the doctor. The doctor is fighting for a theory. The man is fighting for his life. I am anxious that the man should win. But let the whole case be examined into by experts who understand brain-disease, and by people of humane feelings who have still some common-sense and

24. For Major James O. Nelson (1859–1914), see p. 228, n.426 above.

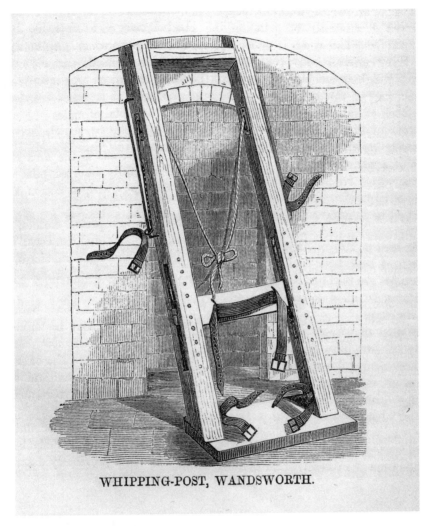

WHIPPING-POST, WANDSWORTH.

Prison whipping post, English, 1860s.

some pity. There is no reason that the sentimentalist should be asked to interfere. He always does harm.

The case is a special instance of the cruelty inseparable from a stupid system, for the present Governor of Reading is a man of gentle and humane character, greatly liked and respected by all the prisoners.[24] He was appointed in July last, and though he cannot alter the rules of the prison

25. Lieutenant-Colonel Henry B. Isaacson (1842–1915).

26. So dated by the *Daily Chronicle*, although the editors of Wilde's correspondence speculate that the letter was begun on or soon after 24 May 1897, when Martin's letter to the *Daily Chronicle* appeared.

system he has altered the spirit in which they used to be carried out under his predecessor.[25] He is very popular with the prisoners and with the warders. Indeed he has quite altered the whole tone of the prison life. Upon the other hand, the system is of course beyond his reach as far as altering its rules is concerned. I have no doubt that he sees daily much of what he knows to be unjust, stupid, and cruel. But his hands are tied. Of course I have no knowledge of his real views of the case of A. 2. 11., nor, indeed, of his views on our present system. I merely judge him by the complete change he brought about in Reading Prison. Under his predecessor the system was carried out with the greatest harshness and stupidity.—I remain, Sir, your obedient servant, OSCAR WILDE.

May 27.[26]

* *The Ballad of Reading Gaol* was begun soon after Wilde's release, in May 1897, "while he was still, psychologically, very much a convict" (Seamus Heaney, "Speranza in Reading: On 'The Ballad of Reading Gaol'" [1993], in his *The Redress of Poetry* [New York: Farrar, Straus and Giroux, 1995], 85), and it relates closely to Wilde's own experiences at Reading. As its dedication implies, it centers on the last days of Charles Thomas Wooldridge, a trooper in the Royal Horse Guards remanded at Reading Prison in April 1896 charged with murdering his wife. After being convicted and sentenced at the Berkshire Assizes on 17 June 1896, Wooldridge was executed by hanging within the prison walls on 7 July 1896.

As described in the Introduction, conditions in British prisons were widely regarded as intolerable in Wilde's day, and a parliamentary committee was established in 1894 to recommend improvements. In prison Wilde was acutely aware of the movement for prison reform and became determined "to write about prison life and to try and change it for others" (*The Complete Letters of Oscar Wilde*, ed. Merlin Holland and Rupert Hart-Davis [New York: Henry Holt, 2000], 798, hereafter cited in annotations as *CL*). Along with his letters to *The Daily Chronicle*, the poem played a small role in bringing about improvements eventually incorporated into the 1898 Prisons Act.

But the poem constitutes much "more … than a pamphlet on prison-reform" (*CL* 1019): it was Wilde's *"chant de cygne"* (swan song) and it "aims at eternity" (*CL* 918). It was first published in February 1898 under Wilde's Reading Prison cell number, C. 3. 3., partly because Wilde's name was felt to be publicly unmentionable. Wilde was quickly identified as the poem's author, but it was not till the seventh edition, published in June 1899, that his name was added to the title page. The first edition sold out within days, and within a few months the poem had run to six editions. It was the most popular of Wilde's books in his own lifetime.

Wilde's spelling "gaol" for "jail" was already becoming archaic in his own day, although this spelling persisted in British statutory and official documents long into the twentieth century.

1. "Obiit H. M. Prison" means "died at Her Majesty's Prison." Wilde originally intended including the following second dedication, to Robert Ross, but was persuaded by Ross to cut it while the book was in proof:

The Ballad of Reading Gaol[*]

In Memoriam
C. T. W.
Sometime Trooper of the Royal Horse Guards.
Obiit H. M. Prison, Reading, Berkshire
July 7th, 1896[1]

I

He did not wear his scarlet coat,[2]
    For blood and wine are red,[3]
And blood and wine were on his hands
    When they found him with the dead,
The poor dead woman whom he loved,
    And murdered in her bed.[4]

He walked amongst the Trial Men
    In a suit of shabby gray;
A cricket cap was on his head,
    And his step seemed light and gay;[5]
But I never saw a man who looked
    So wistfully at the day.

I never saw a man who looked
    With such a wistful eye
Upon that little tent of blue
    Which prisoners call the sky,
And at every drifting cloud that went
    With sails of silver by.

Dedication:
When I came out of prison some met me with garments
And with spices and others with wise counsel.
You met me with love.

2. Wilde employs artistic license here: the tunic of Wooldridge's regiment, the Royal Horse Guards, was blue, not red. When pressed on this point, Wilde purportedly replied, "I could hardly have written 'He did not wear his azure coat / For blood and wine are blue'" (quoted in Richard Ellmann, *Oscar Wilde* [New York: Knopf, 1988], 4). Wooldridge does not wear his regimental tunic because he is dressed in civilian clothes ("a suit of shabby gray"). See also n. 5 below.

3. The conjunction of blood and wine implies Holy Communion, prefiguring Wilde's later characterization of the condemned murderer as a Christlike figure, martyred for the sins of others.

4. Wooldridge murdered his wife on the open road, slashing her throat three times "in a very determined manner, she having excited his jealousy" (*Reading Mercury*, 10 July 1896, quoted in Stuart Mason [Christopher Millard], *Bibliography of Oscar Wilde* [London: T. Werner Laurie, 1914], 426).

5. After 1878 convicted felons wore crudely cut regulation uniforms stamped with broad black arrows, intended as a hindrance to escape and a mark of shame. They also wore a baseball-style cap, called a "Scottish cap," with a low stiff peak to prevent them from seeing or communicating with one another. By contrast, "Trial Men" (remand prisoners, unconvicted and awaiting trial) wore their own clothes and exercised in a different "ring." It is significant that the killer walks among the Trial Men wearing non-regulation clothing, with a cricket cap on his head and a step "light and gay"—details that imply innocence and a carefree spirit.

The

Ballad of Reading Gaol

By

C. 3. 3.

Leonard Smithers
Royal Arcade London W
Mdcccxcviii

"C. 3. 3." [Oscar Wilde], *The Ballad of Reading Gaol* (London: Leonard Smithers, 1898), title page.

6. That is, convicted criminals serving out their sentences, exercising separately from the Trial Men.

7. Prisoners were expected to exercise silently and separately from one another. The whispered remark "That fellow's got to swing" (meaning *that fellow's going to be hanged*) represents the first instance in the poem of the camaraderie among prisoners, as well as the contempt for prison regulations, that will become a marked feature of the poem's second half. The last hanging in Britain took place in 1964, and death by hanging was abolished for murder in 1969. But judicial hanging remained on the statute books in Britain until its abolition in 1998. In the early Victorian period, hangings took place in public. After 1868 they took place behind prison walls.

John Vassos, photolithographic illustration for Oscar Wilde, *The Ballad of Reading Gaol* (New York: E. P. Dutton & Co., Inc., 1928).

I walked, with other souls in pain,[6]
   Within another ring,
And was wondering if the man had done
   A great or little thing,
When a voice behind me whispered low,
   "That fellow's got to swing."[7]

Dear Christ! the very prison walls
   Suddenly seemed to reel,

8. A helmet.

9. "As for the divisions between the separate parts of each canto of the ballad, I want not asterisks, nor lines, but a little design of three flowers, or some decorative motive, simple and severe" (Wilde to his publisher Leonard Smithers, 4 September 1897). Smithers used fleurons in the first edition, not asterisks (as here), to mark divisions between the parts of each canto.

10. The poem's central, paradoxical, refrain echoes elements found in "A New Year's Song," by the Irish nationalist poet Denis MacCarthy (1817–1882), where McCarthy contrasts the bravery of those prepared to die for Ireland with the weakness of the "coward slave." But Wilde's refrain is also one of the frankest expressions in literature of the sadism, heartlessness, and self-destructiveness that often accompany love. A version of it appears as early as 1892 in Wilde's play *Lady Windermere's Fan* ("Love is easily killed! Oh, how easily love is killed!" [act 4, ll. 338–39]), although Wilde may have been thinking too of Anatole France's phrase "Je t'aime par ce que tu m'as perdu [I love you because you have annihilated me]," the penultimate sentence of "L'Humaine Tragédie [The Human Tragedy]," in France's story collection *Le Puits de Sainte-Claire* [*The Well of Saint Clare*] (Paris: Michel Levy, 1895), which Wilde read shortly after his release from prison. France's sentence contains "a terrible symbolic truth," Wilde wrote (*CL* 943). Wilde sometimes felt that his own life had been destroyed by his lover Lord Alfred Douglas—"the mere fact that he wrecked my life makes me love him" (*CL* 943), he wrote while composing the poem—and he was conscious too of the terrible price exacted on his close family members by his pursuit of young men.

11. Wilde finished *The Ballad of Reading Gaol* while he was living with Lord Alfred Douglas at Posillipo, near Naples, in the autumn of 1897: "I love him because he has ruined my life," he stated to friends who criticized him for returning to Douglas.

And the sky above my head became
    Like a casque of scorching steel;[8]
And, though I was a soul in pain,
    My pain I could not feel.

I only knew what hunted thought
    Quickened his step, and why
He looked upon the garish day
    With such a wistful eye;
The man had killed the thing he loved
    And so he had to die.

*[9]

Yet each man kills the thing he loves
    By each let this be heard,
Some do it with a bitter look,
    Some with a flattering word,
The coward does it with a kiss,
    The brave man with a sword![10]

Some kill their love when they are young,
    And some when they are old;
Some strangle with the hands of Lust,
    Some with the hands of Gold:
The kindest use a knife, because
    The dead so soon grow cold.

Some love too little, some too long,[11]
    Some sell, and others buy;
Some do the deed with many tears,
    And some without a sigh:
For each man kills the thing he loves,
    Yet each man does not die.

*

He does not die a death of shame
    On a day of dark disgrace,

12. The first of many mentions of the close supervision under which the condemned man was kept. The warders are on a suicide watch, determined to preserve the man's life in order that he might die at the appointed time.

13. "Exactly at 8 o'clock Wooldridge (who had submitted to the preliminary pinioning with marvellous firmness) was conducted from the condemned cell to the gallows, and took his stand under the beam almost as if he were 'on parade.' . . . The Rev. M. T. Friend [Chaplain], Mr. W. F. Bundy (Under Sheriff), Mr. O. C. Maurice (Surgeon) and Lieut.-Col. H. Isaacson (the Governor of the Gaol) were the only persons present besides the executioner and the warders" (*Reading Mercury*, 10 July 1896, quoted in Mason [Christopher Millard], *Bibliography of Oscar Wilde*, 427).

14. Wilde had originally written "the coarse-mouthed Doctor," but Chiswick Press, printer of *The Ballad of Reading Gaol*, was fearful of a libel action from Dr. Oliver Maurice, the doctor at Reading Gaol, and Wilde agreed to change the line despite insisting "I am describing a general scene with general types" (*CL* 983). The line "simply describes the *type* of prison-doctor in England," Wilde maintained. "As a class," Wilde writes in his second letter to the *Daily Chronicle* (p. 383 below), "I regard, and have always from my earliest youth regarded, doctors as by far the most humane profession in the community. But I must make an exception for prison doctors. They are . . . brutal in manner, coarse in temperament, and utterly indifferent to the health of the prisoners or their comfort."

Nor have a noose about his neck,
    Nor a cloth upon his face,
Nor drop feet foremost through the floor
    Into an empty place

He does not sit with silent men
    Who watch him night and day;[12]
Who watch him when he tries to weep,
    And when he tries to pray;
Who watch him lest himself should rob
    The prison of its prey.

He does not wake at dawn to see
    Dread figures throng his room,
The shivering Chaplain robed in white,
    The Sheriff stern with gloom,
And the Governor all in shiny black,
    With the yellow face of Doom.[13]

He does not rise in piteous haste
    To put on convict-clothes,
While some coarse-mouthed Doctor gloats, and notes
    Each new and nerve-twitched pose,
Fingering a watch whose little ticks
    Are like horrible hammer-blows.[14]

He does not feel that sickening thirst
    That sands one's throat, before
The hangman with his gardener's gloves
    Comes through the padded door,
And binds one with three leathern thongs,
    That the throat may thirst no more.

He does not bend his head to hear
    The Burial Office read,

15. "The shed in which people are hanged is a little shed with a glass roof, like a photographer's studio on the sands at Margate. For eighteen months I thought it *was* the studio for photographing prisoners. There is no adjective to describe it. I call it 'hideous' because it became so to me after I knew its use. In itself, it is a wooden, oblong, narrow shed with a glass roof" (*CL* 956–57). Until 1900, when a special "execution center" was constructed, the execution shed at Reading Prison also served as the photographic studio.

16. Caiaphas was the Roman-appointed Jewish high priest who supervised the Sanhedrin trial of Jesus for blasphemy, prior to handing him over to Pontius Pilate for secular judgment. In the Gospels of Matthew, Mark, and Luke, Judas Iscariot, not Caiaphas, kissed Christ in order to identify him to the Roman authorities. But Wilde meant the kiss of Caiaphas to convey a similar betrayal of intimacy and spiritual trust. "By 'Caiaphas' I do not mean the present Chaplain of Reading: he is a good-natured fool, one of the silliest of God's sheep: a typical clergyman in fact. I mean any priest of God who assists at the unjust and cruel punishments of man" (*CL* 983).

Nor, while the anguish of his soul
    Tells him he is not dead,
Cross his own coffin, as he moves
    Into the hideous shed.

He does not stare upon the air
    Through a little roof of glass:[15]
He does not pray with lips of clay
    For his agony to pass;
Nor feel upon his shuddering cheek
    The kiss of Caiaphas.[16]

II

Six weeks the guardsman walked the yard,
    In a suit of shabby gray:
His cricket cap was on his head,
    And his step was light and gay,
But I never saw a man who looked
    So wistfully at the day.

I never saw a man who looked
    With such a wistful eye
Upon that little tent of blue
    Which prisoners call the sky,
And at every wandering cloud that trailed
    Its ravelled fleeces by.

He did not wring his hands, as do
    Those witless men who dare
To try to rear the changeling Hope
    In the cave of black Despair:
He only looked upon the sun,
    And drank the morning air.

17. The killer, who has not yet been formally condemned, strives for sublimity, "drinking" the air and sun, and walking with a light "gay" step: his life-embracing attitude contrasts strikingly with the other prisoners.

18. Prisoners exercised by walking counterclockwise in concentric rings, organized by age and ability, with the oldest and most infirm in the center. See also Wilde's first letter to the *Daily Chronicle* (p. 305 above), where Wilde says, "Day after day as I tramped the yard, I used to feel ... what Carlyle calls somewhere 'the silent rhythmic charm of human companionship.'"

19. The guardsman's fellow prisoners lose themselves in wonder and sympathy. As Wilde remarks in his first letter to the *Daily Chronicle* (p. 305 above), "The only really humanizing influence in prison is the influence of the prisoners.... Prisoners are, as a class, extremely kind and sympathetic to each other. Suffering and the community of suffering makes people kind."

20. Before the manufacture of a specialized gallows, the condemned were usually hanged from an oak or elm tree, from one bough of which the leaves had been stripped. Wilde figuratively imagines the Reading gallows as such a tree: its leaflessness is a mark of its having been bitten at the root by an adder, and it will bear fruit only once it has borne a corpse.

21. The hangman's noose.

He did not wring his hands nor weep,
  Nor did he peek or pine,
But he drank the air as though it held
  Some healthful anodyne;
With open mouth he drank the sun
  As though it had been wine![17]

And I and all the souls in pain,
  Who tramped the other ring,[18]
Forgot if we ourselves had done
  A great or little thing,
And watched with gaze of dull amaze
  The man who had to swing.[19]

For strange it was to see him pass
  With a step so light and gay,
And strange it was to see him look
  So wistfully at the day,
And strange it was to think that he
  Had such a debt to pay.

*

The oak and elm have pleasant leaves
  That in the spring-time shoot:
But grim to see is the gallows-tree,
  With its adder-bitten root,
And, green or dry, a man must die
  Before it bears its fruit![20]

The loftiest place is the seat of grace
  For which all worldlings try:
But who would stand in hempen band[21]
  Upon a scaffold high,
And through a murderer's collar take
  His last look at the sky?

22. This stanza has often been criticized by readers who admire the poem's grim realism. Shortly after composing it, Wilde told Robert Ross that it was "very good—[although] in the romantic vein that you don't quite approve of, but . . . I can't always be 'banging the tins'" (*CL* 954).

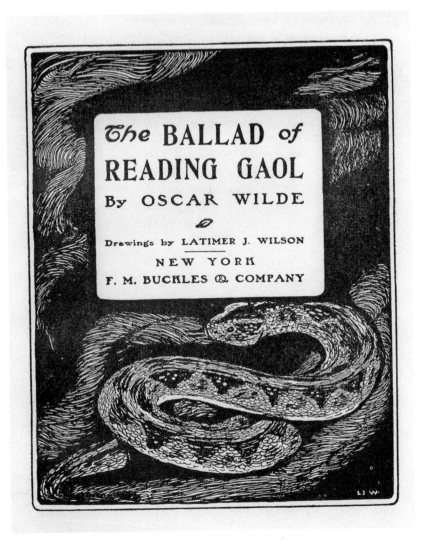

Oscar Wilde, *The Ballad of Reading Gaol,* drawings by Latimer J. Wilson (New York: F. M. Buckles & Co., 1907), title page.

> It is sweet to dance to violins
>   When Love and Life are fair:
> To dance to flutes, to dance to lutes
>   Is delicate and rare:
> But it is not sweet with nimble feet
>   To dance upon the air![22]

23. The day of the killer's trial has arrived: Wooldridge was convicted quickly and sentenced on 17 June 1896.

24. Following his death sentence, the condemned prisoner was isolated from other prisoners. He exercised separately, in a yard previously used for exercising imprisoned debtors, Wilde tells us in the next canto, and he was imprisoned in a separate "condemned cell."

Garrick Palmer, wood-engraved illustration for Oscar Wilde, *The Ballad of Reading Gaol* (Llandogo, Gwent: The Old Stile Press, 1994).

So with curious eyes and sick surmise
    We watched him day by day,
And wondered if each one of us
    Would end the self-same way,
For none can tell to what red Hell
    His sightless soul may stray.

            *

At last the dead man walked no more
    Amongst the Trial Men,
And I knew that he was standing up
    In the black dock's dreadful pen,[23]
And that never would I see his face
    For weal or woe again.[24]

Like two doomed ships that pass in storm
    We had crossed each other's way:
But we made no sign, we said no word,
    We had no word to say;

25. Although imprisoned for a lesser crime, the speaker claims kinship with the murderer: they are both "outcast men," scorned by God and society.

26. A metal trap.

27. Prior to the abolition of imprisonment for debt in 1869, debtors exercised in Reading Prison's A-yard, separately from other categories of prisoner. The yard was later used for stone breaking as a form of hard labor, and its fifty-foot east-facing wall, in almost permanent shadow, would be dripping with condensation and algae (Anthony Stokes, *Pit of Shame: The Real Ballad of Reading Gaol* [Winchester, UK: Waterside, 2007], 109).

28. Wilde capitalized the "w" of "warder" and "warders" here and throughout in the second edition.

29. The 1865 Prison Act, which brought local prisons under central government control, set up an elaborate code of rules for the governance of prisons. Isaacson, the governor of Reading Prison, "believed in the 1865 Act . . . and he had no intention of relaxing discipline" (Ellmann, *Oscar Wilde*, 505).

30. See Wilde's description, in his first letter to the *Daily Chronicle* (p. 311 above), of the "horrible duel" between a fellow prisoner going slowly insane and the Reading prison doctor, who, convinced that he was shamming, repeatedly ordered the prisoner to be flogged: "The doctor is fighting for a theory. The man is fighting for his life. I am anxious that the man should win."

31. As Wilde writes in his second letter to the *Daily Chronicle* (p. 383 below), "Prison chaplains are entirely useless. They are, as a class, well-meaning, but foolish, indeed silly men. They are of no help to any prisoner."

32. Dietary regulations were relaxed, and indulgences such as tobacco and beer were often given to the condemned prisoner awaiting execution. "It would be cruelty to withhold the comfort of a smoke from the man who is on the brink of the grave," remarked Arthur Griffiths, a prison inspector with responsibility for overseeing execution arrangements: "I invariably recommended the issue of tobacco. Stimulants might be and were given, even on the very morning of the dread ceremony" (quoted in Philip Priestley, *Victorian Prison Lives: English Prison Biography 1830–1914* [London: Methuen, 1985], 241).

For we did not meet in the holy night,
    But in the shameful day.

A prison wall was round us both,
    Two outcast men we were:
The world had thrust us from its heart,
    And God from out His care:[25]
And the iron gin[26] that waits for Sin
    Had caught us in its snare.

III

In Debtors' Yard the stones are hard,
    And the dripping wall is high,[27]
So it was there he took the air
    Beneath the leaden sky,
And by each side a warder walked,[28]
    For fear the man might die.

Or else he sat with those who watched
    His anguish night and day;
Who watched him when he rose to weep,
    And when he crouched to pray;
Who watched him lest himself should rob
    Their scaffold of its prey.

The Governor was strong upon
    The Regulations Act:[29]
The Doctor said that Death was but
    A scientific fact:[30]
And twice a day the Chaplain called
    And left a little tract.[31]

And twice a day he smoked his pipe,
    And drank his quart of beer:[32]

33. Wooldridge met his fate with remarkable equanimity. Despite a number of clemency petitions on his behalf (even the jury that convicted him called for leniency), Wooldridge petitioned the home secretary that his execution be allowed to proceed unchallenged.

34. Two warders would accompany the condemned man for twenty-four hours a day, eating and sleeping with him "lest himself should rob / Their scaffold of its prey." A group of six warders would take turns doing this in pairs until twenty minutes before the appointed time of execution, when two new and impartial warders would take over: "this was to prevent the phenomenon known as 'conditioning,' whereby an officer might, through physical proximity to the condemned person, begin to empathise with him ... and thus maybe seek to intervene to prevent the law taking its course" (Stokes, *Pit of Shame*, 57).

His soul was resolute, and held
  No hiding-place for fear;
He often said that he was glad
  The hangman's day was near.[33]

But why he said so strange a thing
  No warder dared to ask:
For he to whom a watcher's doom
  Is given as his task,
Must set a lock upon his lips,
  And make his face a mask.

Or else he might be moved, and try
  To comfort or console:
And what should Human Pity do
  Pent up in Murderers' Hole?
What word of grace in such a place
  Could help a brother's soul?[34]

*

With slouch and swing around the ring
  We trod the Fools' Parade!
We did not care: we knew we were
  The Devil's Own Brigade:
And shaven head and feet of lead
  Make a merry masquerade.

We tore the tarry rope to shreds
  With blunt and bleeding nails;
We rubbed the doors, and scrubbed the floors,
  And cleaned the shining rails:
And, rank by rank, we soaped the plank,
  And clattered with the pails.

We sewed the sacks, we broke the stones,
  We turned the dusty drill:

35. This stanza and the preceding one describe the appalling prison regime of "hard labor, hard board, and hard fare" experienced by Wilde and other prisoners personally. The "tarry rope," "sacks," "drill," and "mill" are the oakum-picking, mail sacks, mechanical crank, and treadmill at which prisoners sentenced to "hard labor" were made to work. (Wilde's own fingernails were broken and bleeding from "tearing the tarry rope," Robert Sherard noticed upon visiting his friend in prison [*Life of Oscar Wilde* (New York: Mitchell Kennerley, 1906), 373]). The "plank" is the hard plank bed on which prisoners were expected to sleep and which, along with everything else in their cells, they were expected to clean upon rising at six each morning. The "tins" are the metal dishes in which coarse bread and "stirabout" (a watery gruel of dubious nutritional value) were served as food. Prisoners "bawl" the hymns because attendance at chapel was mandatory and "just part of one's punishment" (Stuart Wood, *Shades of the Prison House* [1932], quoted in Priestley, *Victorian Prison Lives*, 93). For further details of the punishments exacted on prisoners by hard labor, see H. Montgomery Hyde, *Oscar Wilde: The Aftermath* (New York: Farrar Strauss, 1963), 8–9, and C. Harding et al., *Imprisonment in England and Wales* (London: Croom Helm, 1985), "Appendix 3: A Note on Hard Labor in Nineteenth Century Prisons," 301–3.

36. Wilde implies that the condemned man's sentence is a form of bloodlust.

37. Wilde changed "The fellow" to "Some prisoner" for the second edition.

38. Prisoners were identified by and with the numbered cell ("tomb") in which they spent twenty-three hours each day, in silence and in isolation from one another. For the second edition of the poem, Wilde altered these lines to "And each man trembled as he crept / Into his numbered tomb."

39. Compare with Thomas Hood's "Dream of Eugene Aram" (1831):

> All night I lay in agony,
> In anguish dark and deep,
> My fevered eyes I dared not close,
> But stared aghast at Sleep:
> For Sin had rendered unto her
> The keys of hell to keep.

(*Poems* [New York: Putnam, 1872], 109.)

We banged the tins, and bawled the hymns,
    And sweated on the mill:[35]
But in the heart of every man
    Terror was lying still.

So still it lay that every day
    Crawled like a weed-clogged wave:
And we forgot the bitter lot
    That waits for fool and knave,
Till once, as we tramped in from work,
    We passed an open grave.

With yawning mouth the horrid hole
    Gaped for a living thing;
The very mud cried out for blood
    To the thirsty asphalte ring:[36]
And we knew that ere one dawn grew fair
    The fellow had to swing.[37]

Right in we went, with soul intent
    On Death and Dread and Doom:
The hangman, with his little bag,
    Went shuffling through the gloom
And I trembled as I groped my way
    Into my numbered tomb.[38]

*

That night the empty corridors
    Were full of forms of Fear,
And up and down the iron town
    Stole feet we could not hear,
And through the bars that hide the stars
    White faces seemed to peer.[39]

He lay as one who lies and dreams
    In a pleasant meadow-land,

40. The condemned man's indifference to his fate, like the sweetness of his sleep, raises him to a level above his fellow mortals. He will be likened later in the poem to Christ, suffering crucifixion for the sins of mankind. In some respects he also exemplifies the "pale criminal" whom Friedrich Nietzsche holds to be an *ubermensch* or "superman," transcending mankind's usual self-preserving instincts in order to point a new direction forward for humanity. Nietzsche writes that out of the criminal's eyes "speaks the great contempt," for he judges himself less hypocritically than his accusers do, and "there is no redemption for one who suffers so of himself, except a quick death" (*This Spoke Zarathustra* in *The Portable Nietzsche*, ed. and trans. Walter Kaufmann [Harmondsworth: Penguin, 1976], 149, 150).

41. Warders wore felt-soled shoes so as to maintain the regime of absolute silence.

42. Corpse.

43. Jesus was given a sponge filled with vinegar or "bitter wine" to assuage his thirst while suffering on the cross (Matthew 27:48).

44. According to the Gospels, during the Last Supper Jesus predicted that the Apostle Peter would deny him three times "before the rooster crows twice."

The watcher watched him as he slept,
    And could not understand
How one could sleep so sweet a sleep
    With a hangman close at hand.[40]

But there is no sleep when men must weep
    Who never yet have wept:
So we—the fool, the fraud, the knave—
    That endless vigil kept,
And through each brain on hands of pain
    Another's terror crept.

*

Alas! it is a fearful thing
    To feel another's guilt!
For, right within, the sword of Sin
    Pierced to its poisoned hilt,
And as molten lead were the tears we shed
    For the blood we had not spilt.

The warders with their shoes of felt[41]
    Crept by each padlocked door,
And peeped and saw, with eyes of awe,
    Gray figures on the floor,
And wondered why men knelt to pray
    Who never prayed before.

All through the night we knelt and prayed,
    Mad mourners of a corse![42]
The troubled plumes of midnight shook
    Like the plumes upon a hearse:
And as bitter wine upon a sponge
    Was the savour of Remorse.[43]

*

The gray cock crew, the red cock crew,[44]
    But never came the day:

45. A lively dance in 2/4 time for two people.

46. Grimaces.

47. A slow and stately Spanish dance in triple time.

48. Arabesques are shapes characterized by flowing lines and curving or scroll-like forms. In dance, an arabesque is "a position in which the dancer stands on one leg, with the other leg extended behind with the knee straight and the foot pointed" (*Oxford English Dictonary*).

49. In their "grisly masque," the crooked shapes of Terror recall the ghostly dancers of Wilde's poem "The Harlot's House":

> Like strange mechanical grotesques,
> Making fantastic arabesques,
> The shadows raced across the blind.
>
> We watched the ghostly dancers spin
> To sound of horn and violin,
> Like black leaves wheeling in the wind.
>
> Like wire-pulled automatons,
> Slim silhouetted skeletons
> Went sidling through the slow quadrille.
>
> Then took each other by the hand,
> And danced a stately saraband;
> Their laughter echoed thin and shrill.

(*Poems and Poems in Prose*, ed. Bobby Fong and Karl Beckson, vol. 1 of *The Complete Works of Oscar Wilde* [Oxford: Oxford University Press, 2000], 161.)

50. Wilde had employed the myth of gambling at dice with the devil (or "Sin") less metaphorically in *Dorian Gray*, where he refers to the Renaissance despot Ezzelino da Romano "cheating his father at dice, when gambling with him for his own soul" (*The Picture of Dorian Gray: An Annotated Uncensored Edition*, ed. Nicholas Frankel [Cambridge, MA: Harvard University Press, 2016], 208). He borrowed the myth from Vernon Lee's *Euphorion*, where Lee had expressed skepticism about "such popular legends as gave to Ezzelin the Fiend for a father, and Death and Sin for

And crooked shapes of Terror crouched,
    In the corners where we lay:
And each evil sprite that walks by night
    Before us seemed to play.

They glided past, they glided fast,
    Like travellers through a mist:
They mocked the moon in a rigadoon[45]
    Of delicate turn and twist,
And with formal pace and loathsome grace
    The phantoms kept their tryst.

With mop and mow,[46] we saw them go,
    Slim shadows hand in hand:
About, about, in ghostly rout
    They trod a saraband:[47]
And the damned grotesques made arabesques,[48]
    Like the wind upon the sand!

With the pirouettes of marionettes,
    They tripped on pointed tread:
But with flutes of Fear they filled the ear,
    As their grisly masque they led,
And loud they sang, and long they sang,
    For they sang to wake the dead.[49]

"Oho!" they cried, "The world is wide,
    But fettered limbs go lame!
And once, or twice, to throw the dice
    Is a gentlemanly game,
But he does not win who plays with Sin
    In the secret House of Shame."[50]

                    *

No things of air these antics were
    That frolicked with such glee:

adversaries at dice" (*Euphorion: Being Studies of the Antique and the Medieval in the Renaissance*, 2nd ed. [London: Fisher Unwin, 1885], 105).

51. Shackles.

52. A woman of doubtful reputation.

53. A steward; also a cathedral official.

54. One of several references to the lack of light and color in the prisoner's cell. Wilde wrote from prison that "the very sun and moon seem taken from us. Outside, the day may be blue and gold, but the light that creeps down the thickly-muffled glass of the small iron-barred window beneath which one sits is grey and niggard. It is always twilight in one's cell, as it is always midnight in one's heart" (*CL* 720). Stokes writes that "Wilde's cell was south-facing," and therefore Wilde "would have watched the shadow of his window bars, created by the morning sun, move across its white-washed inner walls, knowing that with every inch the prospect of a man's death came closer" (Stokes, *Pit of Shame*, 112).

To men whose lives were held in gyves,[51]
    And whose feet might not go free,
Ah! wounds of Christ! they were living things,
    Most terrible to see.

Around, around, they waltzed and wound;
    Some wheeled in smirking pairs:
With the mincing step of a demirep[52]
    Some sidled up the stairs:
And with subtle sneer, and fawning leer,
    Each helped us at our prayers.

*

The morning wind began to moan,
    But still the night went on:
Through its giant loom the web of gloom
    Crept till each thread was spun:
And, as we prayed, we grew afraid
    Of the Justice of the Sun.

The moaning wind went wandering round
    The weeping prison-wall:
Till like a wheel of turning-steel
    We felt the minutes crawl:
O moaning wind! what had we done
    To have such a seneschal?[53]

At last I saw the shadowed bars
    Like a lattice wrought in lead,
Move right across the whitewashed wall
    That faced my three-plank bed,
And I knew that somewhere in the world
    God's dreadful dawn was red.[54]

*

At six o'clock we cleaned our cells,
    At seven all was still,

55. A rushing or murmuring sound.

56. Although Reading Prison's execution chamber was fitted with a trapdoor, Wilde may be imagining that execution by hanging involves the removal ("sliding") of a plank or "board."

57. Wooldridge's hangman was James Billington, chief executioner of Great Britain from 1891 to 1901, who showed "a strange fascination with hanging from an early age" (Stokes, *Pit of Shame*, 54).

58. For the brutality inflicted by the good in the name of justice, see p. 296, n.8 above.

59. The murderer of a parent.

60. The Capital Punishment Act of 1868 mandated that hangings took place at eight o'clock on Tuesday mornings.

61. The hangman's noose ran through a metal eyelet so as to avoid friction and ensure a stronger jolt (*The Annotated Oscar Wilde: Poems, Fiction, Plays, Lectures, Essays, and Letters,* ed. H. Montgomery Hyde [New York: Clarkson Potter, 1982], 68, n.25).

62. As the saying "for whom the bell tolls" suggests, the "sign" is the tolling of the local church bell (St. Lawrence's Church, Reading), which began fifteen minutes before an execution. At the eighth toll of the bell, at exactly eight o'clock, the trap door would be sprung.

But the sough[55] and swing of a mighty wing
    The prison seemed to fill,
For the Lord of Death with icy breath
    Had entered in to kill.

He did not pass in purple pomp,
    Nor ride a moon-white steed.
Three yards of cord and a sliding board[56]
    Are all the gallows' need:
So with rope of shame the Herald[57] came
    To do the secret deed.

*

We were as men who through a fen
    Of filthy darkness grope:
We did not dare to breathe a prayer,
    Or give our anguish scope:
Something was dead in each of us,
    And what was dead was Hope.

For Man's grim Justice goes its way,
    And will not swerve aside:
It slays the weak, it slays the strong,
    It has a deadly stride:
With iron heel it slays the strong,[58]
    The monstrous parricide![59]

*

We waited for the stroke of eight:
    Each tongue was thick with thirst:
For the stroke of eight is the stroke of Fate
    That makes a man accursed,[60]
And Fate will use a running noose[61]
    For the best man and the worst.

We had no other thing to do,
    Save to wait for the sign to come:[62]

Frans Masereel, woodcut frontispiece for Oscar Wilde, *The Ballad of Reading Gaol*
(Munich: Drei Masken Verlages, 1923).

So, like things of stone in a valley lone,
    Quiet we sat and dumb:
But each man's heart beat thick and quick
    Like a madman on a drum!

*

With sudden shock the prison-clock
    Smote on the shivering air,
And from all the gaol rose up a wail
    Of impotent despair,
Like the sound the frightened marshes hear
    From some leper in his lair.

And as one sees most fearful things
    In the crystal of a dream,
We saw the greasy hempen rope
    Hooked to the blackened beam,
And heard the prayer the hangman's snare
    Strangled into a scream.

And all the woe that moved him so
    That he gave that bitter cry,
And the wild regrets, and the bloody sweats,
    None knew so well as I:
For he who live more lives than one
    More deaths than one must die.

IV

There is no chapel on the day
    On which they hang a man:
The Chaplain's heart is far too sick,
    Or his face is far too wan,
Or there is that written in his eyes
    Which none should look upon.

63. A reference to the strict separation and cellular division of prisoners. The "terror that seizes and dominates" the prisoner, Wilde writes in his first letter to the *Daily Chronicle* (p. 299 above), "is of course intensified beyond power of expression by the solitary cellular system of our prisons."

64. For the second edition, Wilde changed "happy cloud" to "careless cloud," and "such strange freedom" to "happy freedom."

65. Repeat offenders know themselves to be more culpable than the executed murderer, since they have become indifferent or habituated to a life of crime.

So they kept us close till nigh on noon,
    And then they rang the bell,
And the warders with their jingling keys
    Opened each listening cell,
And down the iron stair we tramped,
    Each from his separate Hell.[63]

Out into God's sweet air we went,
    But not in wonted way,
For this man's face was white with fear,
    And that man's face was gray,
And I never saw sad men who looked
    So wistfully at the day.

I never saw sad men who looked
    With such a wistful eye
Upon that little tent of blue
    We prisoners called the sky,
And at every happy cloud that passed
    In such strange freedom by.[64]

But there were those amongst us all
    Who walked with downcast head,
And knew that, had each got his due,
    They should have died instead:
He had but killed a thing that lived
    Whilst they had killed the dead.[65]

For he who sins a second time
    Wakes a dead soul to pain,
And draws it from its spotted shroud,
    And makes it bleed again,
And makes it bleed great gouts of blood
    And makes it bleed in vain!

*

66. A reference to the notorious broad arrows of Victorian prison uniforms and the red stars that first-time offenders were obliged to wear to differentiate them from recidivists.

Arthur Wragg, photo-engraved illustration for Oscar Wilde, *The Ballad of Reading Gaol* (London: Castle Press, 1948).

> Like ape or clown, in monstrous garb
>   With crooked arrows starred,[66]
> Silently we went round and round
>   The slippery asphalte yard;
> Silently we went round and round,
>   And no man spoke a word.

67. The 1832 Anatomy Act mandated that the executed felon's corpse be buried in unconsecrated ground within the confines of the prison. "Sheet of flame" refers literally to the "burning lime" in which the body of the executed felon was encased for quick decomposition, but Wilde alludes metaphorically to the flames in which early Christian saints were martyred, and perhaps also to the carbonized Shroud of Turin, in which the body of Christ was purportedly wrapped following crucifixion, prior to his burial in Golgotha. "The martyr in his 'shirt of flame' may be looking on the face of God," Wilde writes in *De Profundis* (p. 271 above).

Silently we went round and round,
    And through each hollow mind
The Memory of dreadful things
    Rushed like a dreadful wind,
And Horror stalked before each man,
    And Terror crept behind.

*

The warders strutted up and down,
    And watched their herd of brutes,
Their uniforms were spick and span,
    And they wore their Sunday suits,
But we knew the work they had been at
    By the quicklime on their boots.

For where a grave had opened wide,
    There was no grave at all:
Only a stretch of mud and sand
    By the hideous prison-wall,
And a little heap of burning lime,
    That the man should have his pall.

For he has a pall, this wretched man,
    Such as few men can claim:
Deep down below a prison-yard,
    Naked for greater shame,
He lies, with fetters on each foot,
    Wrapt in a sheet of flame![67]

And all the while the burning lime
    Eats flesh and bone away,
It eats the brittle bone by night,
    And the soft flesh by the day,
It eats the flesh and bones by turns,
    But it eats the heart alway.

68. Here and henceforth, Wilde makes the poem's Christian purpose explicit.

69. Wilde refers in a number of his works to the legend of Tannhäuser's pilgrimage to Rome in search of absolution for his sins. After devoting a full year to the worship of Venus, the legend relates, the knight Tannhäuser journeyed to Rome only to be told by the pope that absolution was as impossible as it would be for the papal staff to sprout into bloom. Tannhäuser returned dejectedly to the Venusberg, but three days after his departure, the pope's staff did indeed sprout blossoms. The pope thereupon sent messengers to retrieve Tannhäuser, but no trace of him could be found and he remained unabsolved. In 1900 Wilde too journeyed to Rome and was blessed as a pilgrim by the pope: "I was deeply impressed," he remarked, "and my walking-stick showed signs of budding; would have budded indeed, only at the door of the chapel it was taken from me. . . . This strange prohibition is, of course, in honour of Tannhäuser" (CL 1180).

*

For three long years they will not sow
  Or root or seedling there:
For three long years the unblessed spot
  Will sterile be and bare,
And look upon the wondering sky
  With unreproachful stare.

They think a murderer's heart would taint
  Each simple seed they sow.
It is not true! God's kindly earth
  Is kindlier than men know,
And the red rose would but blow more red,
  The white rose whiter blow.

Out of his mouth a red, red rose!
  Out of his heart a white!
For who can say by what strange way,
  Christ brings His will to light,[68]
Since the barren staff the pilgrim bore
  Bloomed in the great Pope's sight?[69]

*

But neither milk-white rose nor red
  May bloom in prison air;
The shard, the pebble, and the flint,
  Are what they give us there:
For flowers have been known to heal
  A common man's despair.

So never will wine-red rose or white,
  Petal by petal, fall
On that stretch of mud and sand that lies
  By the hideous prison-wall,

70. For the second edition, Wilde changed "The warders" to "They" and "clothes" to "canvas clothes."

71. Wilde told his publisher, who was worried that the poem might precipitate libel charges, that this is not a literal description of Wooldridge's execution: "The account of the execution is not the account of the Reading scene; it is general" (CL 988).

To tell the men who tramp the yard
    That God's Son died for all.

*

Yet though the hideous prison-wall
    Still hems him round and round,
And a spirit may not walk by night
    That is with fetters bound,
And a spirit may not weep that lies
    In such unholy ground,

He is at peace—this wretched man—
    At peace, or will be soon:
There is no thing to make him mad,
    Nor does Terror walk at noon,
For the lampless Earth in which he lies
    Has neither Sun nor Moon.

They hanged him as a beast is hanged:
    They did not even toll
A requiem that might have brought
    Rest to his startled soul,
But hurriedly they took him out,
    And hid him in a hole.

The warders stripped him of his clothes,[70]
    And gave him to the flies;
They mocked the swollen purple throat
    And the stark and staring eyes:
And with laughter loud they heaped the shroud
    In which the convict lies.[71]

The Chaplain would not kneel to pray
    By his dishonoured grave:
Nor mark it with that blessed Cross
    That Christ for sinners gave,

Frans Masereel, woodcut illustration for Oscar Wilde, *The Ballad of Reading Gaol* (Munich: Drei Masken Verlages, 1923).

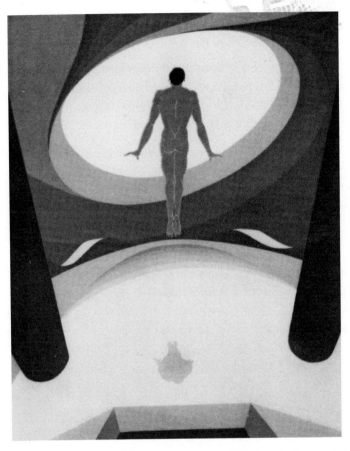

John Vassos, photolithographic illustration for Oscar Wilde, *The Ballad of Reading Gaol* (New York: E. P. Dutton & Co., Inc., 1928).

Because the man was one of those
  Whom Christ came down to save.

Yet all is well; he has but passed
  To Life's appointed bourne:
And alien tears will fill for him
  Pity's long-broken urn,

72. The final four lines of this stanza were chosen by Robert Ross as Wilde's epigraph and inscribed on his tomb at Père Lachaise Cemetery.

73. "You are quite right in saying that the poem should end at 'outcasts always mourn,' but the propaganda which I desire to make begins there" (CL 964). This section and the one following it were written at Naples, where Wilde was living with Douglas in the fall of 1897.

74. An instrument for winnowing grain. According to Matthew 3:12, Christ, "whose fan is in his hand," will "thoroughly purge his floor, and gather his wheat into the garner; but he will burn up the chaff with unquenchable fire."

75. As Wilde observes in his first letter to the *Daily Chronicle* (pp. 293–97 above), "The cruelty that is practised by day and night ... in English prisons is incredible, except to those who have witnessed it and are aware of the brutality of the system. ... Authority is as destructive to those who exercise it as it is to those on whom it is exercised. It is the Prison Board, and the system that carries it out, that is the primary source of the cruelty."

For his mourners will be outcast men,
    And outcasts always mourn.[72]

V[73]

I know not whether Laws be right,
    Or whether Laws be wrong;
All that we know who lie in gaol
    Is that the wall is strong;
And that each day is like a year,
    A year whose days are long.

But this I know, that every Law
    That men have made for Man,
Since first Man took his brother's life,
    And the sad world began,
But straws the wheat and saves the chaff
    With a most evil fan.[74]

This too I know—and wise it were
    If each could know the same—
That every prison that men build
    Is built with bricks of shame,
And bound with bars lest Christ should see
    How men their brothers maim.[75]

With bars they blur the gracious moon,
    And blind the goodly sun:
And they do well to hide their Hell,
    For in it things are done
That Son of God nor son of Man
    Ever should look upon!

*

The vilest deeds like poison weeds
    Bloom well in prison-air:

76. See Wilde's first letter to the *Daily Chronicle* (pp. 293–315 above) for a more exact description of the cruelties inflicted upon children, the sick, and the weak in English jails.

77. Wilde here makes propagandistic poetry out of his own prison experiences: for his fear that in prison he was becoming "the sure prey of morbid passions, and obscene fancies, and thoughts that defile, desecrate and destroy," see p. 47 above. For a detailed overview of Wilde's experiences in prison, see Nicholas Frankel, *Oscar Wilde: The Unrepentant Years* [Cambridge, MA: Harvard University Press, 2017], 36–55.

78. See p. 344, n.54 above.

It is only what is good in Man
  That wastes and withers there:
Pale Anguish keeps the heavy gate,
  And the Warder is Despair

For they starve the little frightened child
  Till it weeps both night and day:
And they scourge the weak, and flog the fool,
  And gibe the old and gray,
And some grow mad, and all grow bad,
  And none a word may say.[76]

Each narrow cell in which we dwell
  Is a foul and dark latrine,
And the fetid breath of living Death
  Chokes up each grated screen,
And all, but Lust, is turned to dust
  In Humanity's machine.[77]

The brackish water that we drink
  Creeps with a loathsome slime,
And the bitter bread they weigh in scales
  Is full of chalk and lime,
And Sleep will not lie down, but walks
  Wild-eyed and cries to Time.

*

But though lean Hunger and green Thirst
  Like asp with adder fight,
We have little care of prison fare,
  For what chills and kills outright
Is that every stone one lifts by day
  Becomes one's heart by night.

With midnight always in one's heart,
  And twilight in one's cell,[78]

79. Perhaps the cruelest element of Victorian prison life was the so-called "silent system," which mandated absolute silence throughout the prison and was designed to prevent communication and enhance the isolation of each prisoner. The ban on speech was rigidly enforced after 1877 and "placed an appalling power in the warders' hands" (George Ives, *A History of Penal Methods* [New York: Stokes, 1914], 214).

80. The title character of Wilde's story "The Happy Prince" (1888) possesses a heart of lead, but even this metal—which won't melt in a furnace—breaks when he learns the value of love and compassion.

81. According to the Gospels, while Jesus was dining in the house of Simon the Leper, a woman came with an alabaster box containing pure nard. She broke the box and poured the costly nard on either Jesus's head or his feet, thereby anointing Jesus in preparation for his crucifixion and eventual burial. See also p. 222, n.412 above.

We turn the crank, or tear the rope,
    Each in his separate Hell,
And the silence is more awful far
    Than the sound of a brazen bell.[79]

And never a human voice comes near
    To speak a gentle word:
And the eye that watches through the door
    Is pitiless and hard:
And by all forgot, we rot and rot,
    With soul and body marred.

And thus we rust Life's iron chain
    Degraded and alone:
And some men curse, and some men weep,
    And some men make no moan:
But God's eternal Laws are kind
    And break the heart of stone.[80]

                    *

And every human heart that breaks,
    In prison-cell or yard,
Is as that broken box that gave
    Its treasure to the Lord,
And filled the unclean leper's house
    With the scent of costliest nard.[81]

Ah! happy they whose hearts can break
    And peace of pardon win!
How else may man make straight his plan
    And cleanse his soul from Sin?
How else but through a broken heart
    May Lord Christ enter in?

                    *

And he of the swollen purple throat.
    And the stark and staring eyes,

82. The holy hands are Christ's. According to Luke 23:39–43, Christ promised the thief who was crucified alongside him, at Gethsemane, that he would be with him in paradise.

83. "A broken and contrite heart, O God, thou wilt not despise" (Psalms 51:17).

84. Compare with Hood's "Dream of Eugene Aram":

> He told how murderers walk the earth
> Beneath the curse of Cain,
> With crimson clouds before their eyes,
> And flames about their brain:
> For blood has left upon their souls
> Its everlasting stain.

(*Poems*, 106.)

By filtering Hood's verse through a biblical lens—in Isaiah 1:18, Christ promises that "though your sins be like scarlet [or] red as crimson," they shall be "as white as snow"—Wilde suggests that the curse of Cain might be cleansed with "tears of blood." Cain was cursed by God with a crimson mark on his forehead, as a sign of shame for killing his brother Abel.

85. See p. 354, n.67 above.

Waits for the holy hands that took
    The Thief to Paradise;[82]
And a broken and a contrite heart
    The Lord will not despise.[83]

The man in red who reads the Law
    Gave him three weeks of life,
Three little weeks in which to heal
    His soul of his soul's strife,
And cleanse from every blot of blood
    The hand that held the knife.

And with tears of blood he cleansed the hand,
    The hand that held the steel:
For only blood can wipe out blood,
    And only tears can heal:
And the crimson stain that was of Cain
    Became Christ's snow-white seal.[84]

VI

In Reading gaol by Reading town
    There is a pit of shame,
And in it lies a wretched man
    Eaten by teeth of flame,
In a burning winding-sheet he lies,[85]
    And his grave has got no name.

And there, till Christ call forth the dead,
    In silence let him lie:
No need to waste the foolish tear,
    Or heave the windy sigh:
The man had killed the thing he loved,
    And so he had to die.

86. Although Wooldridge cut his wife's throat with a razor, Wilde's insistence that only the brave man kills his love with a sword imputes a level of bravery to the murderer that raises him above the common man. Like Nietzsche in *Beyond Good and Evil* (1886), Wilde inverts traditional moral categories (good / bad, cowardice / bravery) so that a frank assertion of the murderous violence lurking within all humans becomes less repulsive than the "cowardice" of a kiss or the hypocritical bloodlust of the judicial system.

87. In prison Wilde was identified by guards and fellow prisoners alike not by name but rather by his cell number. As he writes in *De Profundis*, "In the great prison where I was then incarcerated I was merely the figure and letter of a little cell in a long gallery, one of a thousand lifeless numbers, as of a thousand lifeless lives" (p. 135 above). Wilde's decision to publish *The Ballad of Reading Gaol* under his Reading cell number has been seen as a pragmatic one, since he was a social pariah after his release and his real name was anathema. But as Wilde observed to his publisher when insisting that the number should appear at the poem's end, "the pseudonym C.3.3. at the end ... is not a mere literary caprice, but the actual name for eighteen months of the man who wrote the poem" (*CL* 1004). By inscribing his cell number as a signature at the end of the poem, Wilde underscored his identity as both writer and narrator of *The Ballad of Reading Gaol*, even while masking it under the guise of anonymity. Nevertheless, one contemporary reviewer observed, the poem's authorship was "not difficult to guess." Wilde and his publisher knew that he would quickly be identified as the poem's author—indeed they were counting on it.

And all men kill the thing they love,
    By all let this be heard,
Some do it with a bitter look,
    Some with a flattering word,
The coward does it with a kiss,
    The brave man with a sword![86]

C. 3. 3.[87]

THE ANNOTATED PRISON WRITINGS OF OSCAR WILDE

* This letter appeared in the *Daily Chronicle* under the headline "Don't Read This If You Want to Be Happy Today," on 24 March 1898, the date on which the House of Commons began debating the second reading of the Prisons Bill. Wilde left Reading determined to write about prison life and to try to change it for others. He followed the prison reform movement closely, and his letter was clearly timed to affect parliamentary debate. According to Christopher Millard (who was informed of it "on undeniable authority," he claimed), "the Commissioners appointed to inquire into the question of Prison Reform ... spent three days considering the suggestions made [by Wilde in this letter]" (Millard, "Oscar Wilde's Letters on Prison Reform," *The Athenaeum*, 23 May 1908, 638). While it is hard to gauge the exact effect of Wilde's letter on the reform debate, some MPs who spoke in the wake of its appearance—in particular, the Irish MPs Michael Davitt, T. P. O'Connor, and John Redmond—echoed Wilde in spirit, while two of them quoted or cited Wilde's "Ballad of Reading Gaol." The chief effect of the 1898 Prisons Act was to give the home secretary more discretion in the administration of prisons, but many of the improvements suggested by Wilde were taken up early in the twentieth century.

1. The "present stupid and barbarous system" to which Wilde alludes is the harshly punitive regime of "hard labour, hard board, and hard fare" mandated by the 1865 and 1877 Prison Acts (these Acts centralized and standardized the administration of British prisons) and which remained in place until the Prisons Act of 1898. From 1877 until 1895, this regime was ruthlessly overseen by the first chairman of the Prison Commission, Major-General Sir Edmund Du Cane. As the prison historian Sean McConville writes, Du Cane "fashioned ... a national penology for the last quarter of the nineteenth century" by refining and legitimizing dietary, labor, and living arrangements that amounted to "scarcely veiled torture" (Sean McConville, "The Victorian Prison: England 1865–1965," in *The Oxford History of the Prison*, ed. N. Morris and D. J. Rothman [Oxford: Oxford University Press, 1995], 146–47). The system, which was designed to break the spirit of even the toughest offenders and drove many prisoners insane, had come under severe criticism even before Wilde's imprisonment, leading to Du Cane's resignation in April 1895 and his replacement by the more liberal-minded Sir Evelyn Ruggles-Brise. But Ruggles-Brise's hands were tied by Parliament, and as Wilde laments of the governor of Reading Prison in his earlier letter to the *Daily Chronicle*, while Ruggles-Brise might

Letter to the *Daily Chronicle**

23 March 1898

S<small>IR</small>,—I understand that the Home Secretary's Prison Reform Bill is to be read this week for the first or second time, and as your journal has been the one paper in England that has taken a real and vital interest in this important question, I hope that you will allow me, as one who has had long personal experience of life in an English gaol, to point out what reforms in our present stupid and barbarous system are urgently necessary.[1]

From a leading article that appeared in your columns about a week ago, I learn that the chief reform proposed is an increase in the number of inspectors and official visitors that are to have access to our English prisons.

Such a reform as this is entirely useless. The reason is extremely simple. The inspectors and justices of the peace that visit prisons come there for the purpose of seeing that the prison regulations are duly carried out. They come for no other purpose, nor have they any power, even if they had the desire, to alter a single clause in the regulations. And what is cruel and ignorant is this very code of regulations. No prisoner has ever had the smallest relief, or attention, or care from any of the official visitors. The visitors arrive not to help the prisoners, but to see that the rules are carried out. Their object in coming is to ensure the enforcement of a foolish and inhuman code. And, as they must have some occupation, they take very good care to do it. A prisoner who has been allowed the smallest privilege dreads the arrival of the inspectors. And on the day of any prison

have countenanced some alteration in the spirit in which the regulations were carried out, he could not alter the prison rules, which were legislated by the Prison Acts. While Wilde's own imprisonment and writings helped foster the groundswell of support for legislative change between 1895 and 1898, it was Wilde's misfortune that the legal changes necessary for some relaxation of existing English prison rules did not take place till after his release. Even given these legislative changes, twentieth- and twenty-first-century imprisonment in England "has been marked by a tenacious Victorian inheritance" (McConville, "The Victorian Prison," 154).

inspection the prison officials are more than usually brutal to the prisoners. Their object is, of course, to show the splendid discipline they maintain.

The necessary reforms are very simple. They concern the needs of the body and the needs of the mind of each unfortunate prisoner.

With regard to the first, there are three permanent punishments authorised by law in English prisons:—

1. Hunger.
2. Insomnia.
3. Disease.

The food supplied to prisoners is entirely inadequate. Most of it is revolting in character. All of it is insufficient. Every prisoner suffers day and night from hunger. A certain amount of food is carefully weighed out ounce by ounce for each prisoner. It is just enough to sustain, not life exactly, but existence. But one is always racked by the pain and sickness of hunger.

The result of the food—which in most cases consists of weak gruel, badly-baked bread, suet, and water—is disease in the form of incessant diarrhœa. This malady, which ultimately with most prisoners becomes a permanent disease, is a recognised institution in every prison. At Wandsworth Prison, for instance—where I was confined for two months, till I had to be carried into hospital, where I remained for another two months—the warders go round twice or three times a day with astringent medicines, which they serve out to the prisoners as a matter of course. After about a week of such treatment it is unnecessary to say that the medicine produces no effect at all. The wretched prisoner is then left a prey to the most weakening, depressing, and humiliating malady that can be conceived; and if, as often happens, he fails, from physical weakness, to complete his required revolutions at the crank or the mill he is reported for idleness, and punished with the greatest severity and brutality. Nor is this all.

Nothing can be worse than the sanitary arrangements of English prisons. In old days each cell was provided with a form of latrine. These

Jean-Gabriel Daragnès, wood-engraved illustration for *Ballade de La Geôle de Reading, par C.3.3.*, trans. Henry-D. Davray (Paris: Léon Pichon, 1918).

latrines have now been suppressed. They exist no longer. A small tin vessel is supplied to each prisoner instead. Three times a day a prisoner is allowed to empty his slops. But he is not allowed to have access to the prison lavatories, except during the one hour when he is at exercise. And after five o'clock in the evening he is not allowed to leave his cell under any pretence, or for any reason. A man suffering from diarrhœa is consequently placed in a position so loathsome that it is unnecessary to dwell on it, that it would be unseemly to dwell on it. The misery and tortures that prisoners go through in consequence of the revolting sanitary arrangements are quite indescribable. And the foul air of the prison cells, increased by a system of ventilation that is utterly ineffective, is so sickening and unwholesome that it is no uncommon thing for warders, when they come in the morning out of the fresh air and open and inspect each cell, to be violently sick. I have seen this myself on more than three occasions, and several of the warders have mentioned it to me as one of the disgusting things that their office entails on them.

The food supplied to prisoners should be adequate and wholesome. It should not be of such a character as to produce the incessant diarrhœa that, at first a malady, becomes a permanent disease.

The sanitary arrangements in English prisons should be entirely altered. Every prisoner should be allowed to have access to the lavatories when necessary, and to empty his slops when necessary. The present system of ventilation in each cell is utterly useless. The air comes through choked-up gratings, and through a small ventilator in the tiny barred window, which is far too small, and too badly constructed, to admit any adequate amount of fresh air. One is only allowed out of one's cell for one hour out of the twenty-four that compose the long day, and so for twenty-three hours one is breathing the foulest possible air.

With regard to the punishment of insomnia, it only exists in Chinese and in English prisons. In China it is inflicted by placing the prisoner in a small bamboo cage; in England by means of the plank bed. The object of the plank bed is to produce insomnia. There is no other object in it, and it invariably succeeds. And even when one is subsequently allowed

Jean-Gabriel Daragnès, wood-engraved illustration for *Ballade de La Geôle de Reading, par C.3.3.*, trans. Henry-D. Davray (Paris: Léon Pichon, 1918).

a hard mattress, as happens in the course of imprisonment, one still suffers from insomnia. For sleep, like all wholesome things, is a habit. Every prisoner who has been on a plank bed suffers from insomnia. It is a revolting and ignorant punishment.

With regard to the needs of the mind, I beg that you will allow me to say something.

The present prison system seems almost to have for its aim the wrecking and the destruction of the mental faculties. The production of insanity is, if not its object, certainly its result. That is a well-ascertained fact. Its causes are obvious. Deprived of books, of all human intercourse, isolated from every humane and humanising influence, condemned to eternal silence, robbed of all intercourse with the external world, treated like an unintelligent animal, brutalised below the level of any of the brute creation, the wretched man who is confined in an English prison can hardly escape becoming insane. I do not wish to dwell on these horrors; still less to excite any momentary sentimental interest in these matters. So I will merely, with your permission, point out what should be done.

Every prisoner should have an adequate supply of good books. At present, during the first three months of imprisonment, one is allowed no books at all, except a Bible, prayer-book, and hymn-book. After that one is allowed one book a week. That is not merely inadequate, but the books that compose an ordinary prison library are perfectly useless. They consist chiefly of third-rate, badly-written, religious books, so-called, written apparently for children, and utterly unsuitable for children or for anyone else. Prisoners should be encouraged to read, and should have whatever books they want, and the books should be well chosen. At present the selection of books is made by the prison chaplain.

Under the present system a prisoner is only allowed to see his friends four times a year, for twenty minutes each time. This is quite wrong. A prisoner should be allowed to see his friends once a month, and for a reasonable time. The mode at present in vogue of exhibiting a prisoner to his friends should be altered. Under the present system the prisoner is either locked up in a large iron cage or in a large wooden box, with a small aperture, covered with wire netting, through which he is allowed to peer.

His friends are placed in a similar cage, some three or four feet distant, and two warders stand between to listen to, and, if they wish, stop or interrupt the conversation, such as it may be. I propose that a prisoner should be allowed to see his relatives or friends in a room. The present regulations are inexpressibly revolting and harassing. A visit from our relatives or friends is to every prisoner an intensification of humiliation and mental distress. Many prisoners, rather than support such an ordeal, refuse to see their friends at all. And I cannot say I am surprised. When one sees one's solicitor, one sees him in a room with a glass door, on the other side of which stands the warder. When a man sees his wife and children, or his parents, or his friends, he should be allowed the same privilege. To be exhibited, like an ape in a cage, to people who are fond of one, and of whom one is fond, is a needless and horrible degradation.

Every prisoner should be allowed to write and receive a letter at least once a month. At present one is allowed to write only four times a year. This is quite inadequate. One of the tragedies of prison life is that it turns a man's heart to stone. The feelings of natural affection, like all other feelings, require to be fed. They die easily of inanition. A brief letter, four times a year, is not enough to keep alive the gentler and more humane affections by which ultimately the nature is kept sensitive to any fine or beautiful influences that may heal a wrecked and ruined life.

The habit of mutilating and expurgating prisoners' letters should be stopped. At present, if a prisoner in a letter makes any complaint of the prison system, that portion of his letter is cut out with a pair of scissors. If, upon the other hand, he makes any complaint when he speaks to his friends through the bars of the cage, or the aperture of the wooden box, he is brutalised by the warders, and reported for punishment every week till his next visit comes round, by which time he is expected to have learned, not wisdom, but cunning, and one always learns that. It is one of the few things that one does learn in prison. Fortunately, the other things are, in some instances, of higher import.

If I may trespass for a little longer, may I say this? You suggested in your leading article that no prison chaplain should be allowed to have any care or employment outside the prison itself. But this is a matter of

2. This signature carried considerable weight at the time of publication and also hinted at Wilde's brief rebirth as a prominent literary figure in his own lifetime. *The Ballad of Reading Gaol* had been published to great acclaim six weeks prior to this letter's publication. The poem had already run through four editions, representing 3,100 copies, and a fifth edition (representing another 1,000 copies) had been printed days earlier. Two further editions, representing another 3,000 copies, were to be printed before Wilde's death in 1900. The *Ballad* was the best-selling of Wilde's books in his own lifetime. Wilde's letter capitalized on this success, and the poem was twice quoted or cited in parliamentary debate of the Prisons Bill in the days after the letter's appearance.

no moment. The prison chaplains are entirely useless. They are, as a class, well-meaning, but foolish, indeed silly, men. They are of no help to any prisoner. Once every six weeks or so a key turns in the lock of one's cell door, and the chaplain enters. One stands, of course, at attention. He asks one whether one has been reading the Bible. One answers "Yes" or "No," as the case may be. He then quotes a few texts, and goes out and locks the door. Sometimes he leaves a tract.

The officials who should not be allowed to hold any employment outside the prison, or to have any private practice, are the prison doctors. At present the prison doctors have usually, if not always, a large private practice, and hold appointments in other institutions. The consequence is that the health of the prisoners is entirely neglected, and the sanitary condition of the prison entirely overlooked. As a class I regard, and have always from my earliest youth regarded, doctors as by far the most humane profession in the community. But I must make an exception for prison doctors. They are as far as I came across them, and from what I saw of them in hospital and elsewhere, brutal in manner, coarse in temperament, and utterly indifferent to the health of the prisoners or their comfort. If prison doctors were prohibited from private practice they would be compelled to take some interest in the health and sanitary condition of the people under their charge. I have tried to indicate in my letter a few of the reforms necessary to our English prison system. They are simple, practical, and humane. They are, of course, only a beginning. But it is time that a beginning should be made, and it can only be started by a strong pressure of public opinion formularised in your powerful paper, and fostered by it.

But to make even these reforms effectual, much has to be done. And the first, and perhaps the most difficult task is to humanise the governors of prisons, to civilise the warders, and to Christianise the chaplains.—Yours, etc.,

The Author of "The Ballad of Reading Gaol"[2]

Further Reading

EDITIONS

The Complete Letters of Oscar Wilde. Edited by Merlin Holland and Rupert Hart-Davis. New York: Henry Holt, 2000.

De Profundis; "Epistola: In Carcere et Vinculis." Edited by Ian Small. Vol. 2 of *The Complete Works of Oscar Wilde.* Oxford: Oxford University Press, 2005.

De Profundis: A Facsimile. Introduction by Merlin Holland. London: British Library, 2000.

Poems and Poems in Prose. Edited by Bobby Fong and Karl Beckson. Vol. 1 of *The Complete Works of Oscar Wilde.* Oxford: Oxford University Press, 2000.

BIOGRAPHICAL

Ackroyd, Peter. *The Last Testament of Oscar Wilde.* 1983. Reprint, London: Abacus, 1988.

Bristow, Joseph. "The Blackmailer and the Sodomite: Oscar Wilde on Trial." *Feminist Theory* 17, no. 1 (2016): 41–62.

———. *Oscar Wilde on Trial: The Criminal Proceedings.* New Haven, CT: Yale University Press, forthcoming.

Ellmann, Richard. *Oscar Wilde.* New York: Knopf, 1988.

Frankel, Nicholas. *Oscar Wilde: The Unrepentant Years.* Cambridge, MA: Harvard University Press, 2017.

Hyde, H. Montgomery. *Oscar Wilde: The Aftermath.* New York: Farrar Strauss, 1963.

———. *The Trials of Oscar Wilde.* 2nd ed. 1962. Reprint, New York: Dover, 1973.

Lee, Laura. *Oscar's Ghost: The Battle for Oscar Wilde's Legacy.* Stroud, UK: Amberley, 2017.

McKenna, Neil. *The Secret Life of Oscar Wilde.* New York: Basic Books, 2005.

Oscar Wilde: Interviews and Recollections. Edited by E. H. Mikhail. 2 vols. London: Macmillan, 1979.

Oscar Wilde, Trial and Punishment: 1895–1897. London: Public Record Office, 1997.

The Real Trial of Oscar Wilde. Introduction and commentary by Merlin Holland. New York: Fourth Estate, 2003.

Robins, Ashley H. *Oscar Wilde: The Great Drama of His Life.* Brighton, UK: Sussex Academic, 2011.

BIBLIOGRAPHICAL

Beckson, Karl, ed. *Oscar Wilde: The Critical Heritage.* London: Routledge and Kegan Paul, 1970.

Fletcher, Ian, and John Stokes. "Oscar Wilde." In *Anglo-Irish Literature: A Review of Research*, edited by Richard Finneran, 48–137. New York: MLA, 1976.

———. "Oscar Wilde." In *Recent Research on Anglo-Irish Writers*, edited by Richard Finneran, 21–47. New York: MLA, 1983.

Horodisch, Abraham. *Oscar Wilde's "Ballad of Reading Gaol": A Bibliographical Study.* New York: Aldus, 1954.

Mikhail, E. H. *Oscar Wilde: An Annotated Bibliography of Criticism.* London: Macmillan, 1978.

Mikolyzk, Thomas A. *Oscar Wilde: An Annotated Bibliography.* Westport, CT: Greenwood Press, 1993.

Stuart Mason [Christopher Millard]. *Bibliography of Oscar Wilde.* London: T. Werner Laurie, 1914.

HISTORICAL AND CONTEXTUAL

Cocks, H. G. *Nameless Offences: Homosexual Desire in the Nineteenth Century.* London: I. B. Tauris, 2003.

Cohen, Ed. *Talk on the Wilde Side: Toward a Genealogy of Discourses on Male Sexualities.* London: Routledge, 1993.

Dollimore, Jonathan. *Sexual Dissidence: Augustine to Wilde, Freud to Foucault.* Oxford: Clarendon Press, 1991.

Field, Rev. J. *Prison Discipline; and the Advantages of the Separate System of Imprisonment, with a Detailed Account of the Discipline now pursued at the new County Gaol at Reading*. London: Longman, Brown, Green, and Longmans, 1846.

Foucault, Michel. *Discipline and Punish: The Birth of the Prison*. Translated by A. Sheridan. New York: Pantheon, 1978.

———. *History of Sexuality*. Vol. 1. Translated by R. Hurley. 1978. Reprint, New York: Vintage, 1990.

Ireland, Richard W. *"A Want of Order and Good Discipline": Rules, Discretion, and the Victorian Prison*. Cardiff: University of Wales Press, 2007.

McConville, Sean. *English Local Prisons 1860–1900: Next Only to Death*. New York: Routledge, 1995.

———. "The Victorian Prison: England 1865–1965." In *The Oxford History of the Prison,* edited by N. Morris and D. J. Rothman, 131–67. Oxford: Oxford University Press, 1995.

Priestley, Philip. *Victorian Prison Lives: English Prison Biography 1830–1914*. London: Methuen, 1985.

Stokes, Anthony. *Pit of Shame: The Real Ballad of Reading Gaol*. Winchester, UK: Waterside, 2007.

Stoneley, Peter. " 'Looking at the Others': Oscar Wilde and the Reading Gaol Archive." *Journal of Victorian Culture* 19 (2014): 457–80.

Weeks, Jeffrey. *Sex, Politics, Society: The Regulation of Sexuality since 1800*. London: Longman, 1981.

———. *Sexuality*. 4th ed. London: Routledge, 2017.

Wiener, Martin J. *Reconstructing the Criminal: Culture, Law, and Policy in England, 1830–1914*. Cambridge: Cambridge University Press, 1990.

CRITICAL

Alkalay-Gut, Karen. "The Thing He Loves: Murder as Aesthetic Experience in 'The Ballad of Reading Gaol.' " *Victorian Poetry* 35 (1997): 349–66.

Arata, Stephen. "Oscar Wilde and Jesus Christ." In *Wilde Writings: Contextual Conditions*, edited by Joseph Bristow, 254–72. Toronto: University of Toronto Press, 2003.

Bristow, Joseph. " 'All Men Kill the Thing They Love': Romance, Realism, and *The Ballad of Reading Gaol*." In *Approaches to Teaching the Works of Oscar Wilde,* edited by Philip E. Smith II, 230–47. New York: MLA, 2008.

———. "Oscar Wilde's Poetic Traditions: From Aristophanes's *Clouds* to *The Ballad of Reading Gaol*." In *Oscar Wilde in Context,* edited by Kerry Powell and Peter Raby, 73–87. Cambridge: Cambridge University Press, 2014.

Frankel, Nicholas. "Manuscript, Typescript, Print: Embodiments of Authorship [on *De Profundis*]." *The Wildean: A Journal of Oscar Wilde Studies* 28 (January 2006): 67–77.

———. "The Typewritten Self: Media Technology and Identity in Oscar Wilde's *De Profundis.*" In *Masking the Text: Essays on Literature and Mediation in the 1890s,* 83–100. High Wycombe, UK: Rivendale Press, 2009.

Gagnier, Regenia. "*De Profundis:* An Audience of Peers." In *Idylls of the Marketplace: Oscar Wilde and the Victorian Public,* 177–95. Stanford, CA: Stanford University Press, 1986.

Hanson, Ellis. *Decadence and Catholicism.* Cambridge, MA: Harvard University Press, 1997.

———. "Wilde's Exquisite Pain." In *Wilde Writings: Contextual Conditions,* edited by Joseph Bristow, 101–23. Toronto: University of Toronto Press, 2003.

Heaney, Seamus. "Speranza in Reading: On 'The Ballad of Reading Gaol'" (1993). In *The Redress of Poetry.* New York: Farrar, Straus and Giroux, 1995.

Nathan, Leonard. "The Ballads of Reading Gaol: At the Limits of the Lyric." In *Critical Essays on Oscar Wilde,* edited by Regenia Gagnier, 213–22. New York: G. K. Hall, 1991.

Small, Ian. "Love Letter, Spiritual Autobiography, or Prison Writing? Identity and Value in *De Profundis.*" In *Wilde Writings: Contextual Conditions,* edited by Joseph Bristow, 86–100. Toronto: University of Toronto Press, 2003.

Willoughby, Guy. *Art as Christhood: The Aesthetics of Oscar Wilde.* London: Associated University Presses, 1993.

Illustration Credits

page 3
Reading Prison, exterior, circa 1900. Published in *The Real Oscar Wilde: To be used as a Supplement to and in Illustration of "The Life of Oscar Wilde"* by Robert Harborough Sherard (London: T. Werner Laurie Ltd., 1916), opposite p. 258.

page 10
Lord Alfred Douglas, c. 1892, shortly after Wilde first met him. Published in *Oscar Wilde and Myself* by Lord Alfred Douglas (New York: Duffield and Co., 1914), opposite p. 30.

page 17
Oscar Wilde, untitled manuscript letter to Lord Alfred Douglas, composed in Reading Prison, 1896–1897, published posthumously as *De Profundis*. British Library (Add MS 50141 A) / Granger.

page 90
Frans Masereel, woodcut illustration for Oscar Wilde, *The Ballad of Reading Gaol* (Munich: Drei Masken Verlages, 1923). © 2017 Artists Rights Society (ARS), New York / VG Bild-Kunst, Bonn.

page 129
Jean-Gabriel Daragnès, wood-engraved illustration for *Ballade de la Geôle de Reading, par C.3.3.,* trans. Henry-D. Davray (Paris: Léon Pichon, 1918). © 2017 Artists Rights Society (ARS), New York / ADAGP, Paris.

page 145
John Vassos, photolithographic illustration for Oscar Wilde, *The Ballad of Reading Gaol* (New York: E. P. Dutton & Co., Inc., 1928).

page 193
Garrick Palmer, wood-engraved frontispiece for Oscar Wilde, *The Ballad of Reading Gaol* (Llandogo, Gwent: The Old Stile Press, 1994). Courtesy of the artist.

page 237
Jean-Gabriel Daragnès, wood-engraved illustration for *Ballade de la Geôle de Reading, par C.3.3.*, trans. Henry-D. Davray (Paris: Léon Pichon, 1918). © 2017 Artists Rights Society (ARS), New York / ADAGP, Paris.

page 276
Jean-Gabriel Daragnès, wood-engraved illustration for *Ballade de la Geôle de Reading, par C.3.3.*, trans. Henry-D. Davray (Paris: Léon Pichon, 1918). © 2017 Artists Rights Society (ARS), New York / ADAGP, Paris.

page 302
W. F. Poulton, lithograph of interior of Reading Prison (East Wing), 1846. Drawing by W. F. Poulton, lithograph by T. J. Rawlins. Published in John Field, *Prison Discipline: The Advantages of the Separate System of Imprisonment, as established in the New County Gaol of Reading; with a description of the former prisons, and a detailed account of the discipline now pursued* (London: Longman and Co., 1846).

page 313
Prison whipping post, English, 1860s. Published in Henry Mayhew and John Binney, *The Criminal Prisons of London and Scenes of Prison Life, with numerous illustrations from photographs* (London: Griffin, Bohn, and Co., 1862), p. 570.

page 319
"C. 3. 3." [Oscar Wilde], *The Ballad of Reading Gaol* (London: Leonard Smithers, 1898), title page.

page 321
John Vassos, photolithographic illustration for Oscar Wilde, *The Ballad of Reading Gaol* (New York: E. P. Dutton & Co., Inc., 1928).

page 331
Oscar Wilde, *The Ballad of Reading Gaol*, drawings by Latimer J. Wilson (New York: F. M. Buckles & Co., 1907), title page.

page 333
Garrick Palmer, wood-engraved illustration for Oscar Wilde, *The Ballad of Reading Gaol* (Llandogo, Gwent: The Old Stile Press, 1994). Courtesy of the artist.

page 348
Frans Masereel, woodcut frontispiece for Oscar Wilde, *The Ballad of Reading Gaol* (Munich: Drei Masken Verlages, 1923). © 2017 Artists Rights Society (ARS), New York / VG Bild-Kunst, Bonn.

page 353
Arthur Wragg, photo-engraved illustration for Oscar Wilde, *The Ballad of Reading Gaol* (London: Castle Press, 1948).

page 360
Frans Masereel, woodcut illustration for Oscar Wilde, *The Ballad of Reading Gaol* (Munich: Drei Masken Verlages, 1923). © 2017 Artists Rights Society (ARS), New York / VG Bild-Kunst, Bonn.

page 361
John Vassos, photolithographic illustration for Oscar Wilde, *The Ballad of Reading Gaol* (New York: E. P. Dutton & Co., Inc., 1928).

page 376
Jean-Gabriel Daragnès, wood-engraved illustration for *Ballade de la Geôle de Reading, par C.3.3.,* trans. Henry-D. Davray (Paris: Léon Pichon, 1918). © 2017 Artists Rights Society (ARS), New York / ADAGP, Paris.

page 378
Jean-Gabriel Daragnès, wood-engraved illustration for *Ballade de la Geôle de Reading, par C.3.3.,* trans. Henry-D. Davray (Paris: Léon Pichon, 1918). © 2017 Artists Rights Society (ARS), New York / ADAGP, Paris.

Acknowledgments

This book owes a great debt to many individuals—to Merlin Holland, for generous assistance with the text of *De Profundis,* as well as kind permission to reproduce this and other material in which he owns the copyright; to Jerome McGann, for a series of eye-opening conversations about *De Profundis,* stretching over many years; to Susan Barstow, my wife—and always my first editor—for reading my drafts with eyes of love and acumen; to Joseph Bristow, for generously sharing his own ongoing research and insight; to Laura Lee, for invaluable feedback on the Introduction; to Michael Boetius Sullivan, for expert assistance with Wilde's Greek; to J'Aimee Cronin and the Artists Rights Society, for generous permission to reproduce Frans Masereel's woodcuts; and to Garrick Palmer, for the warm kindness with which he granted me permission to reproduce the two wood engravings by him that appear in these pages.

At Harvard University Press, I owe much to John Kulka, who commissioned the book and set it on its way; to Andrew Kinney, who edited it in its final stages and saw it into production; to two anonymous readers, whose probing, attentive reviews resulted in a number of improvements to the manuscript; to Christine Thorsteinsson, project manager; to Stephanie Vyce and (especially) Scarlett Wilkes, for advice and assistance arranging permissions; to Dean Bornstein, designer, and Tim Jones, who patiently put up with my obstinacy; also to Kate Brick, Mihaela-Andreea Pacurar, and Olivia Woods. I owe much too to John Donohue at Westchester Publishing Services, who prepared the manuscript with consummate expertise.

Closer to home, my work could not flourish without the support of David Latané, Chair of the English Department at Virginia

Commonwealth University (VCU); Ginnie Schmitz and Margret Schluer in the English office; Montse Fuentes, Dean of the College of Humanities and Sciences at VCU; and the staff of Cabell Library, especially the Interlibrary Loan and Document Delivery office. Debts of a more purely scholarly nature will be clear from my Note on the Texts, annotations, and endnotes.